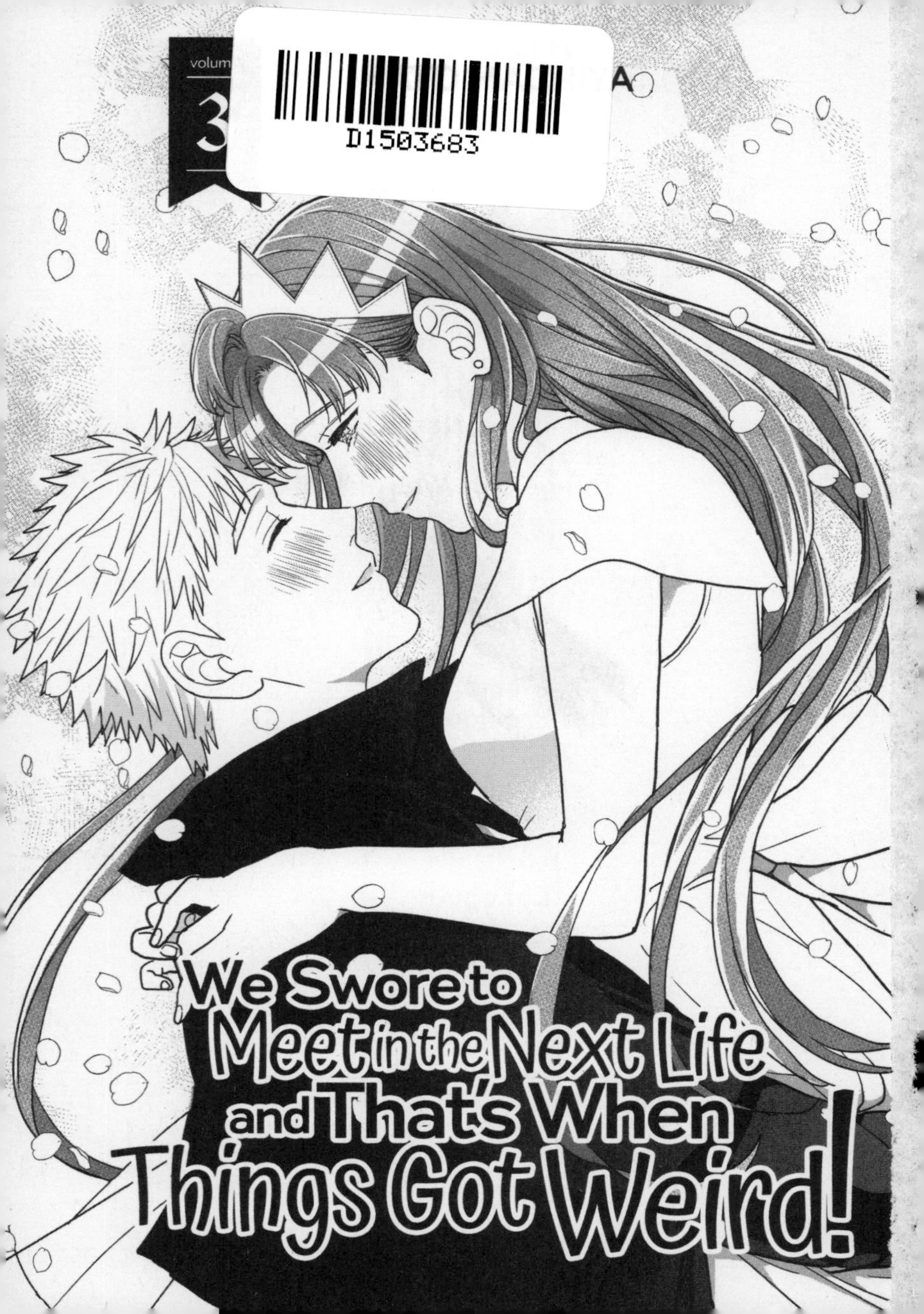
volume 3
We Swore to Meet in the Next Life and That's When Things Got Weird!

contents

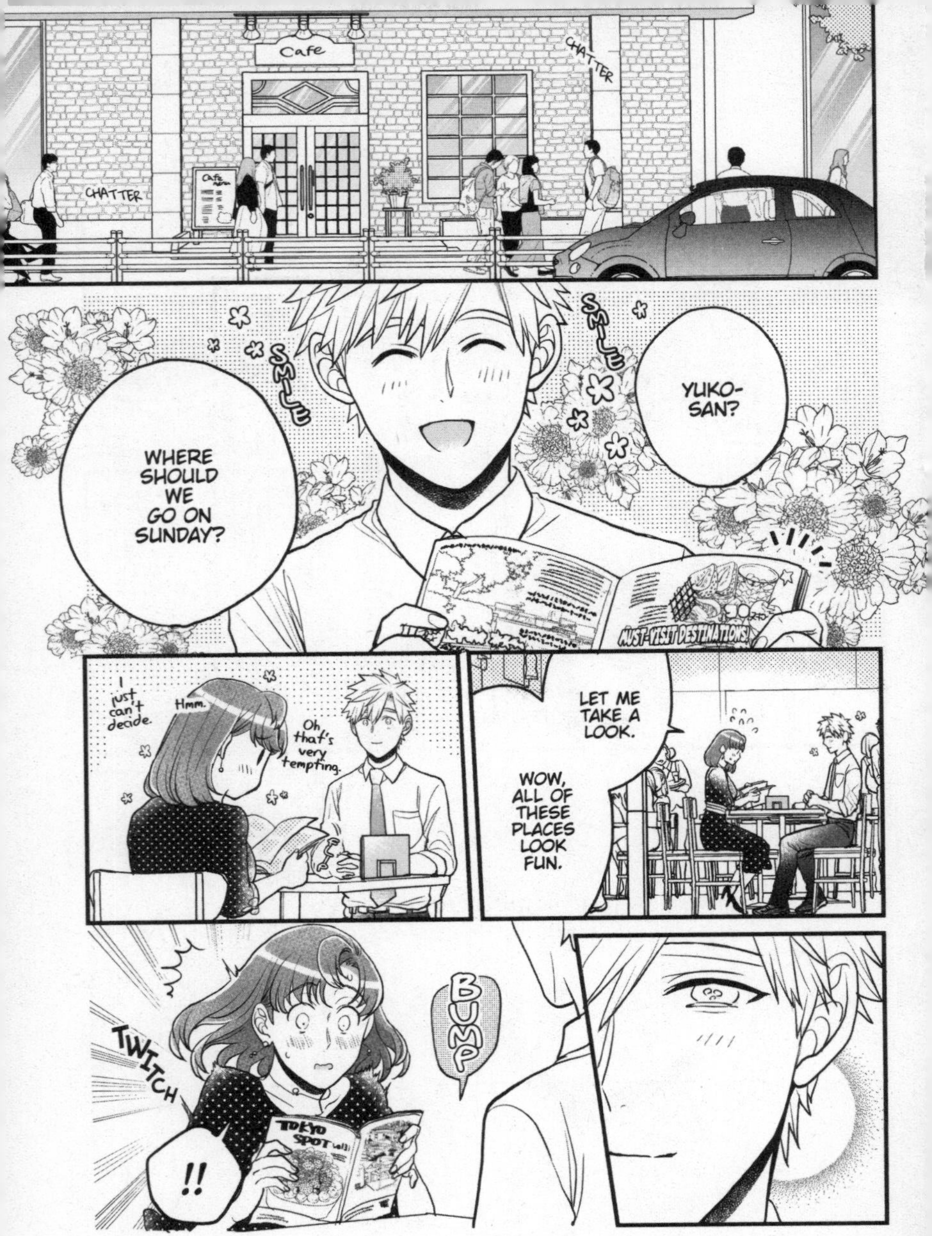

Cafe
CHATTER
CHATTER
YUKO-SAN?
SMILE
SMILE
WHERE SHOULD WE GO ON SUNDAY?
MUST-VISIT DESTINATIONS!
LET ME TAKE A LOOK.
WOW, ALL OF THESE PLACES LOOK FUN.
I just can't decide.
Hmm.
Oh that's very tempting.
BUMP
TWITCH
!!
TOKYO SPOT

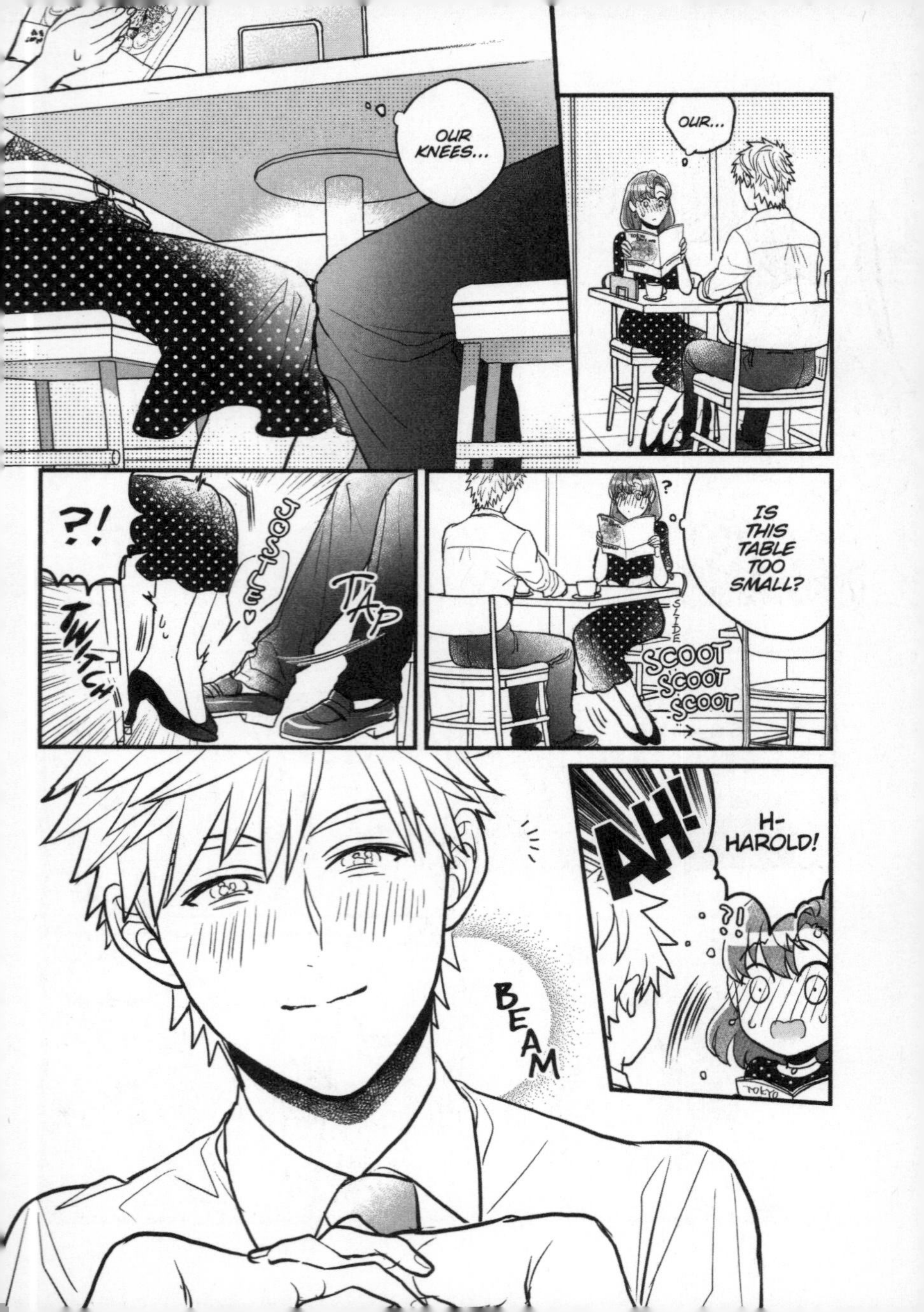

OUR...
OUR KNEES...
?
IS THIS TABLE TOO SMALL?
SLIDE
SCOOT SCOOT SCOOT
?!
JOSTLE
TAP
TWITCH
AH!
H-HAROLD!
?!
BEAM

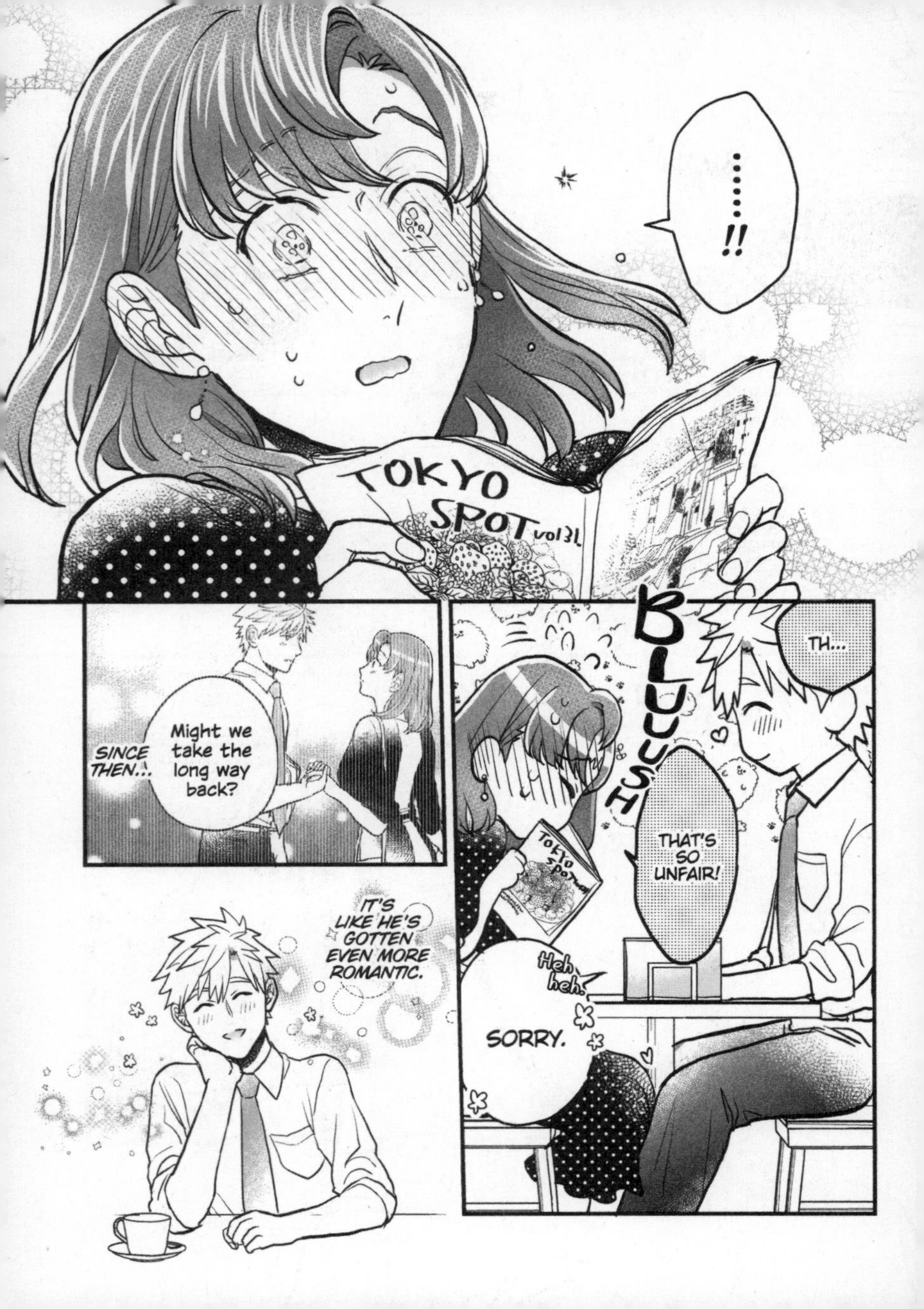
......!!
TOKYO SPOT
TH...
BLUUUSH
THAT'S SO UNFAIR!
Heh heh.
SORRY.
SINCE THEN...
Might we take the long way back?
IT'S LIKE HE'S GOTTEN EVEN MORE ROMANTIC.

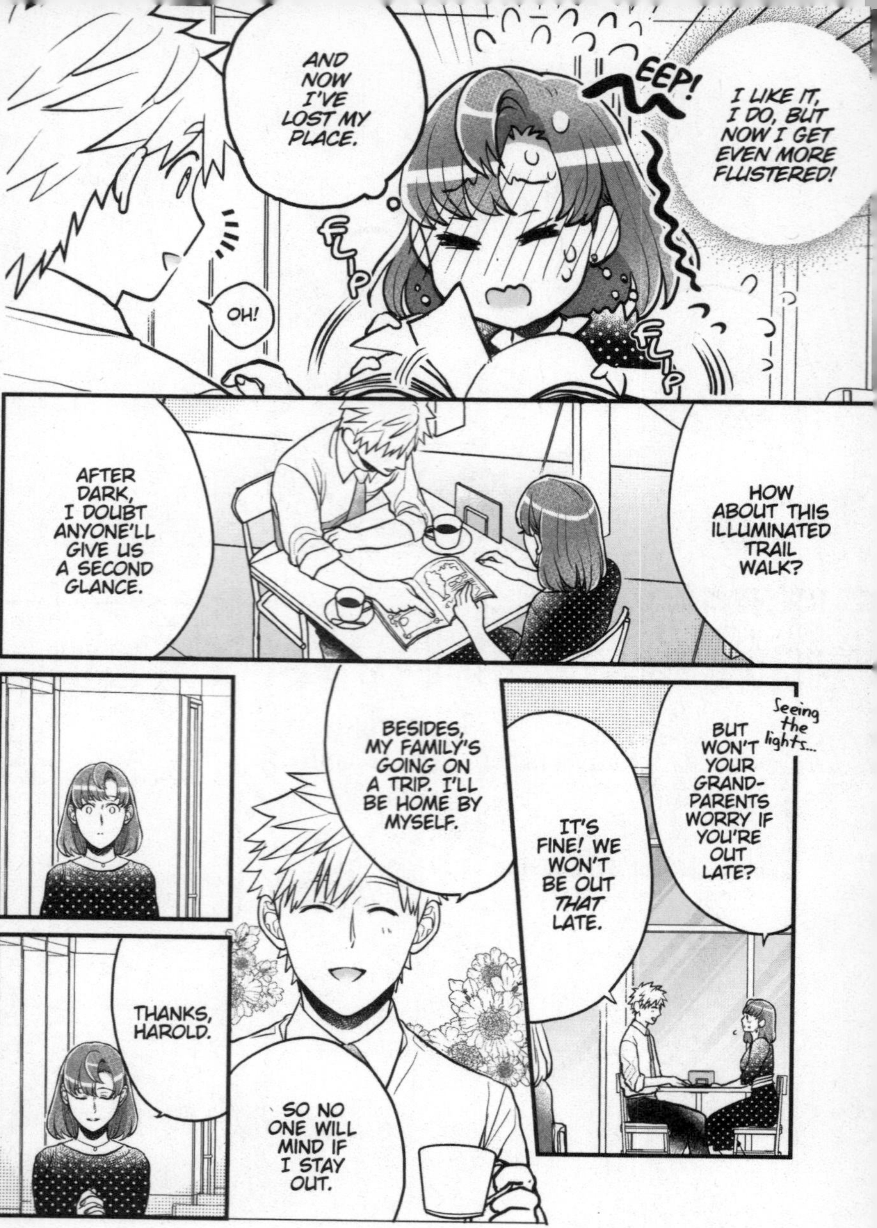
I LIKE IT, I DO, BUT NOW I GET EVEN MORE FLUSTERED!
EEP!
AND NOW I'VE LOST MY PLACE.
FLIP
FLIP
OH!
HOW ABOUT THIS ILLUMINATED TRAIL WALK?
AFTER DARK, I DOUBT ANYONE'LL GIVE US A SECOND GLANCE.
BUT WON'T YOUR GRANDPARENTS WORRY IF YOU'RE OUT LATE?
Seeing the lights...
IT'S FINE! WE WON'T BE OUT THAT LATE.
BESIDES, MY FAMILY'S GOING ON A TRIP. I'LL BE HOME BY MYSELF.
SO NO ONE WILL MIND IF I STAY OUT.
THANKS, HAROLD.

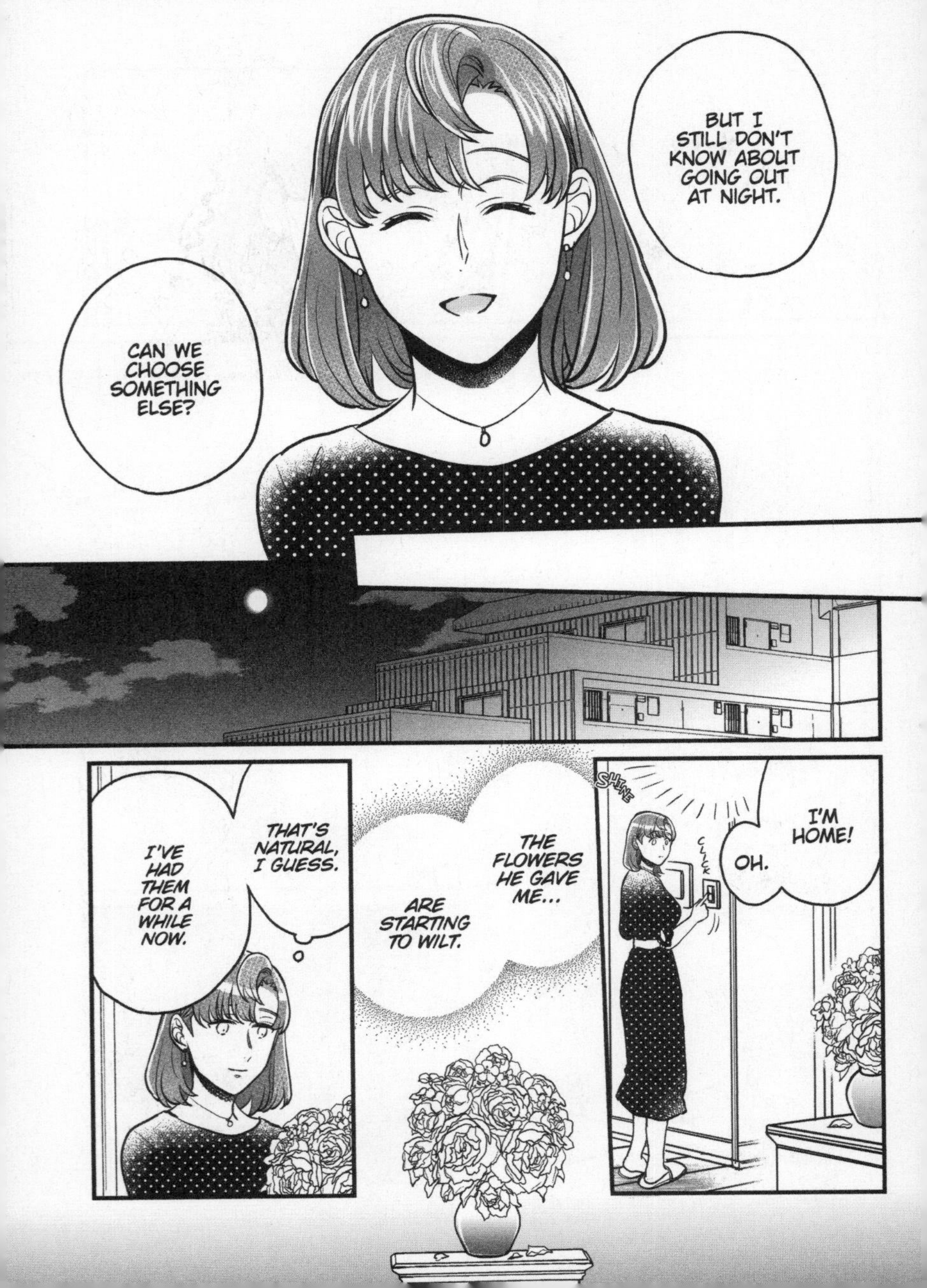
BUT I STILL DON'T KNOW ABOUT GOING OUT AT NIGHT.
CAN WE CHOOSE SOMETHING ELSE?
SHINE
I'M HOME!
CLICK
OH.
THE FLOWERS HE GAVE ME...
ARE STARTING TO WILT.
THAT'S NATURAL, I GUESS.
I'VE HAD THEM FOR A WHILE NOW.

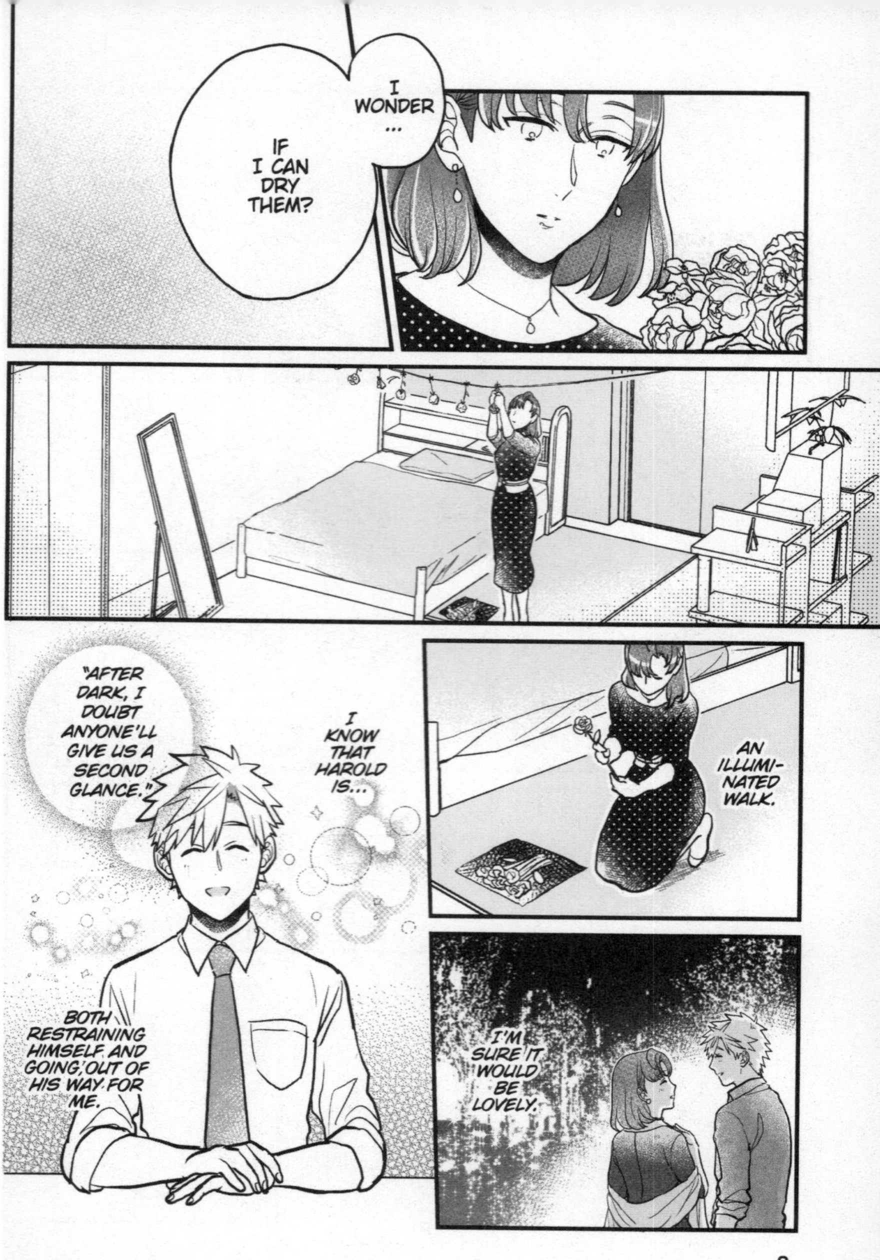
I WONDER ...
IF I CAN DRY THEM?
AN ILLUMINATED WALK.
"AFTER DARK, I DOUBT ANYONE'LL GIVE US A SECOND GLANCE."
I KNOW THAT HAROLD IS...
BOTH RESTRAINING HIMSELF AND GOING OUT OF HIS WAY FOR ME.
I'M SURE IT WOULD BE LOVELY.

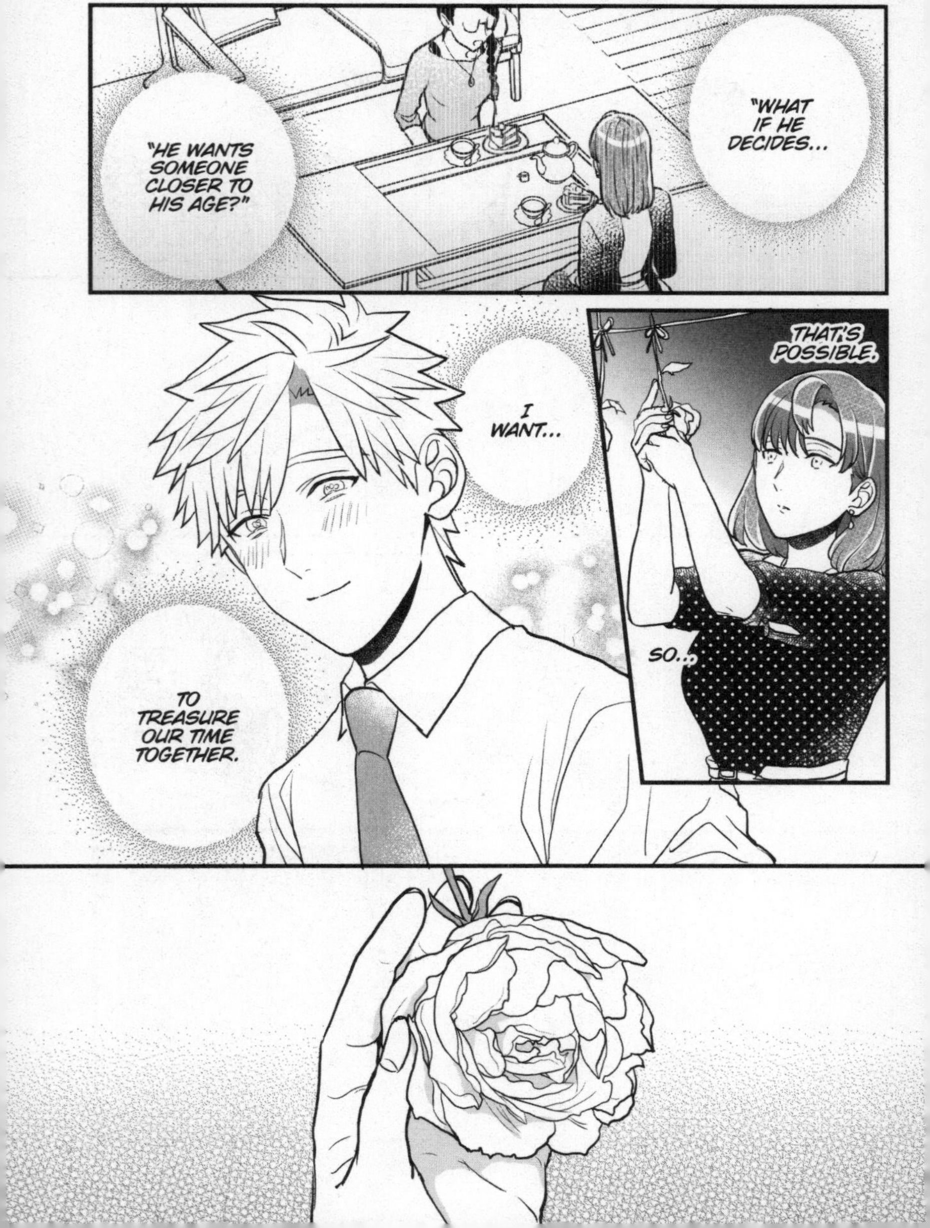
"WHAT IF HE DECIDES...
"HE WANTS SOMEONE CLOSER TO HIS AGE?"
THAT'S POSSIBLE.
SO...
I WANT...
TO TREASURE OUR TIME TOGETHER.

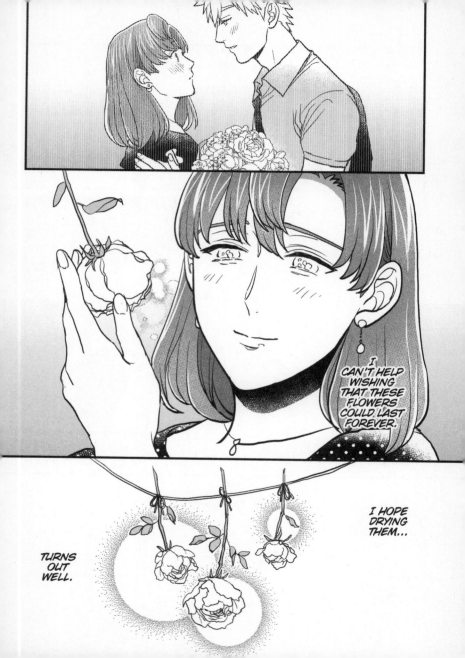

I CAN'T HELP WISHING THAT THESE FLOWERS COULD LAST FOREVER.

I HOPE DRYING THEM...

TURNS OUT WELL.

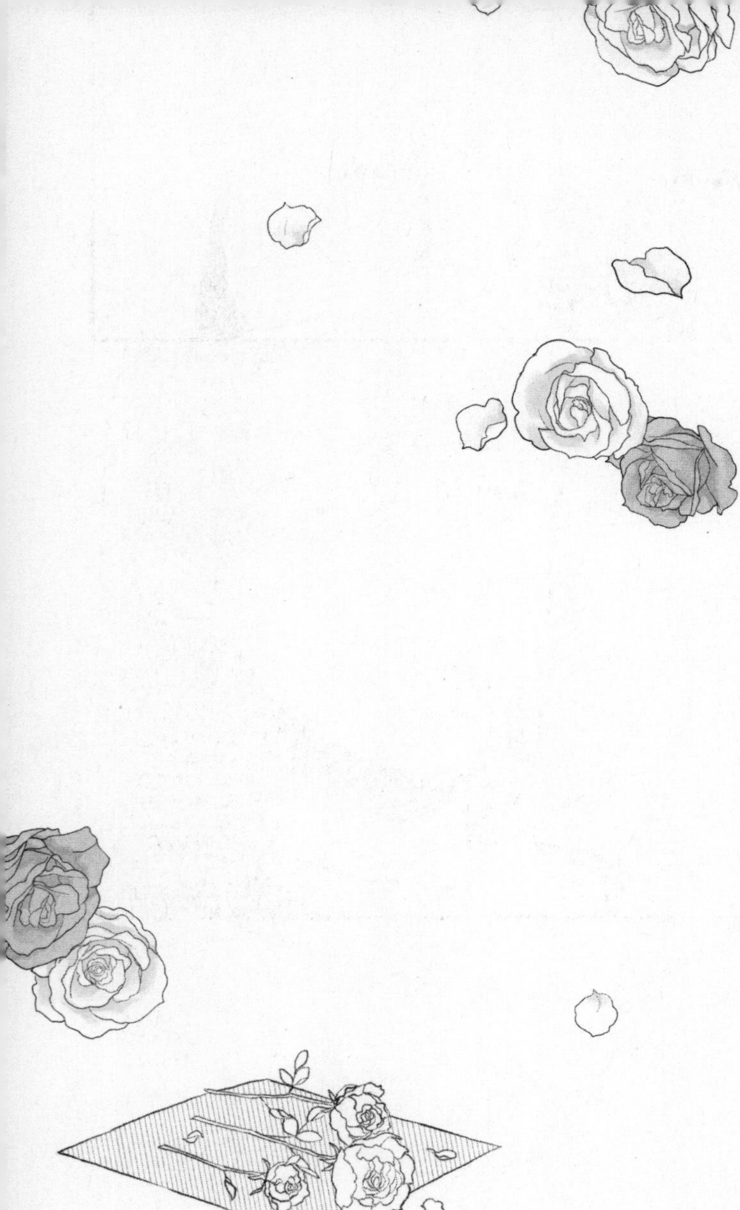

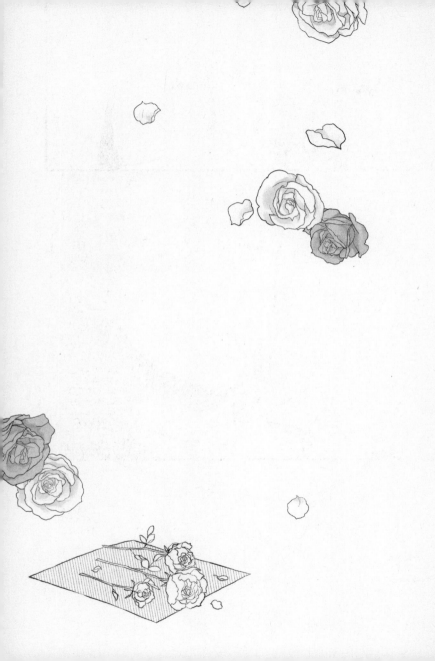

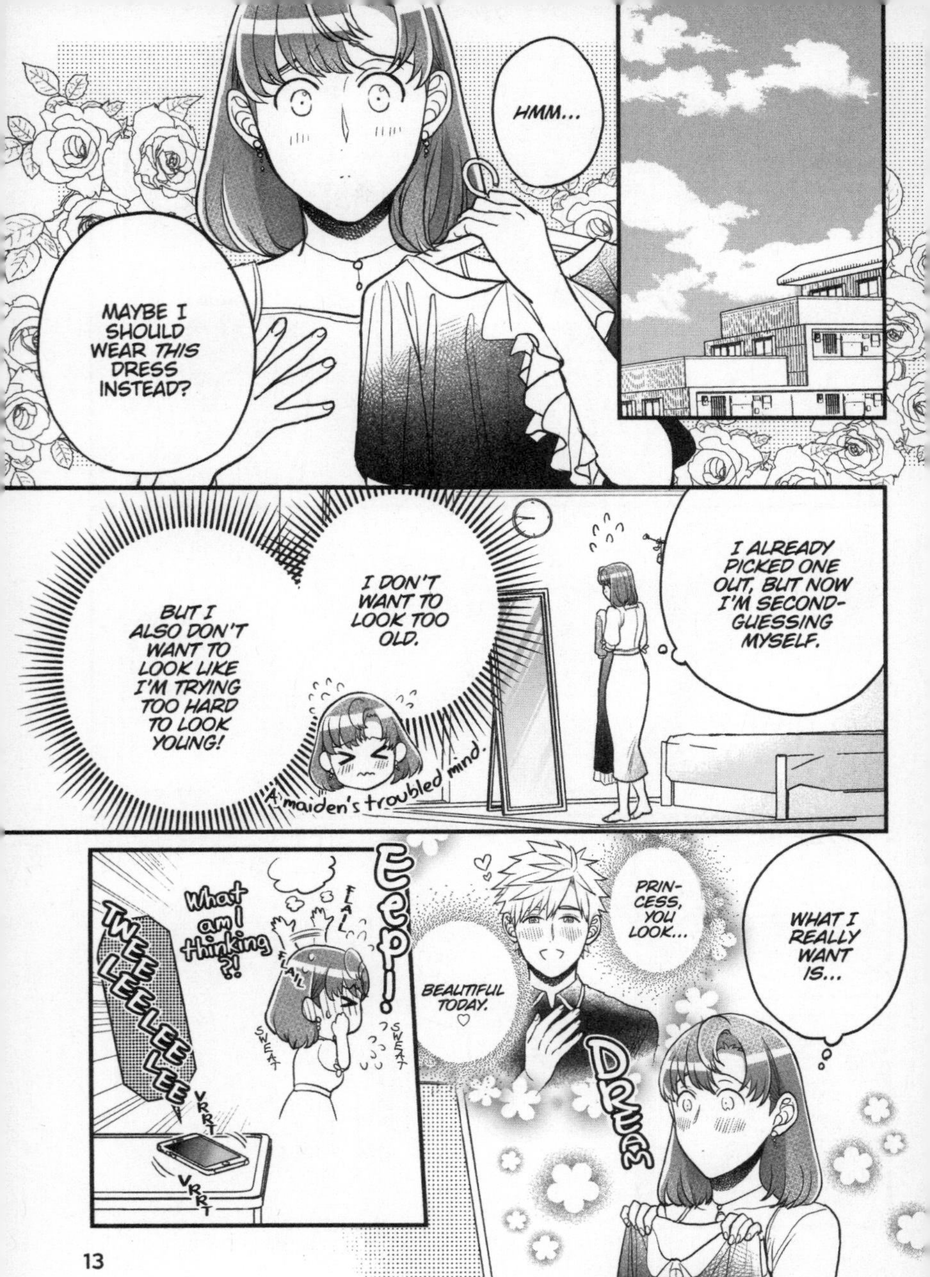
HMM...
MAYBE I SHOULD WEAR THIS DRESS INSTEAD?
I ALREADY PICKED ONE OUT, BUT NOW I'M SECOND-GUESSING MYSELF.
I DON'T WANT TO LOOK TOO OLD.
BUT I ALSO DON'T WANT TO LOOK LIKE I'M TRYING TOO HARD TO LOOK YOUNG!
A maiden's troubled mind.
WHAT I REALLY WANT IS...
PRINCESS, YOU LOOK...
BEAUTIFUL TODAY.
DREAMS
Eep!
FLAIL
FLAIL
What am I thinking?!
SWEAT
SWEAT
TWEELEELEELEELEE
VRRT
VRRT

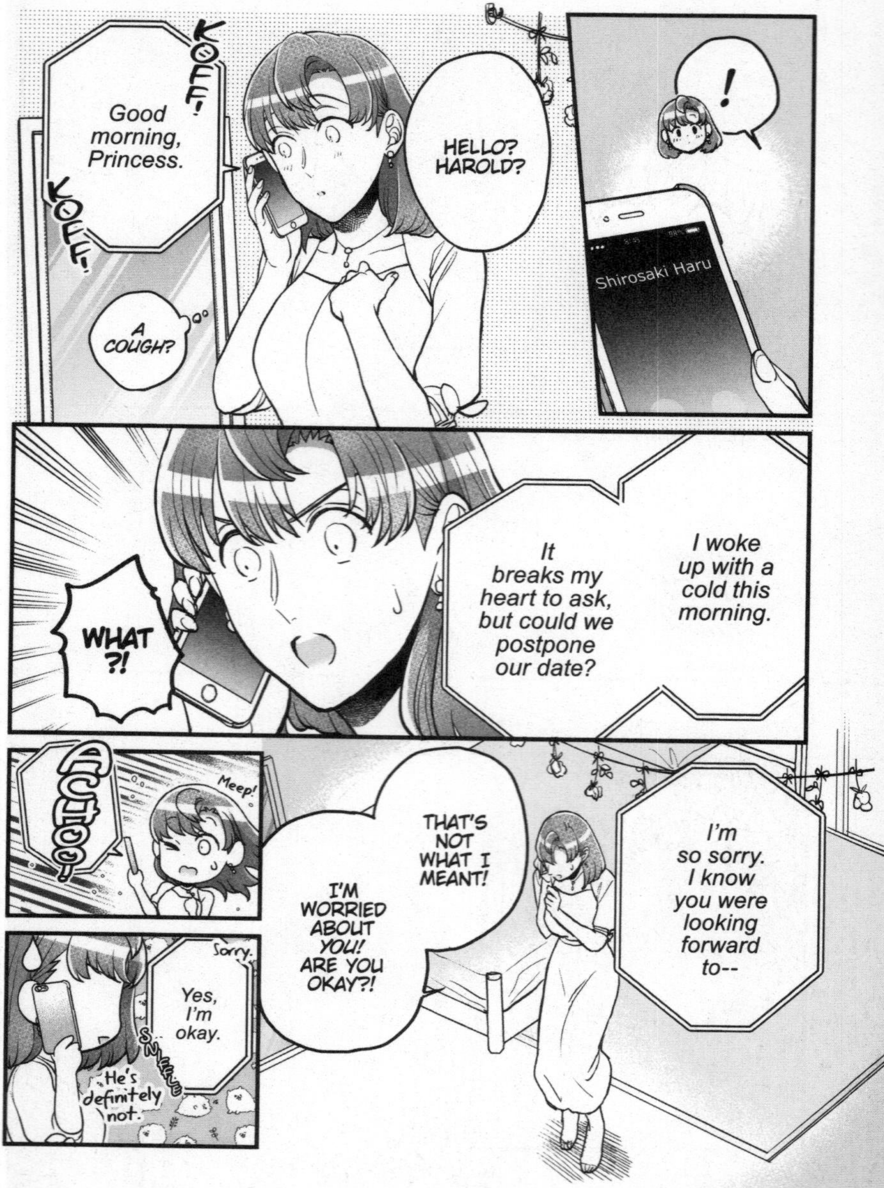
!
Shirosaki Haru
HELLO? HAROLD?
KOFF!
Good morning, Princess.
KOFF!
A COUGH?
I woke up with a cold this morning.
It breaks my heart to ask, but could we postpone our date?
WHAT ?!
I'm so sorry. I know you were looking forward to--
THAT'S NOT WHAT I MEANT!
I'M WORRIED ABOUT YOU! ARE YOU OKAY?!
ACHOO!
Meep!
Sorry.
Yes, I'm okay.
SNIFFLE
He's definitely not.

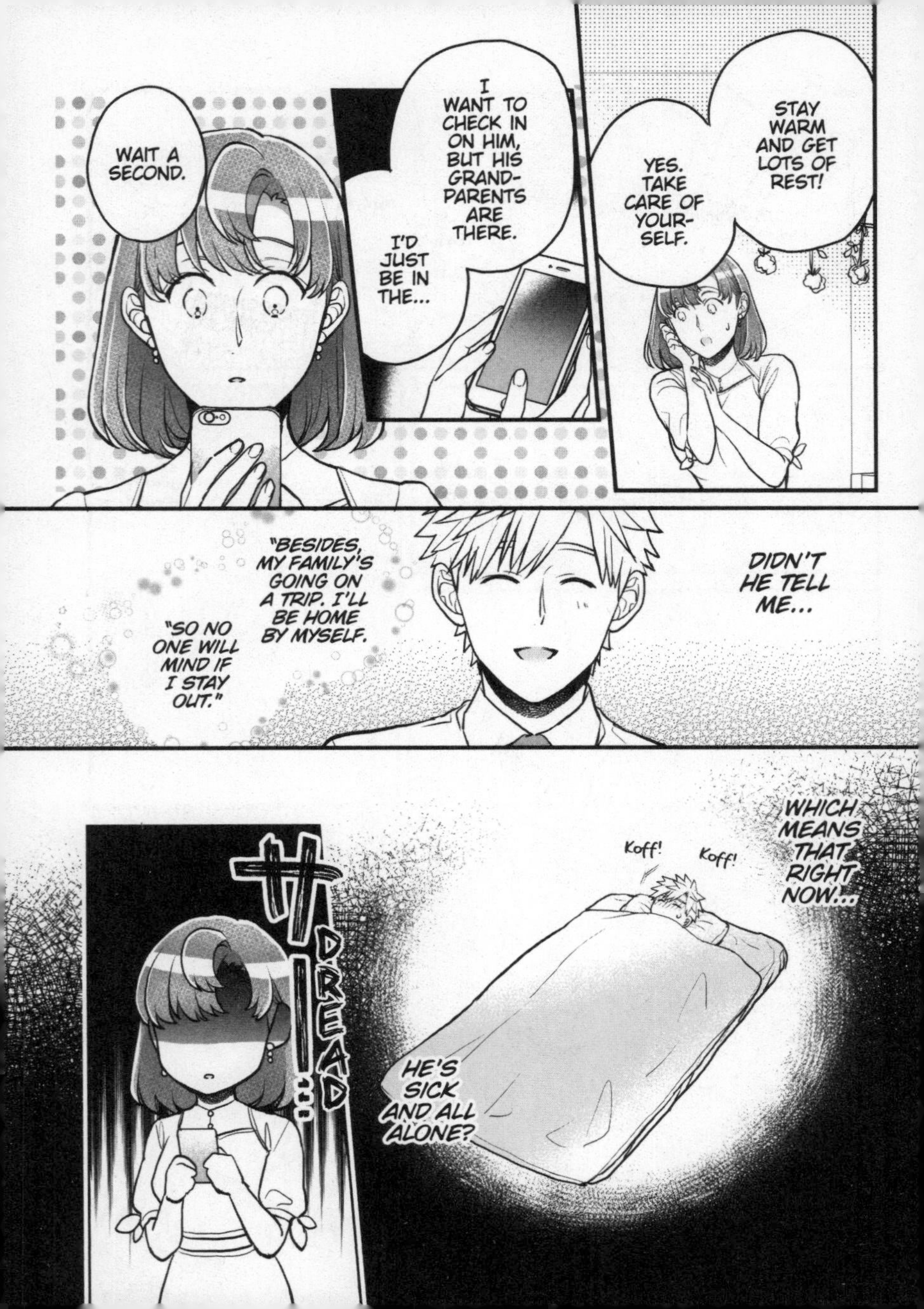
STAY WARM AND GET LOTS OF REST!
YES. TAKE CARE OF YOUR-SELF.
I WANT TO CHECK IN ON HIM, BUT HIS GRAND-PARENTS ARE THERE.
I'D JUST BE IN THE...
WAIT A SECOND.
DIDN'T HE TELL ME...
"BESIDES, MY FAMILY'S GOING ON A TRIP. I'LL BE HOME BY MYSELF.
"SO NO ONE WILL MIND IF I STAY OUT."
WHICH MEANS THAT RIGHT NOW...
Koff!
Koff!
HE'S SICK AND ALL ALONE?
DREAD...

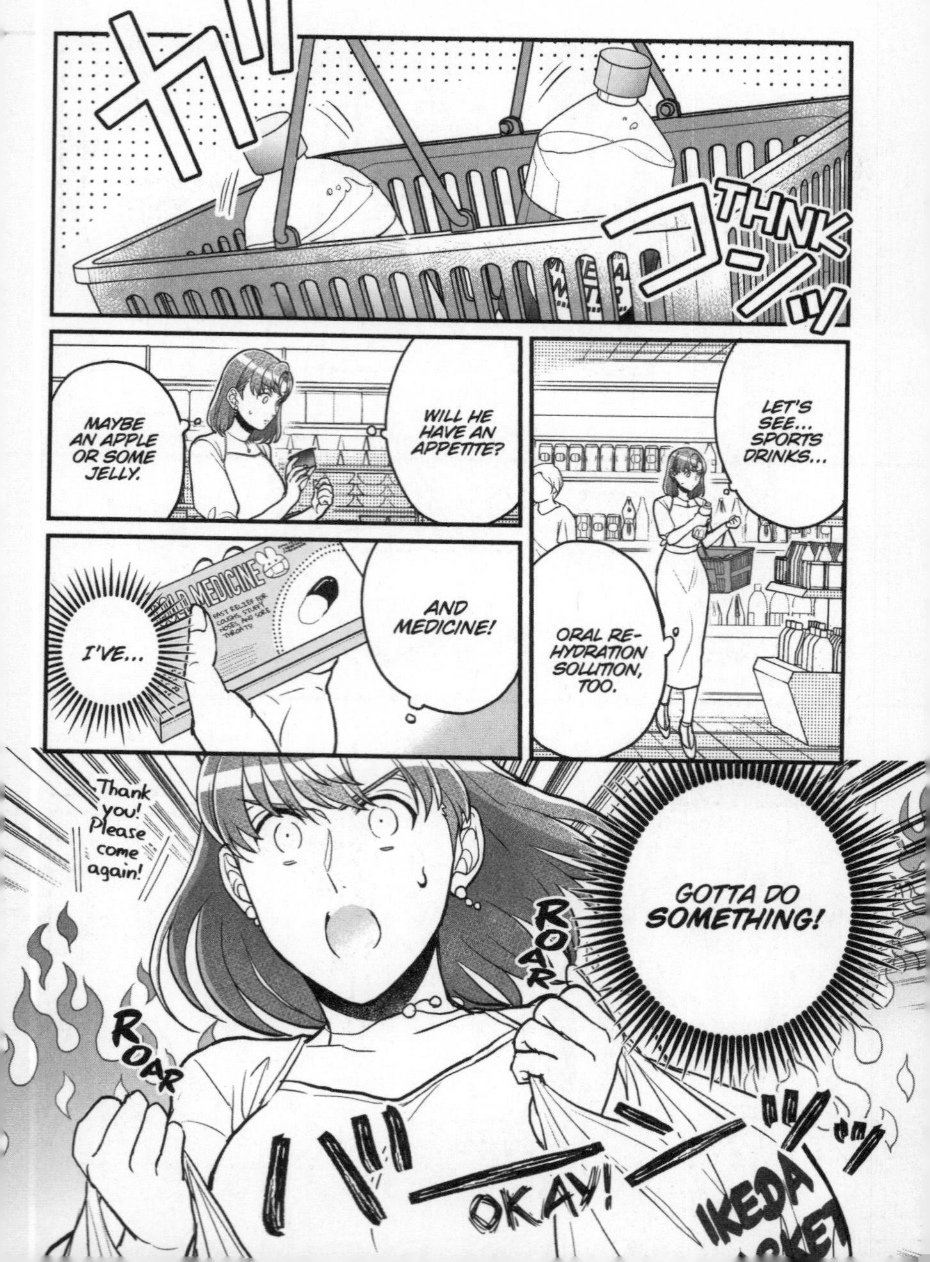
THNK
LET'S SEE... SPORTS DRINKS...
ORAL RE-HYDRATION SOLUTION, TOO.
WILL HE HAVE AN APPETITE?
MAYBE AN APPLE OR SOME JELLY.
COLD MEDICINE
FAST RELIEF FOR COUGHS, STUFFY NOSES, AND SORE THROATS!
AND MEDICINE!
I'VE...
GOTTA DO SOMETHING!
ROAR
ROAR
Thank you! Please come again!
OKAY!
IKEDA

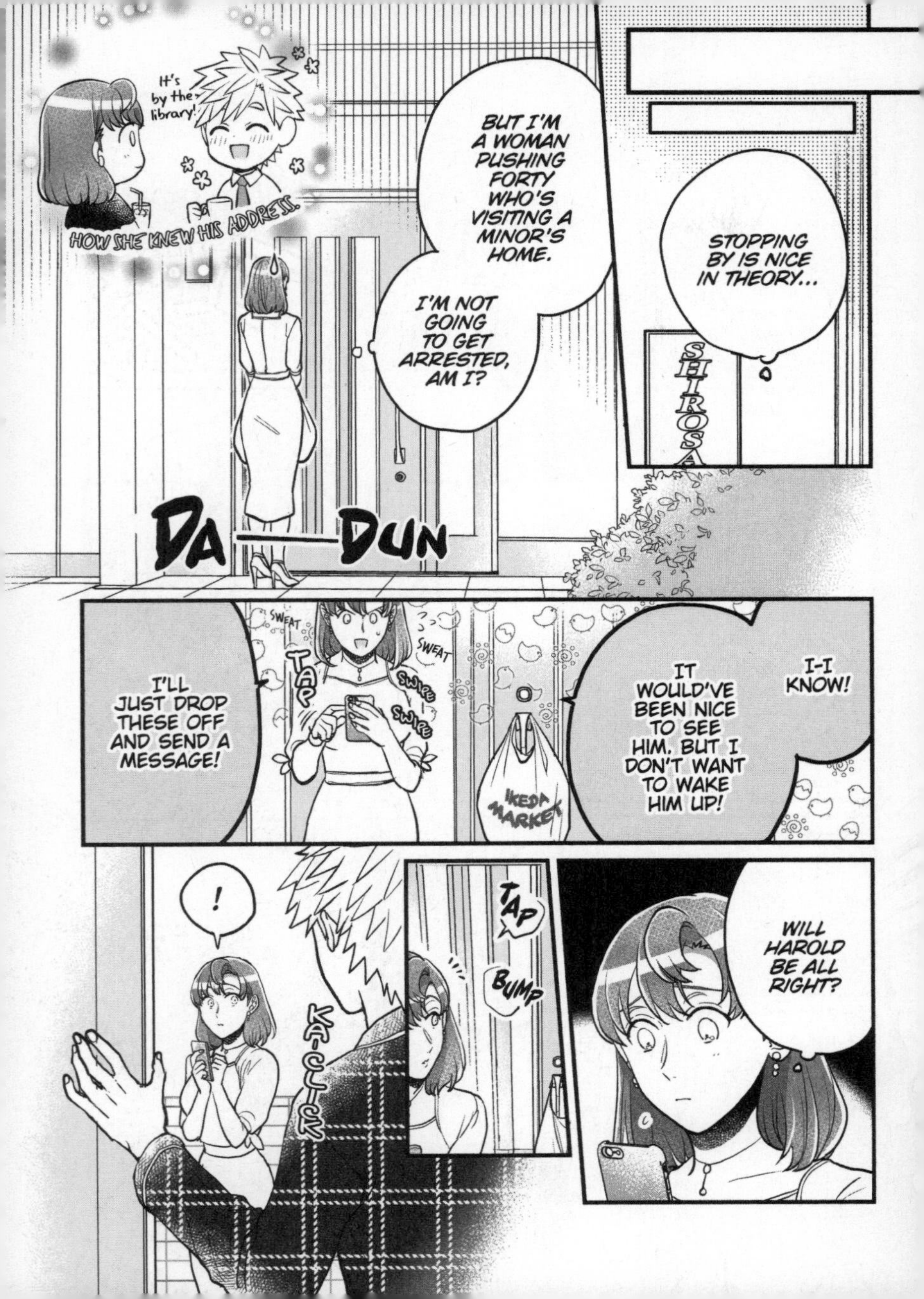
SHIROSA
STOPPING BY IS NICE IN THEORY...
BUT I'M A WOMAN PUSHING FORTY WHO'S VISITING A MINOR'S HOME.
I'M NOT GOING TO GET ARRESTED, AM I?
It's by the library!
HOW SHE KNEW HIS ADDRESS.
DA—DUN
I-I KNOW!
IT WOULD'VE BEEN NICE TO SEE HIM, BUT I DON'T WANT TO WAKE HIM UP!
SWEAT
SWEAT
SWIPE
SWIPE
TAP
I'LL JUST DROP THESE OFF AND SEND A MESSAGE!
IKEDA MARKET
WILL HAROLD BE ALL RIGHT?
TAP
BUMP
KA-CLICK
!

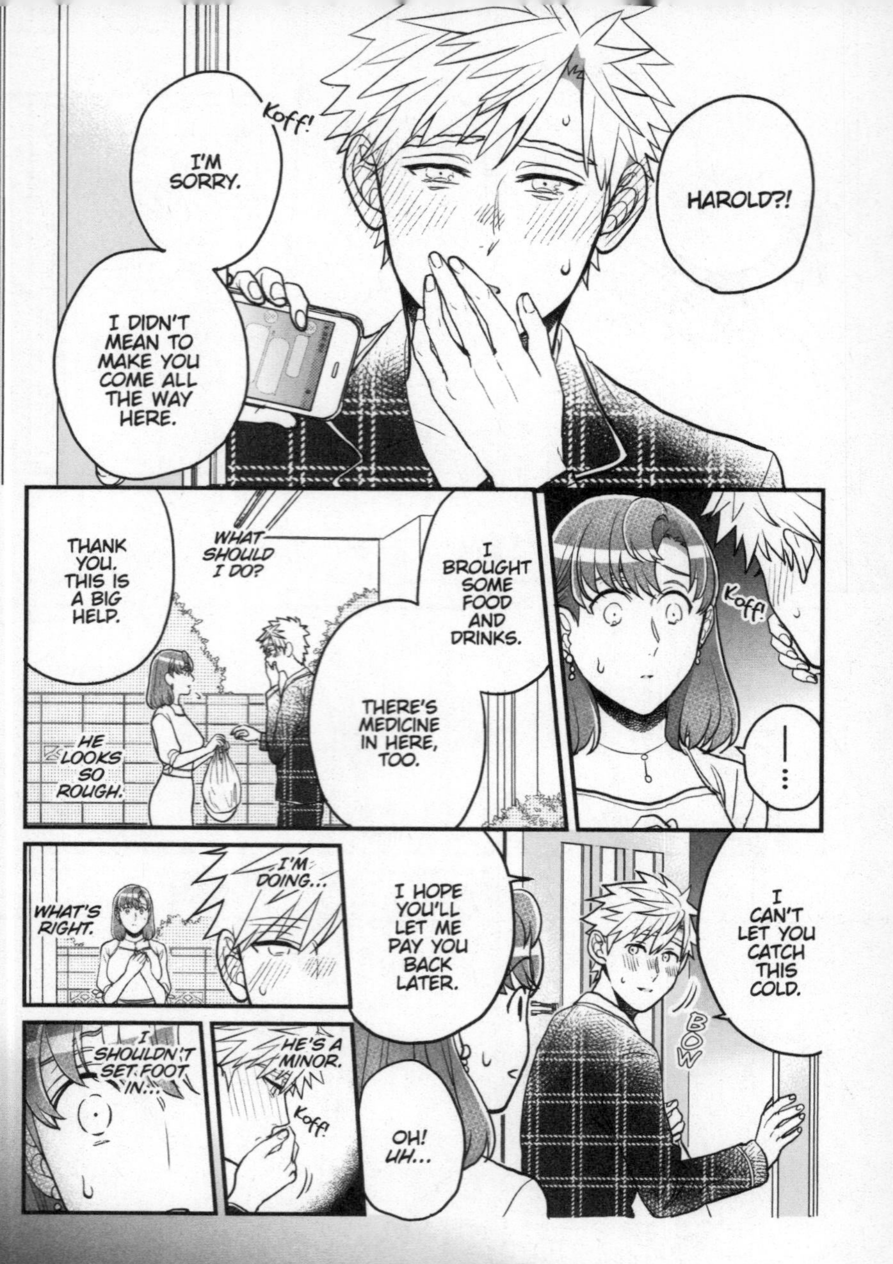
HAROLD?!
Koff!
I'M SORRY.
I DIDN'T MEAN TO MAKE YOU COME ALL THE WAY HERE.
Koff!
—...
I BROUGHT SOME FOOD AND DRINKS.
THERE'S MEDICINE IN HERE, TOO.
THANK YOU. THIS IS A BIG HELP.
WHAT SHOULD I DO?
HE LOOKS SO ROUGH.
I CAN'T LET YOU CATCH THIS COLD.
BOW
I HOPE YOU'LL LET ME PAY YOU BACK LATER.
I'M DOING...
WHAT'S RIGHT.
OH! UH...
HE'S A MINOR.
Koff!
I SHOULDN'T SET FOOT IN...

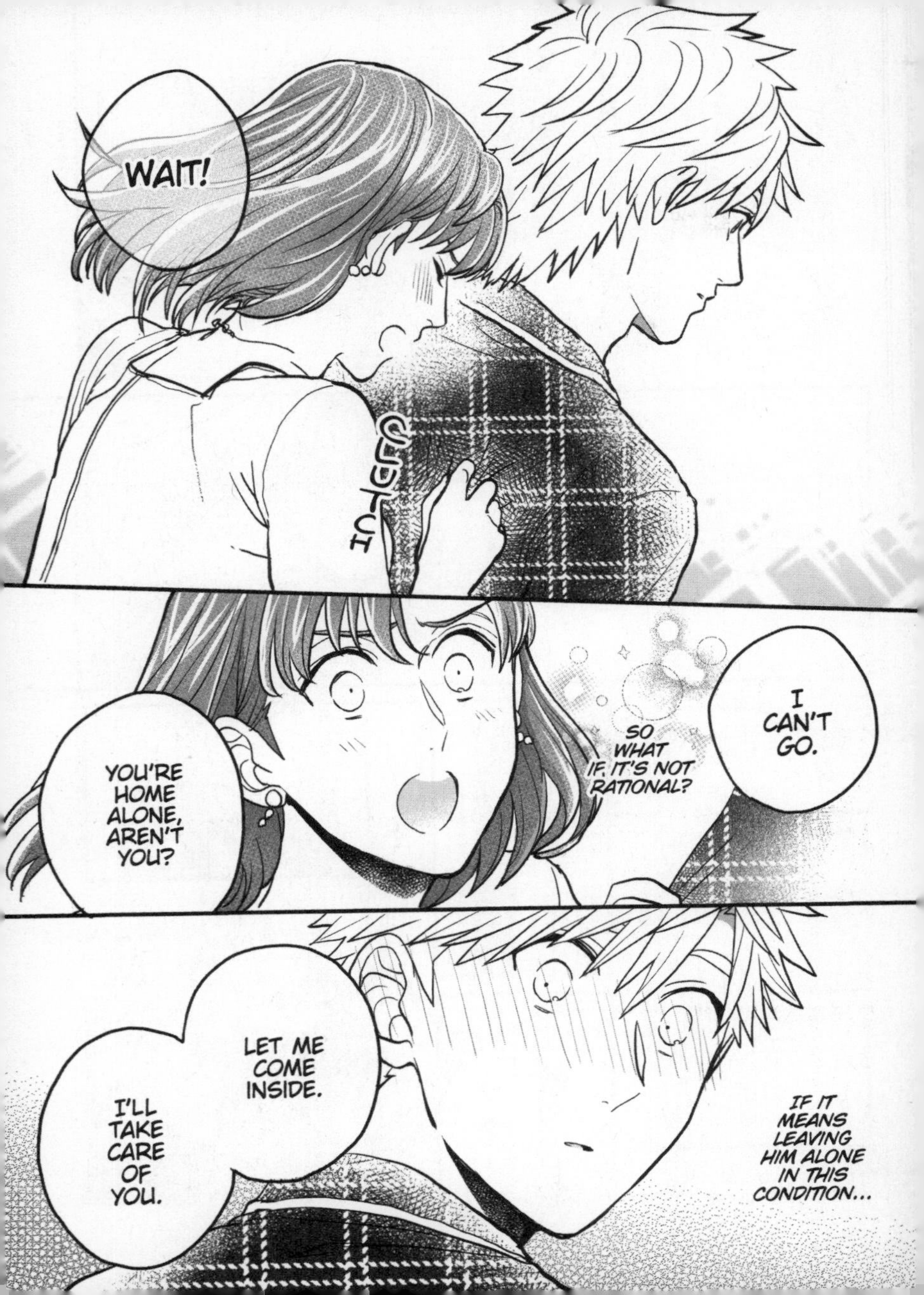
WAIT!
CLUTCH
I CAN'T GO.
SO WHAT IF IT'S NOT RATIONAL?
YOU'RE HOME ALONE, AREN'T YOU?
IF IT MEANS LEAVING HIM ALONE IN THIS CONDITION...
LET ME COME INSIDE.
I'LL TAKE CARE OF YOU.

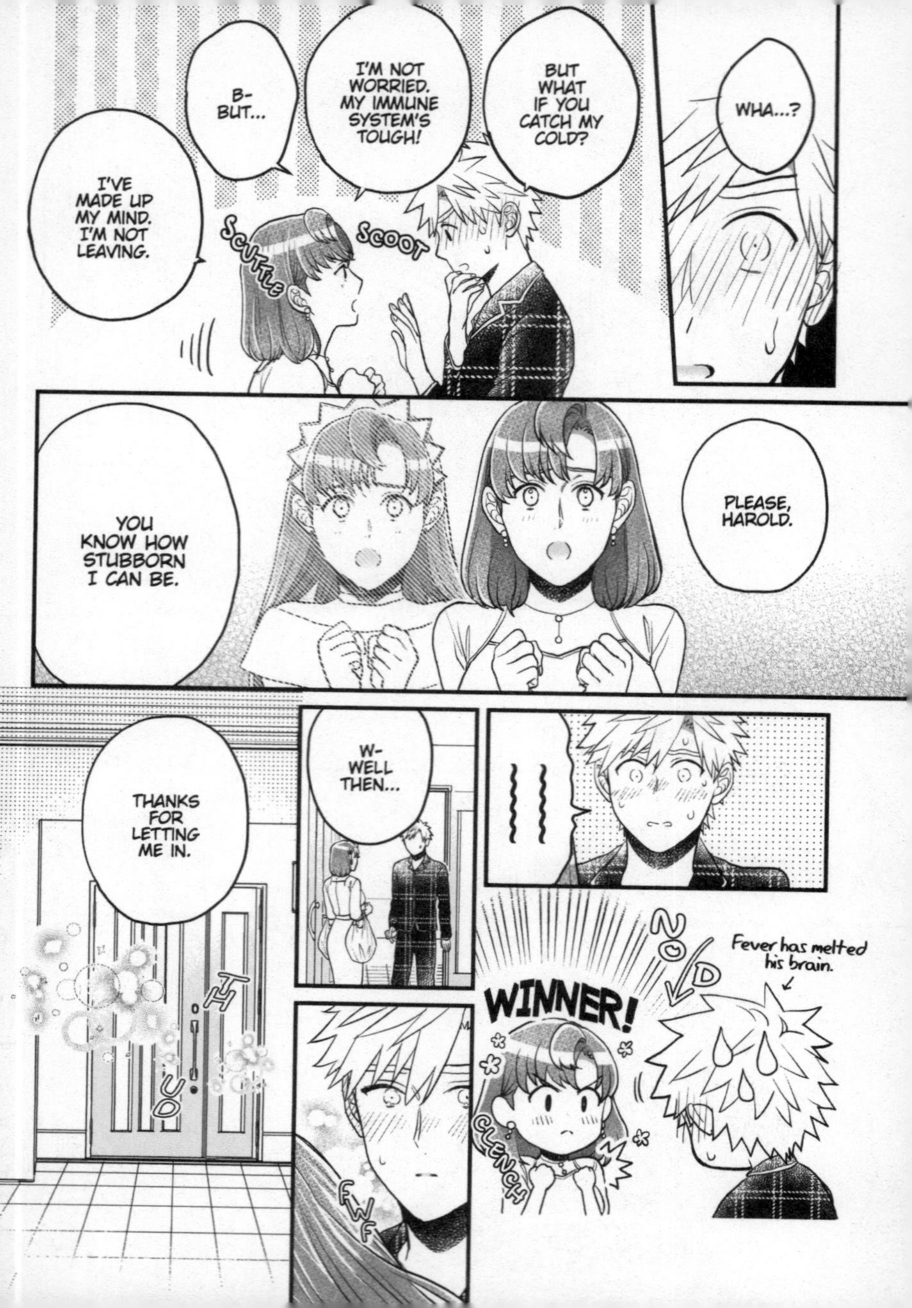
WHA...?
BUT WHAT IF YOU CATCH MY COLD?
I'M NOT WORRIED. MY IMMUNE SYSTEM'S TOUGH!
B-BUT...
SCOOT
SCUTTLE
I'VE MADE UP MY MIND. I'M NOT LEAVING.
PLEASE, HAROLD.
YOU KNOW HOW STUBBORN I CAN BE.
W-WELL THEN...
NOD
WINNER!
Fever has melted his brain.
CLENCH
FWF
THUD
THANKS FOR LETTING ME IN.

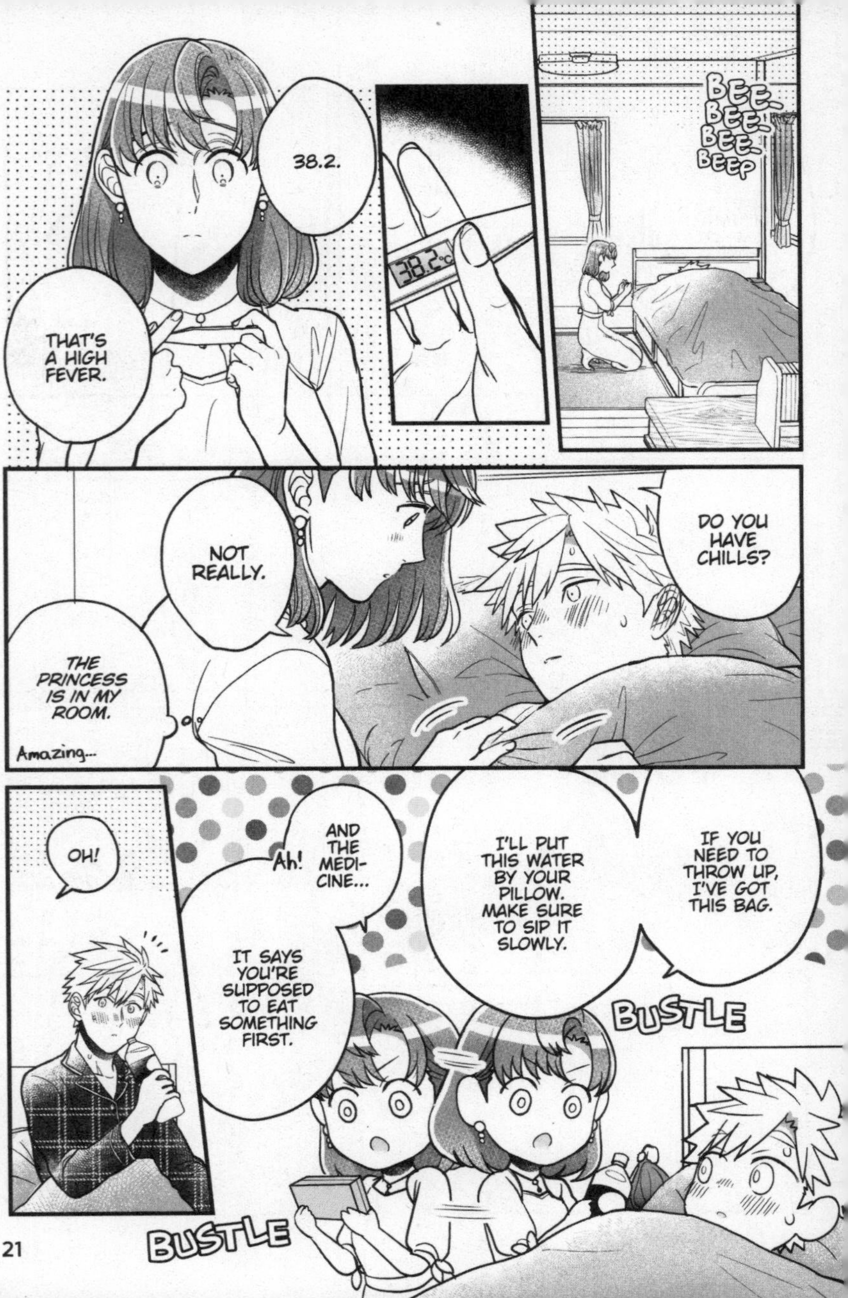

BEE-BEE-BEE-BEEP
38.2°C
38.2.
THAT'S A HIGH FEVER.
DO YOU HAVE CHILLS?
NOT REALLY.
THE PRINCESS IS IN MY ROOM.
Amazing...
IF YOU NEED TO THROW UP, I'VE GOT THIS BAG.
I'LL PUT THIS WATER BY YOUR PILLOW. MAKE SURE TO SIP IT SLOWLY.
Ah!
AND THE MEDICINE...
IT SAYS YOU'RE SUPPOSED TO EAT SOMETHING FIRST.
BUSTLE
BUSTLE
OH!

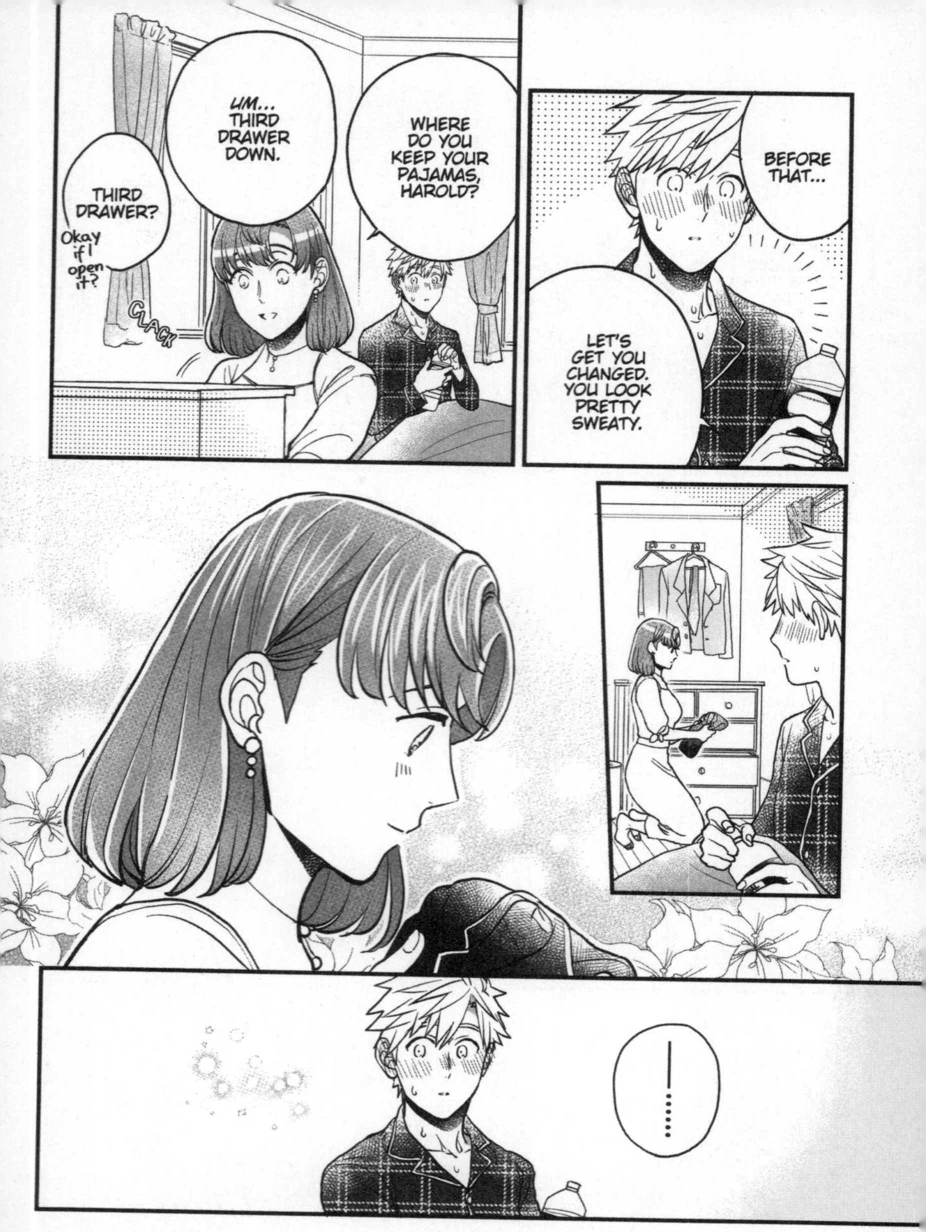
BEFORE THAT...
LET'S GET YOU CHANGED. YOU LOOK PRETTY SWEATY.
WHERE DO YOU KEEP YOUR PAJAMAS, HAROLD?
UM... THIRD DRAWER DOWN.
THIRD DRAWER?
Okay if I open it?
CLACK
—......

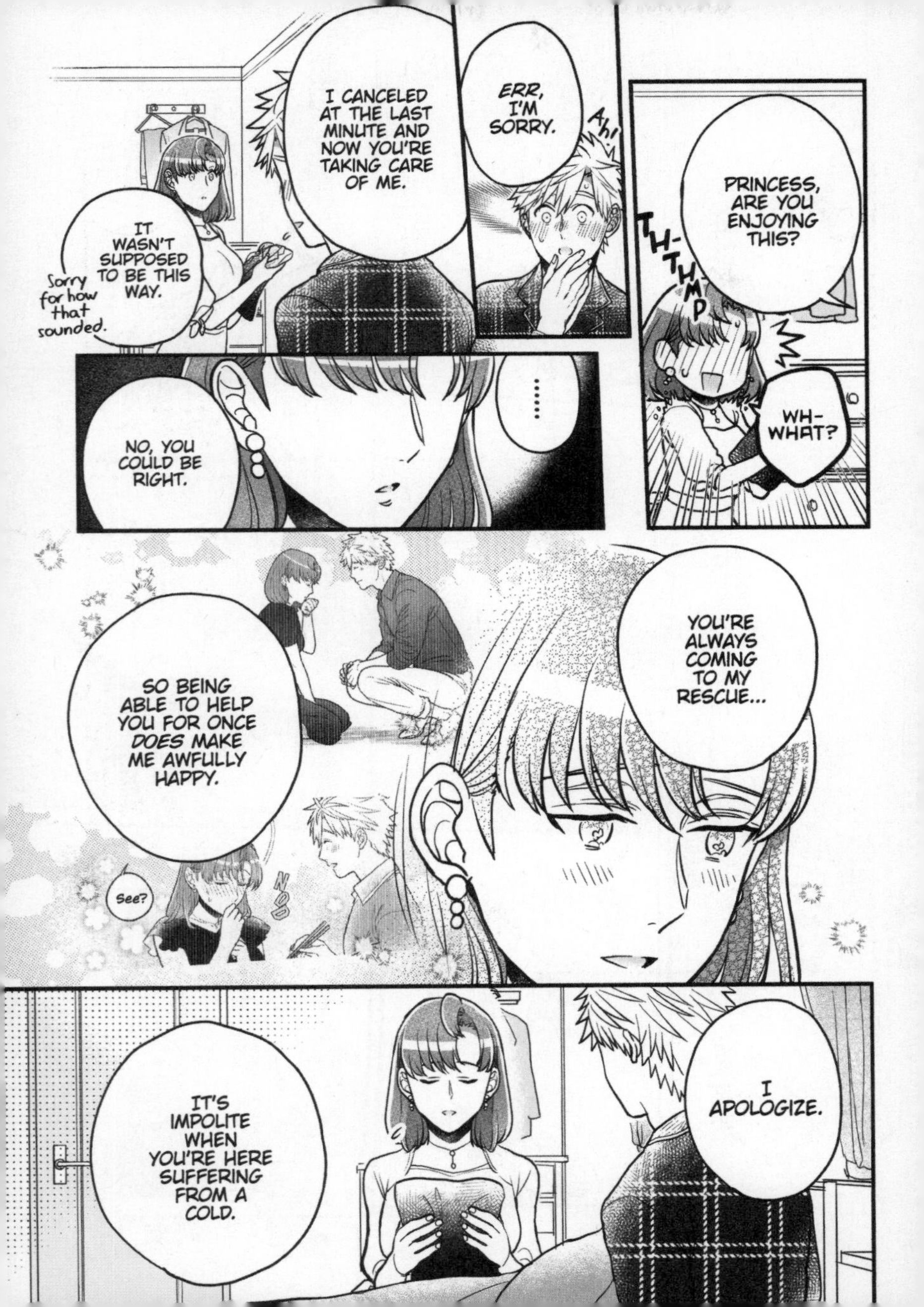
I CANCELED AT THE LAST MINUTE AND NOW YOU'RE TAKING CARE OF ME.
IT WASN'T SUPPOSED TO BE THIS WAY.
Sorry for how that sounded.
ERR, I'M SORRY.
Ah!
PRINCESS, ARE YOU ENJOYING THIS?
TH-THUMP
WH-WHAT?
......
NO, YOU COULD BE RIGHT.
YOU'RE ALWAYS COMING TO MY RESCUE...
SO BEING ABLE TO HELP YOU FOR ONCE DOES MAKE ME AWFULLY HAPPY.
See?
NOD
I APOLOGIZE.
IT'S IMPOLITE WHEN YOU'RE HERE SUFFERING FROM A COLD.

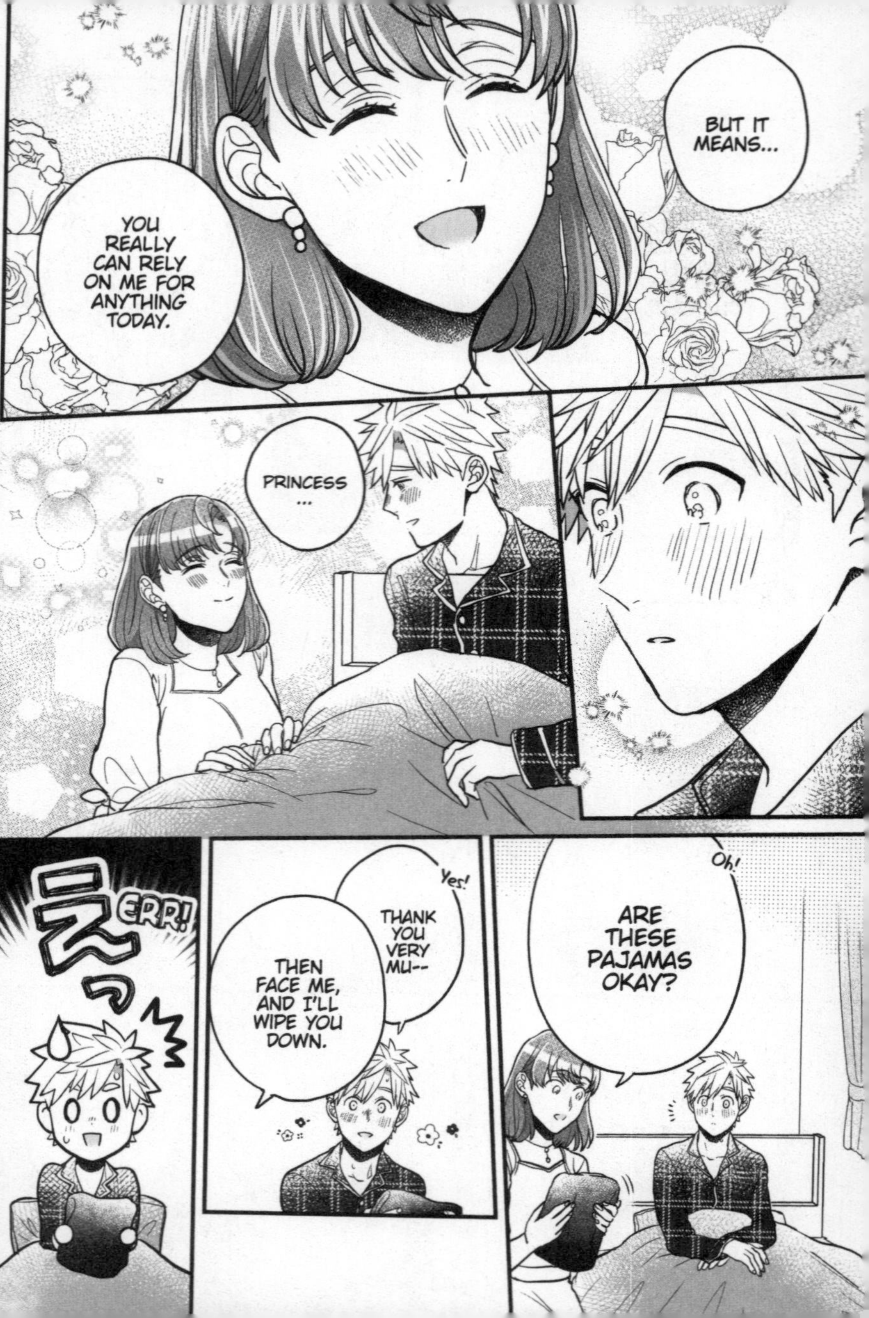
BUT IT MEANS...
YOU REALLY CAN RELY ON ME FOR ANYTHING TODAY.
PRINCESS ...
Oh!
ARE THESE PAJAMAS OKAY?
Yes!
THANK YOU VERY MU--
THEN FACE ME, AND I'LL WIPE YOU DOWN.
えっ
ERR!

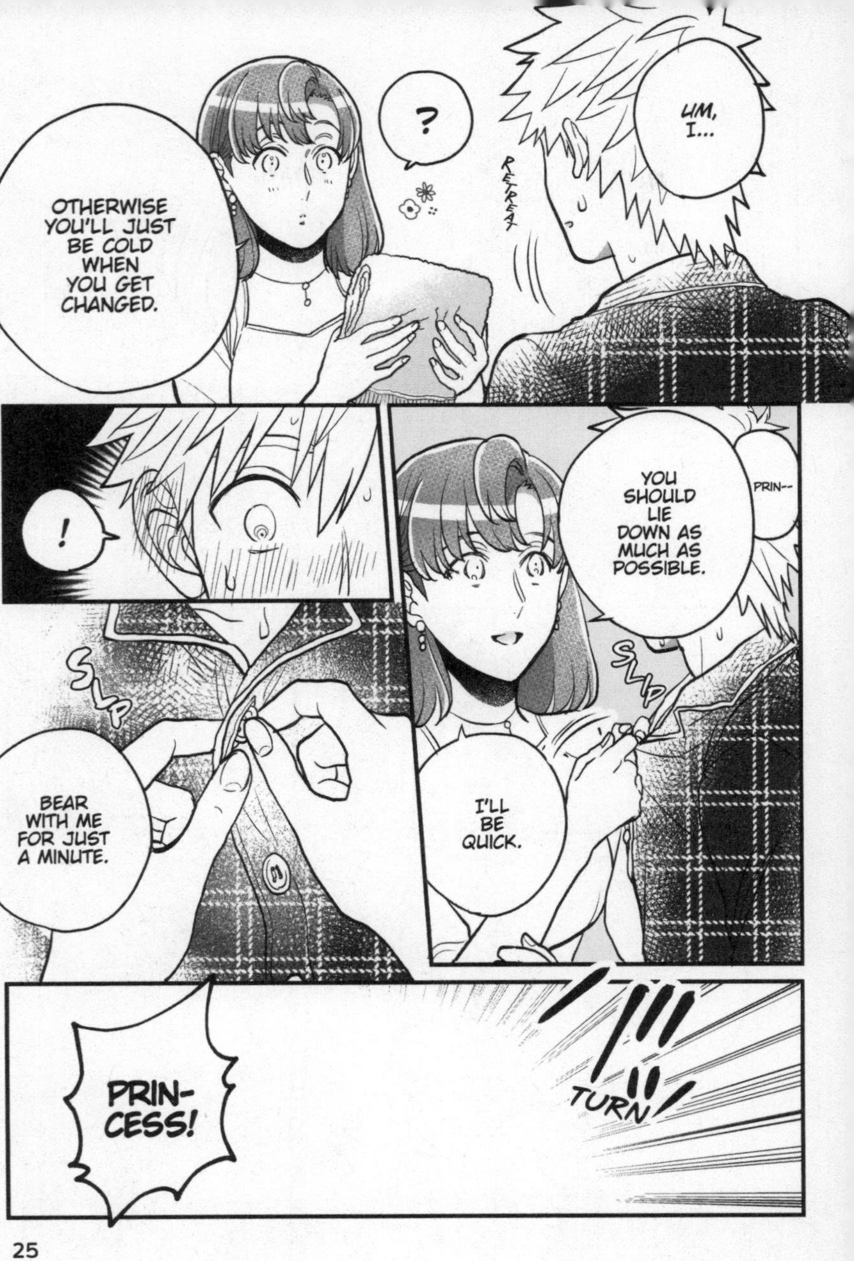
UM, I...
RETREAT
?
OTHERWISE YOU'LL JUST BE COLD WHEN YOU GET CHANGED.
PRIN--
YOU SHOULD LIE DOWN AS MUCH AS POSSIBLE.
SLIP
I'LL BE QUICK.
!
SLIP
BEAR WITH ME FOR JUST A MINUTE.
TURN
PRIN-CESS!

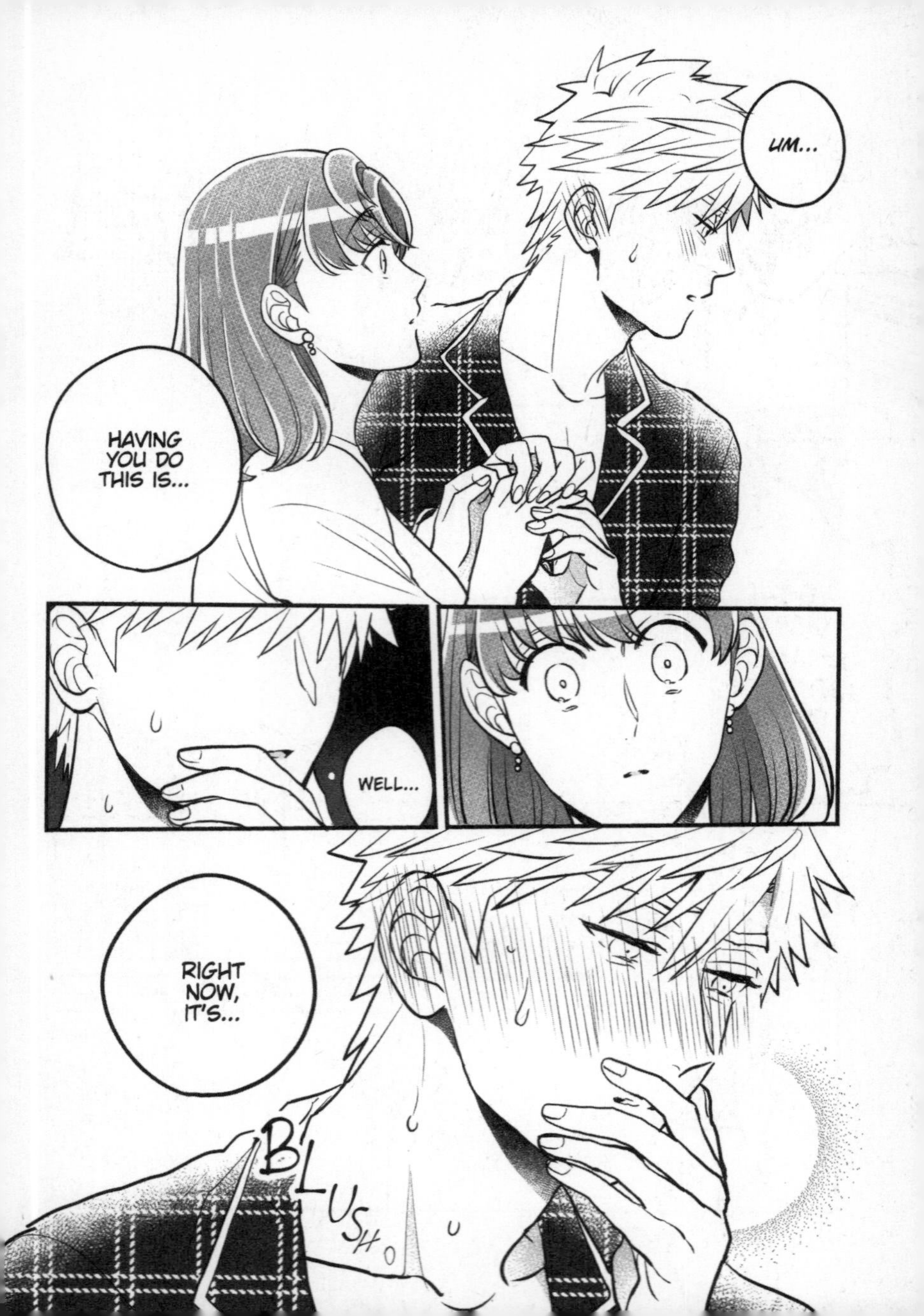
UM...
HAVING YOU DO THIS IS...
WELL...
RIGHT NOW, IT'S...
BLUSH

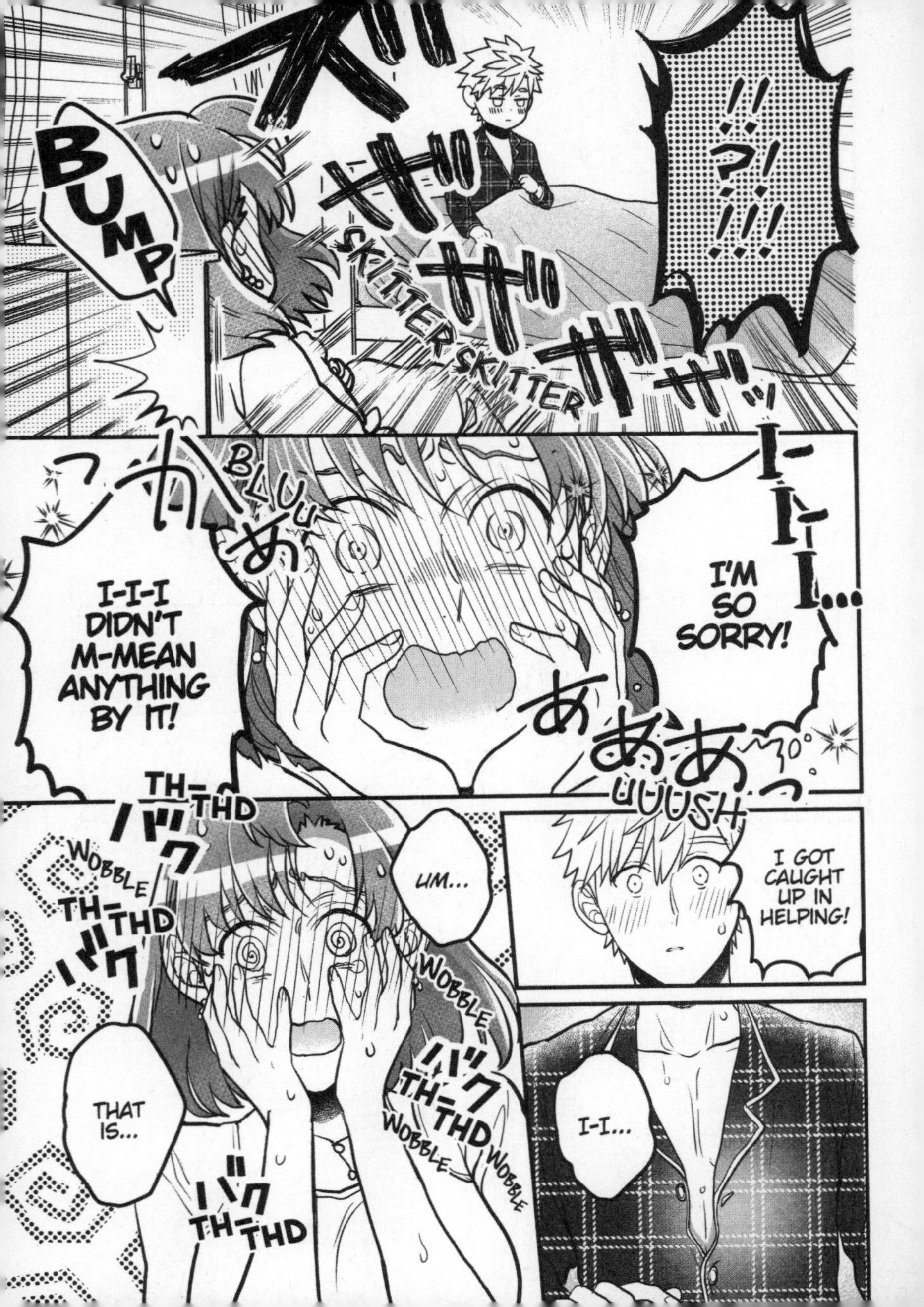

!!?!!!
ズ
BUMP
ザザ
ザザ
SKITTER SKITTER
ザザ
ザザッ
I-I-I...
I'M SO SORRY!
I-I-I DIDN'T M-MEAN ANYTHING BY IT!
わあああああっ
BLUUUUSH
TH-THD
バク
WOBBLE
UM...
I GOT CAUGHT UP IN HELPING!
THAT IS...
I-I...
WOBBLE

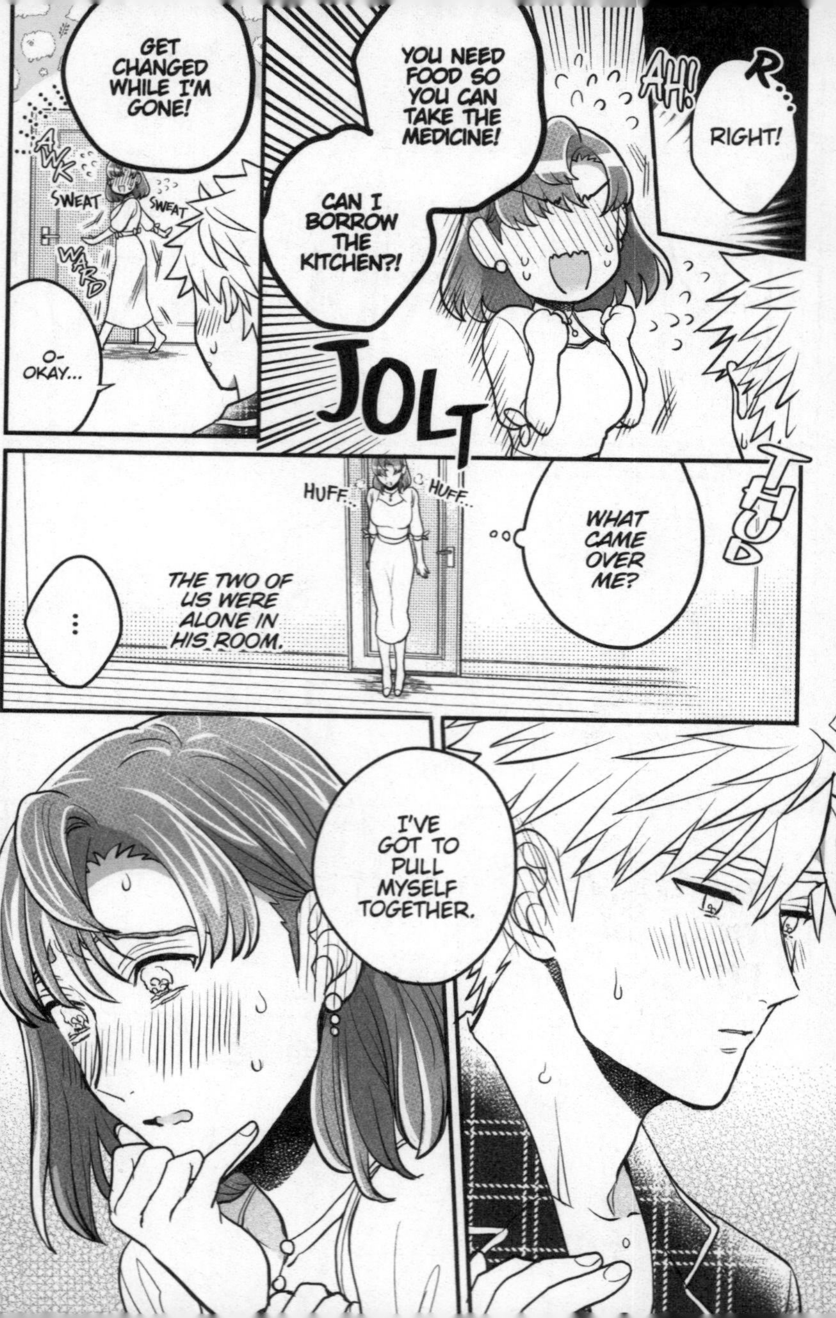
AH!
R... RIGHT!
YOU NEED FOOD SO YOU CAN TAKE THE MEDICINE!
CAN I BORROW THE KITCHEN?!
JOLT
GET CHANGED WHILE I'M GONE!
AWKWARD
SWEAT
SWEAT
O-OKAY...
THUD
WHAT CAME OVER ME?
HUFF...
HUFF...
THE TWO OF US WERE ALONE IN HIS ROOM.
...
I'VE GOT TO PULL MYSELF TOGETHER.

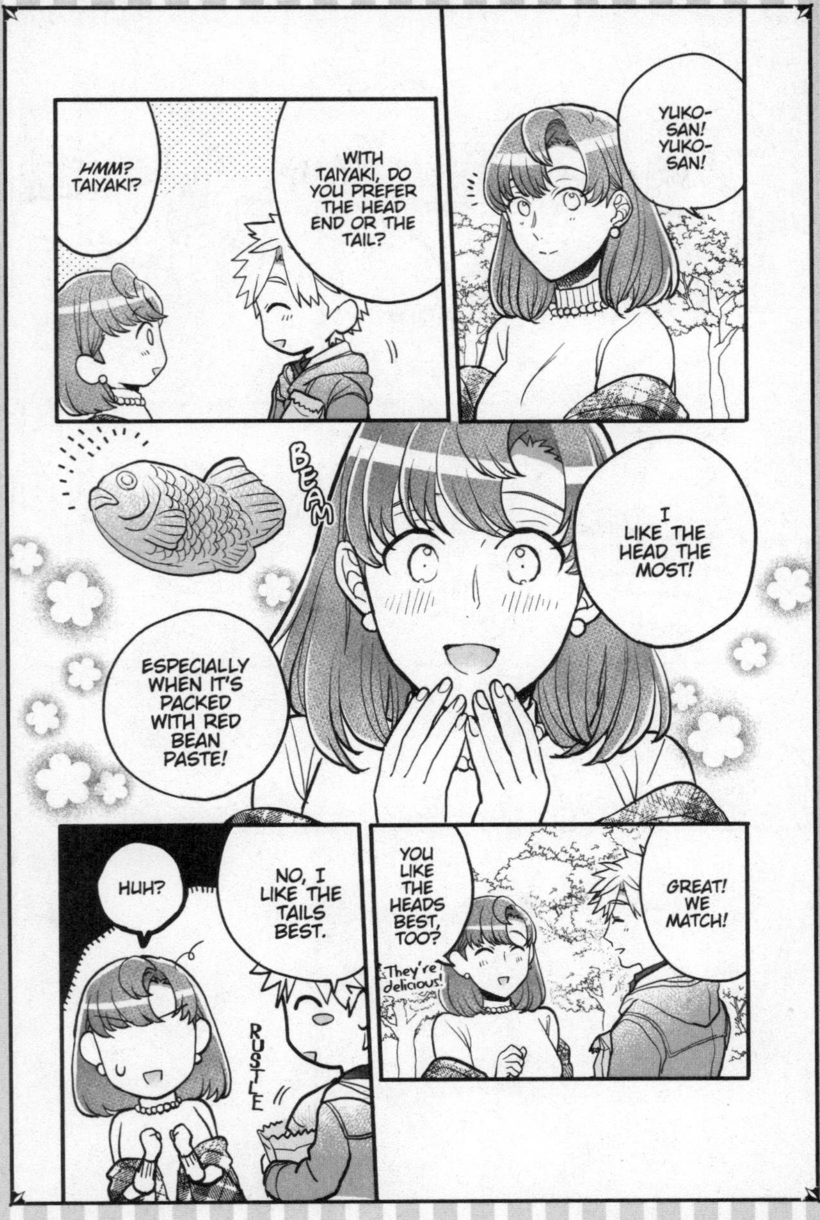
YUKO-SAN! YUKO-SAN!
WITH TAIYAKI, DO YOU PREFER THE HEAD END OR THE TAIL?
HMM? TAIYAKI?
BEAM
I LIKE THE HEAD THE MOST!
ESPECIALLY WHEN IT'S PACKED WITH RED BEAN PASTE!
GREAT! WE MATCH!
YOU LIKE THE HEADS BEST, TOO?
They're delicious!
NO, I LIKE THE TAILS BEST.
HUH?
RUSTLE

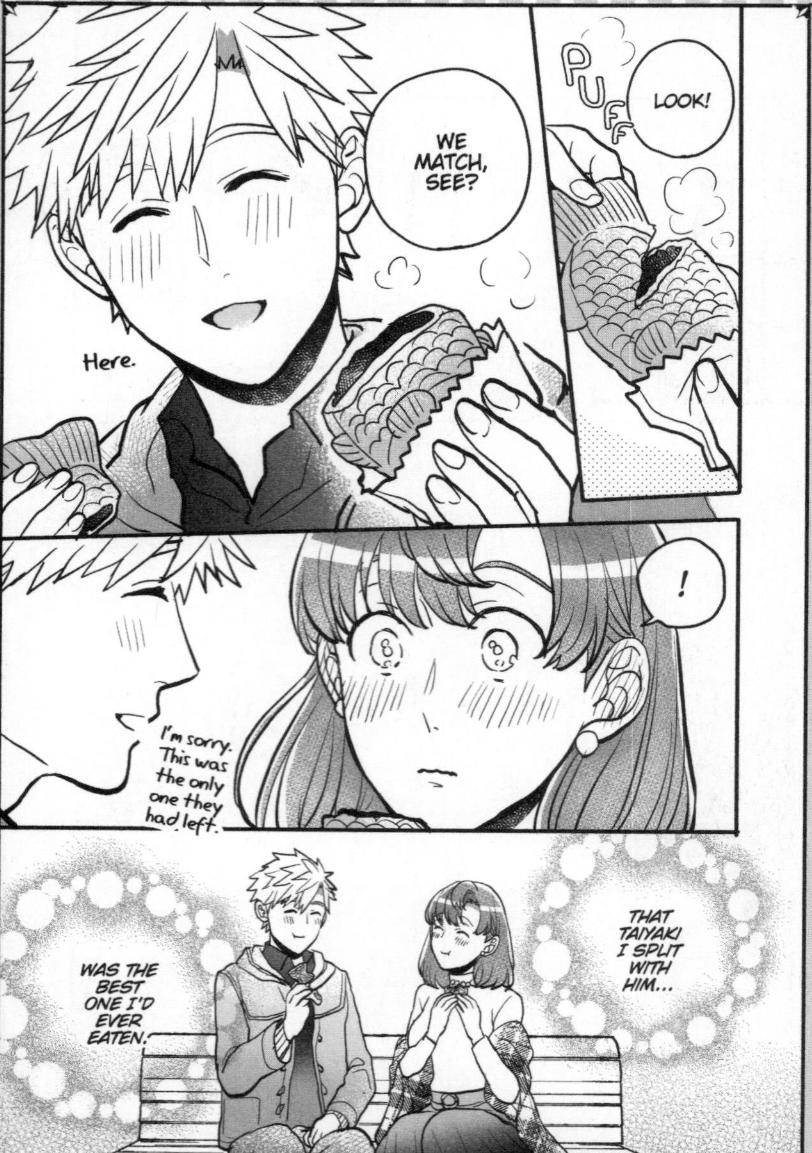
LOOK!
PUFF
WE MATCH, SEE?
Here.
!
I'm sorry. This was the only one they had left.
THAT TAIYAKI I SPLIT WITH HIM...
WAS THE BEST ONE I'D EVER EATEN.

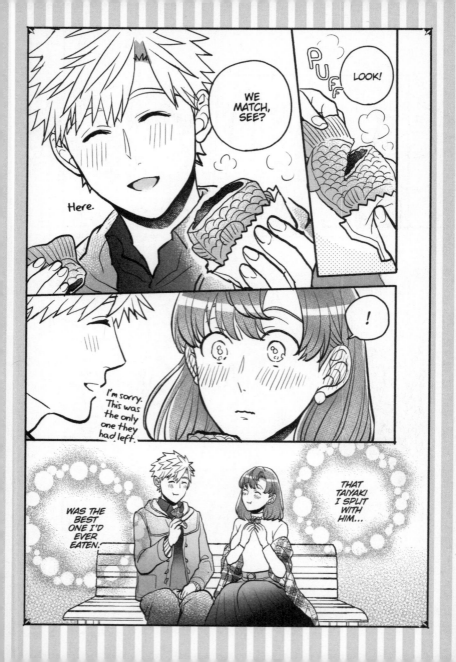

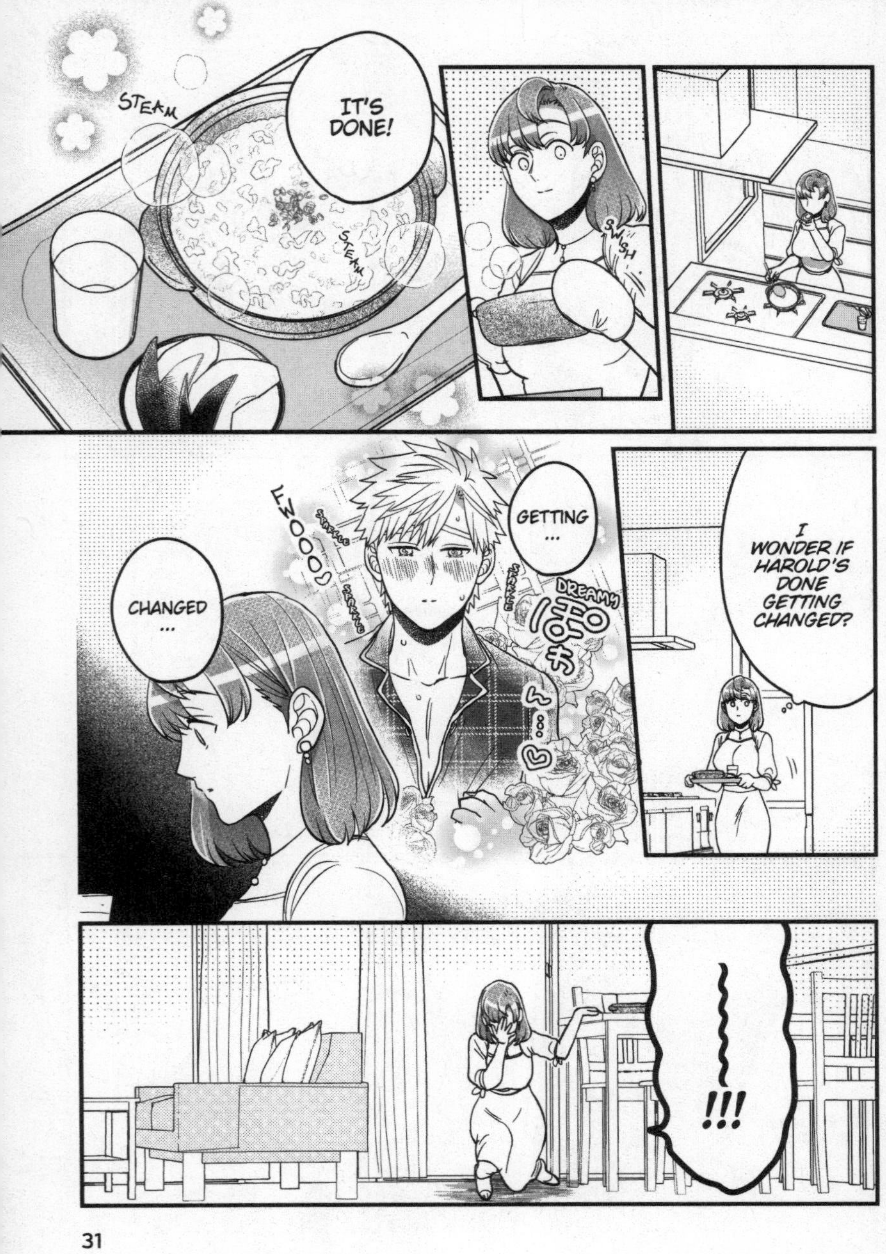
SWISH
IT'S DONE!
STEAM
STEAM
I WONDER IF HAROLD'S DONE GETTING CHANGED?
GETTING ...
CHANGED ...
FWOOOO♡
SPARKLE
SPARKLE
SPARKLE
DREAMY
ぽおん…♡
~~~~!!!
~~~~

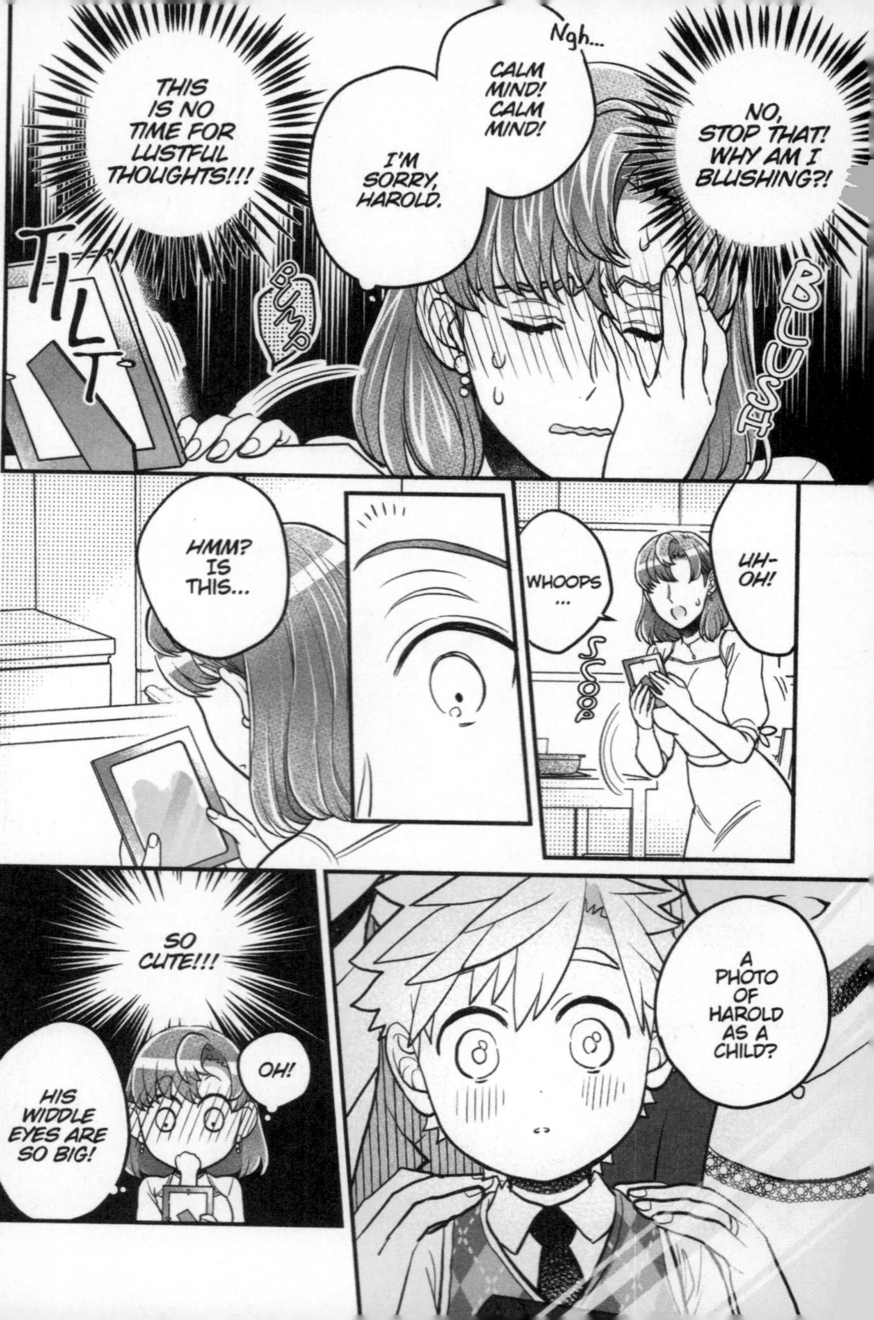
NO, STOP THAT! WHY AM I BLUSHING?!
Ngh...
CALM MIND! CALM MIND!
I'M SORRY, HAROLD.
THIS IS NO TIME FOR LUSTFUL THOUGHTS!!!
BLUSH
BUMP
TILT
UH-OH!
WHOOPS ...
SLOOP
HMM? IS THIS...
A PHOTO OF HAROLD AS A CHILD?
SO CUTE!!!
OH!
HIS WIDDLE EYES ARE SO BIG!

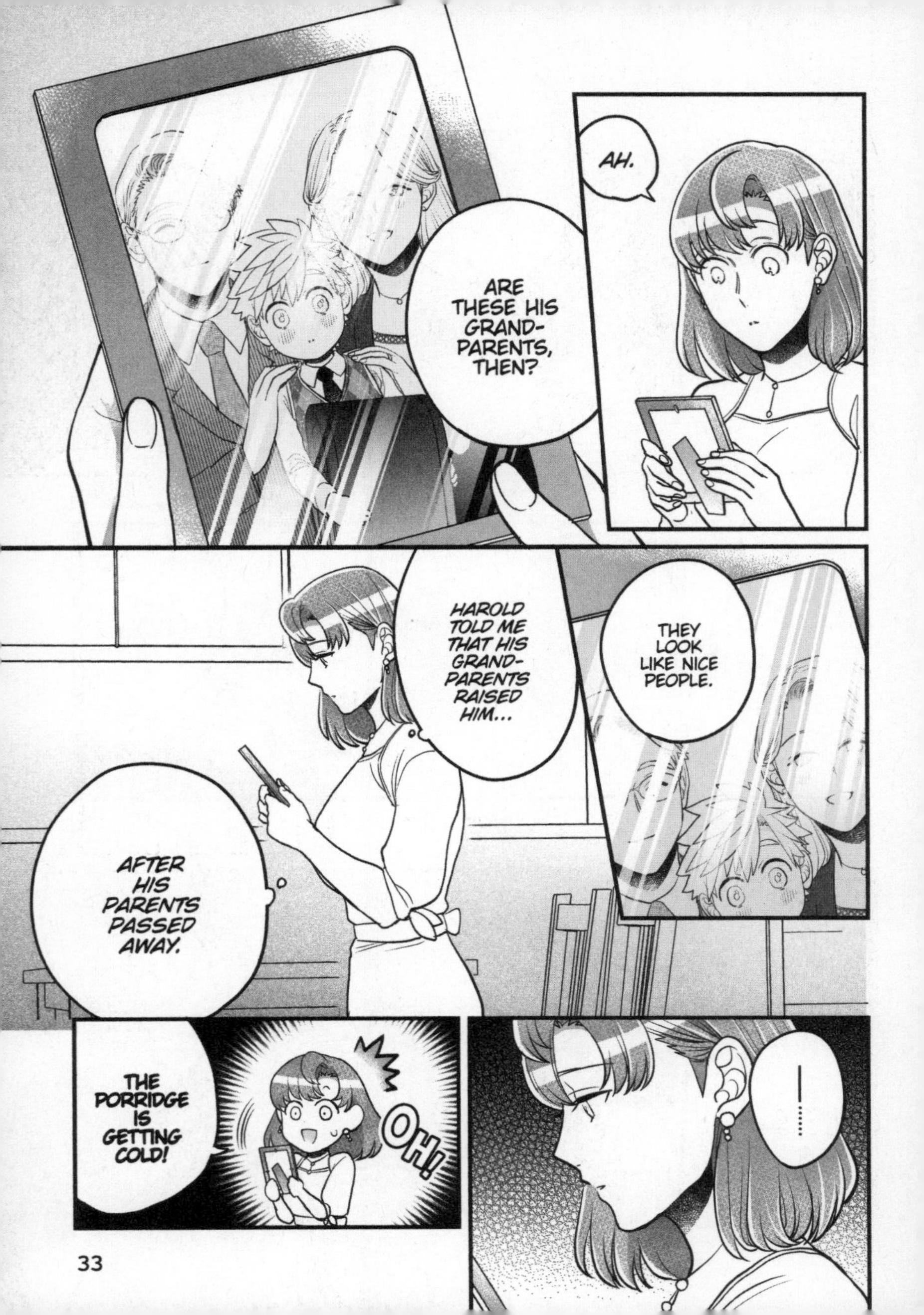
ARE THESE HIS GRAND-PARENTS, THEN?
AH.
HAROLD TOLD ME THAT HIS GRAND-PARENTS RAISED HIM...
THEY LOOK LIKE NICE PEOPLE.
AFTER HIS PARENTS PASSED AWAY.
—......
OH!
THE PORRIDGE IS GETTING COLD!

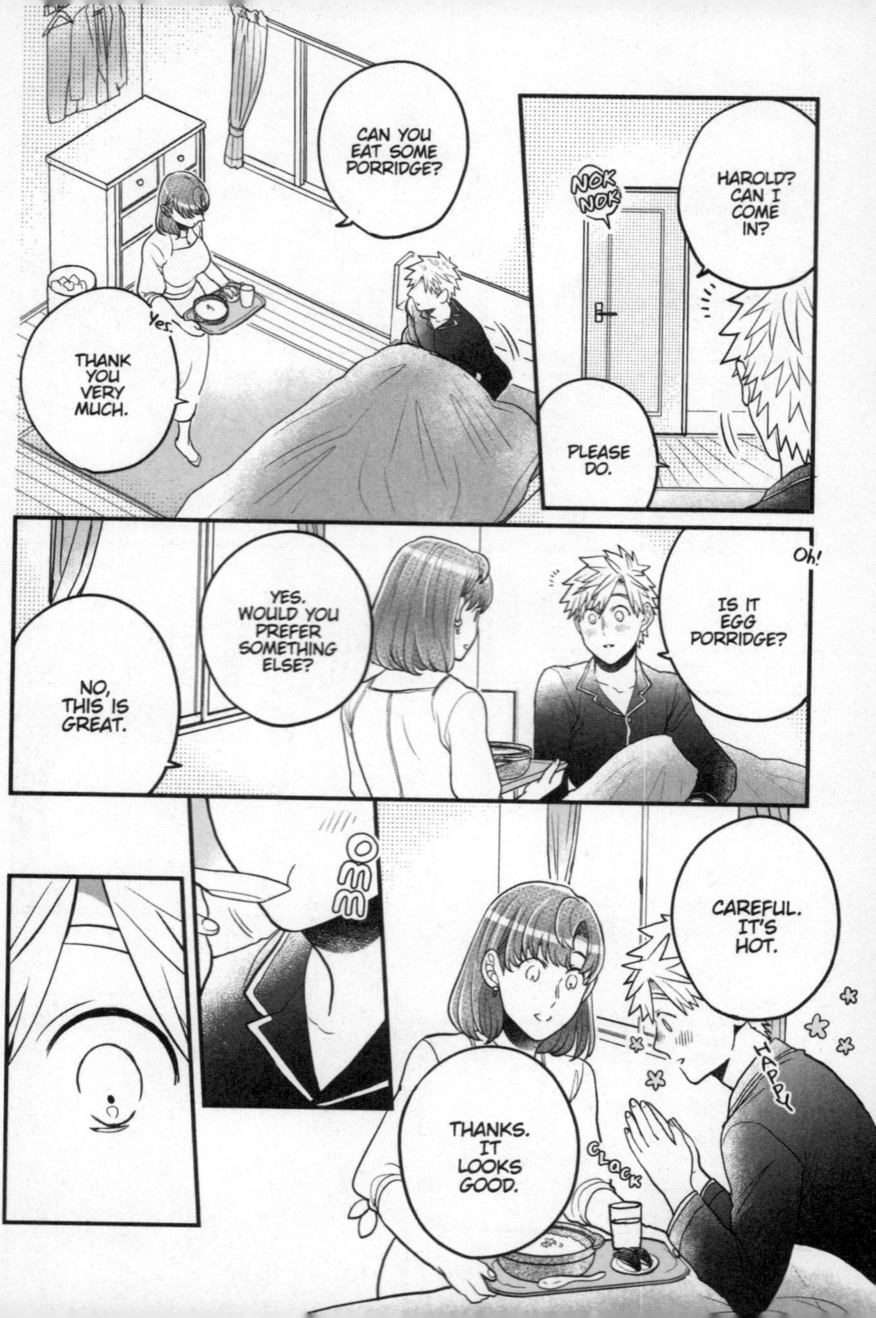
NOK NOK
HAROLD? CAN I COME IN?
PLEASE DO.
CAN YOU EAT SOME PORRIDGE?
Yes.
THANK YOU VERY MUCH.
Oh!
IS IT EGG PORRIDGE?
YES. WOULD YOU PREFER SOMETHING ELSE?
NO, THIS IS GREAT.
CAREFUL. IT'S HOT.
HAPPY
THANKS. IT LOOKS GOOD.
CLACK

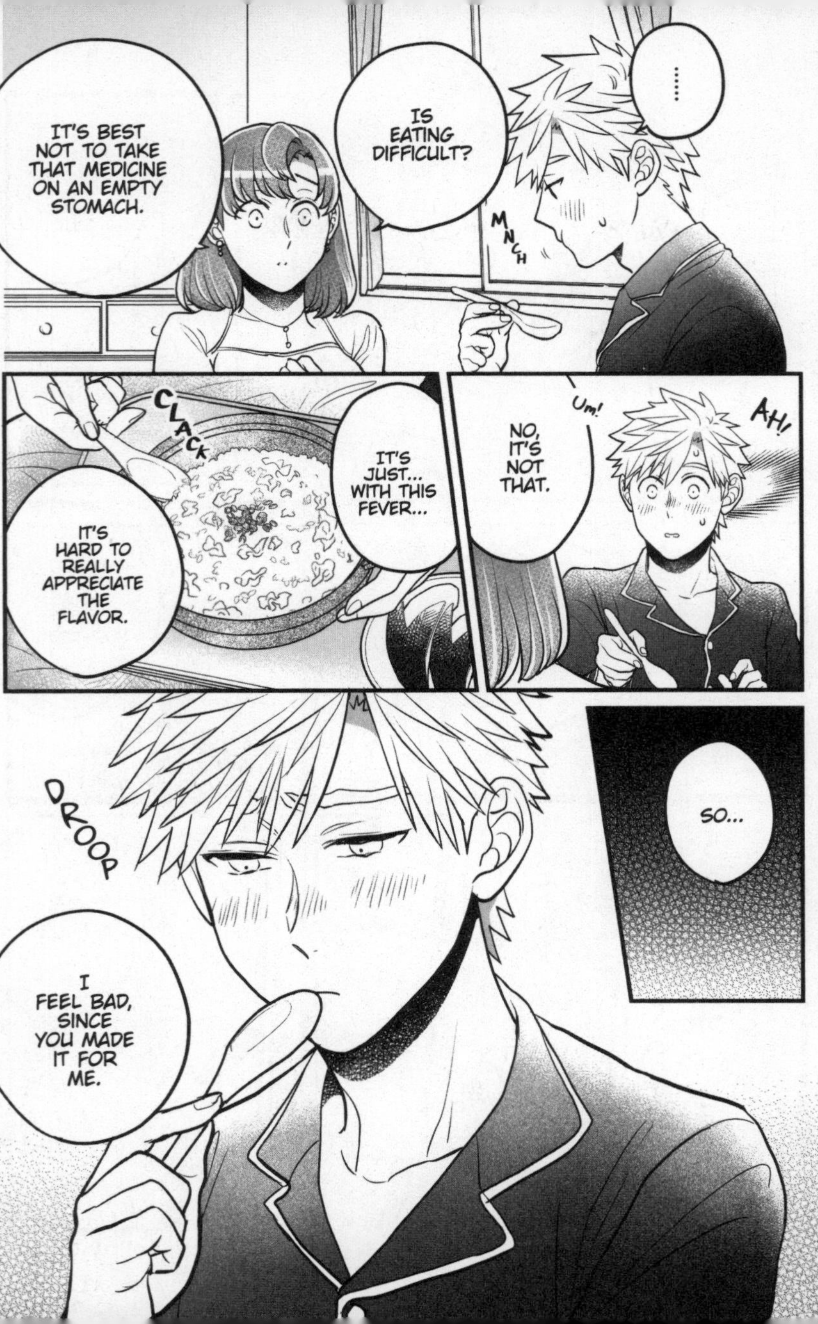
......
MNCH
IS EATING DIFFICULT?
IT'S BEST NOT TO TAKE THAT MEDICINE ON AN EMPTY STOMACH.
AH!
Um!
NO, IT'S NOT THAT.
IT'S JUST... WITH THIS FEVER...
CLACK
IT'S HARD TO REALLY APPRECIATE THE FLAVOR.
SO...
DROOP
I FEEL BAD, SINCE YOU MADE IT FOR ME.

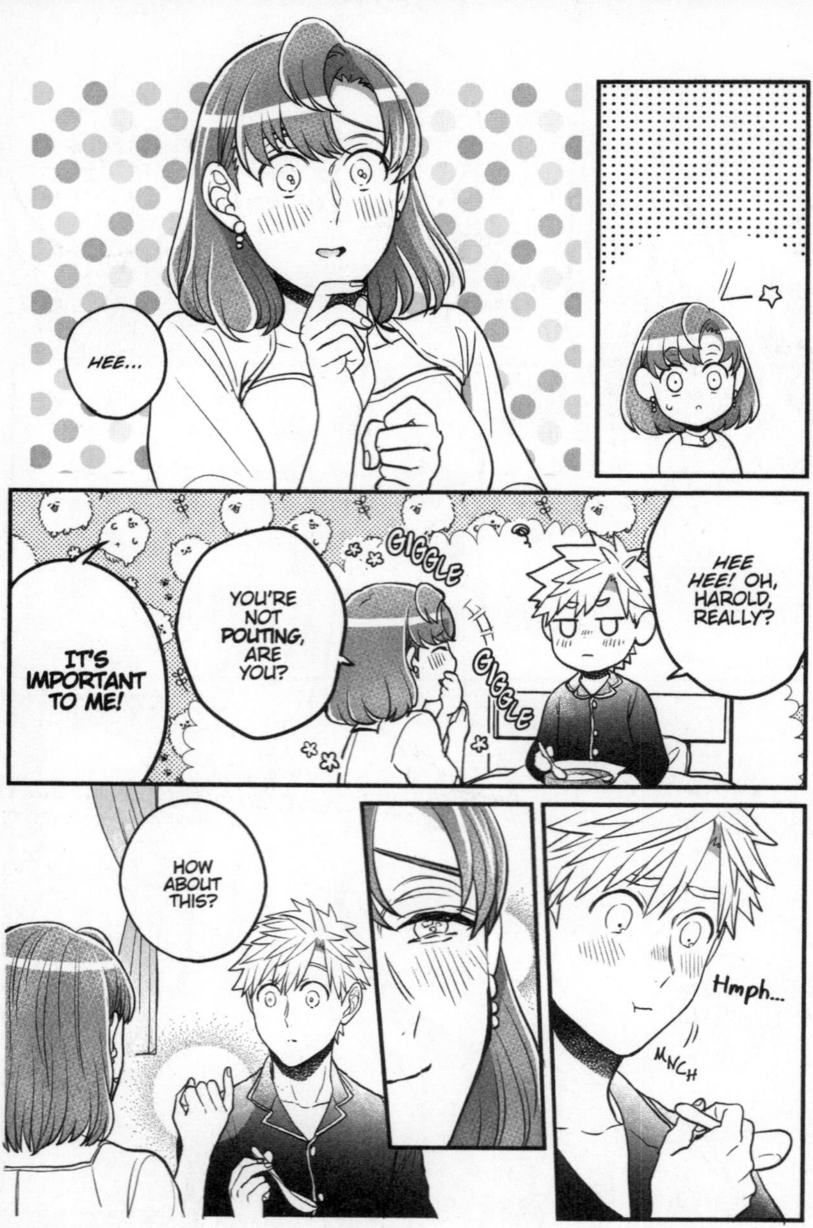
HEE...
HEE HEE! OH, HAROLD, REALLY?
GIGGLE
GIGGLE
GIGGLE
YOU'RE NOT POUTING, ARE YOU?
IT'S IMPORTANT TO ME!
HOW ABOUT THIS?
Hmph...
MNCH

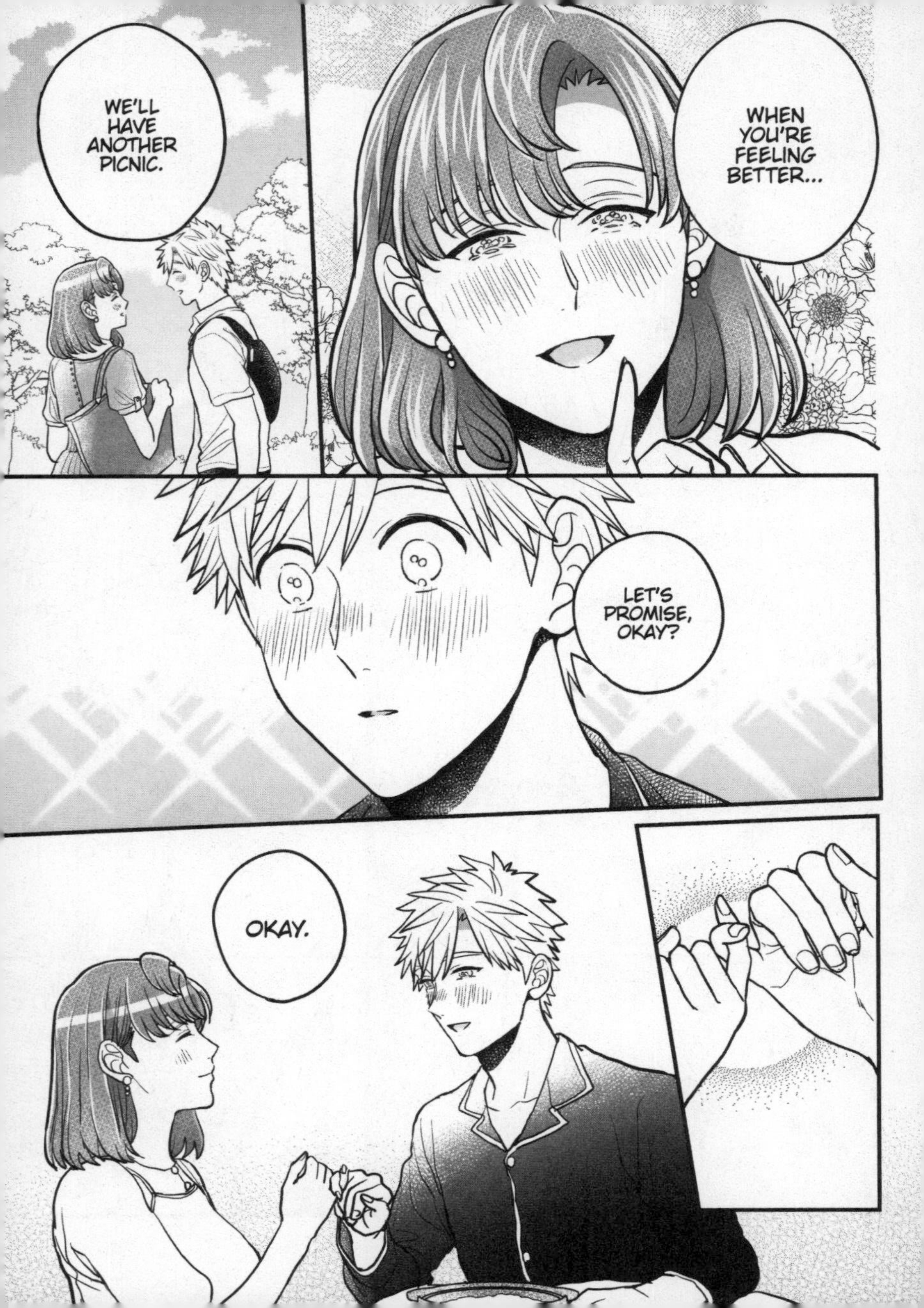
WHEN YOU'RE FEELING BETTER...
WE'LL HAVE ANOTHER PICNIC.
LET'S PROMISE, OKAY?
OKAY.

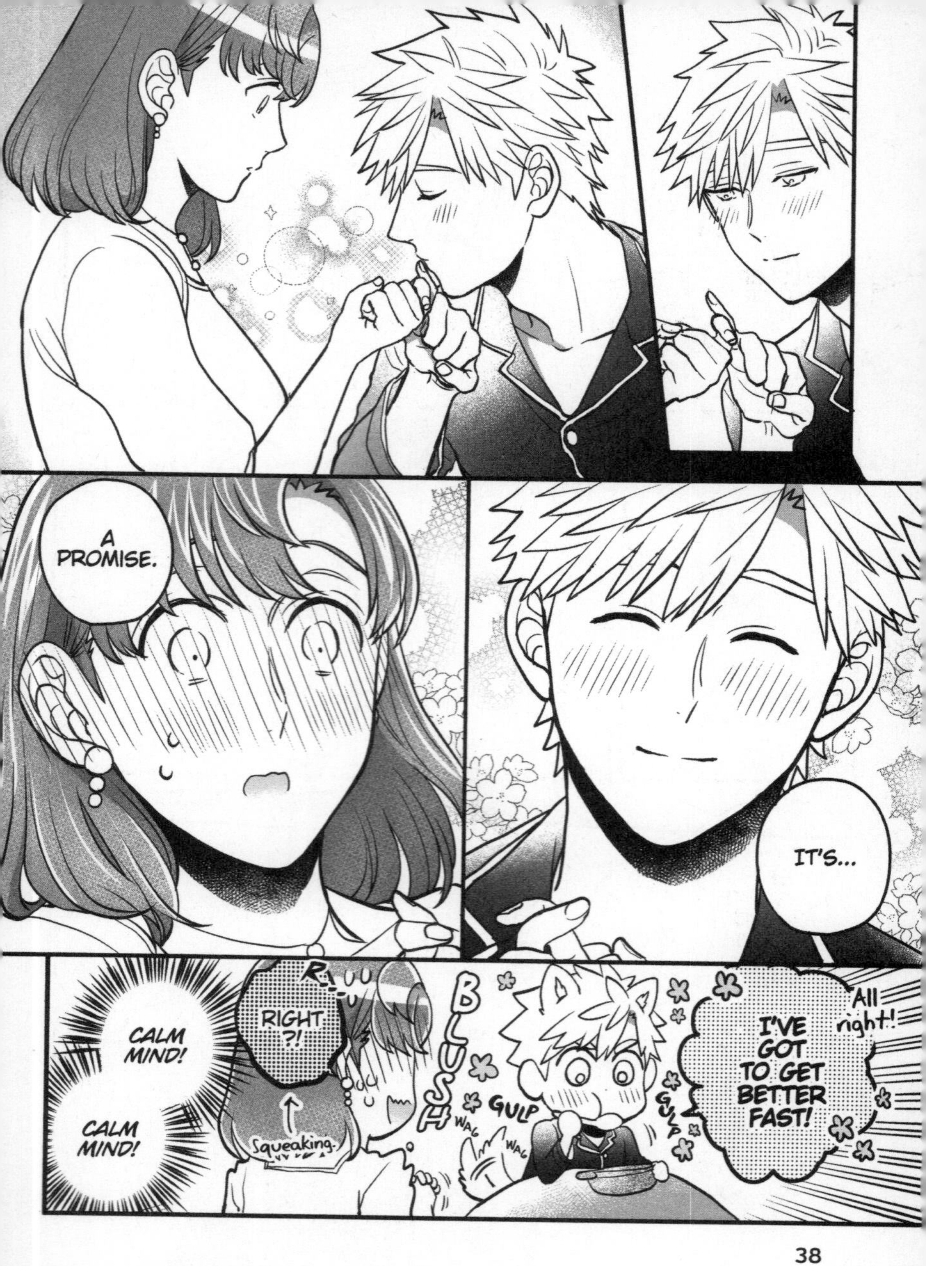
IT'S...
A PROMISE.
All right!
I'VE GOT TO GET BETTER FAST!
GULP
GULP
WAG
WAG
BLUSH
R-
RIGHT?!
Squeaking.
CALM MIND!
CALM MIND!

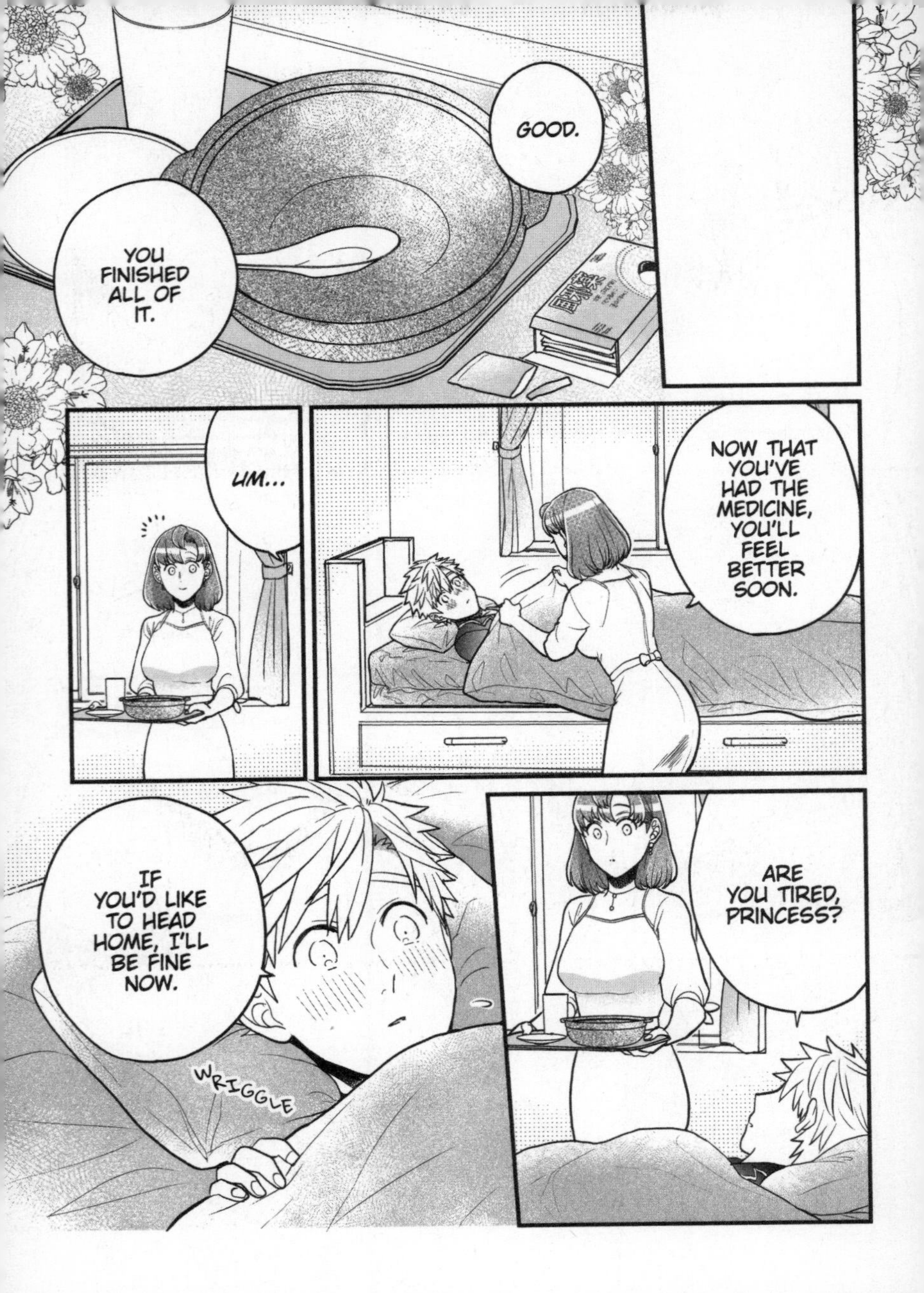
GOOD.
YOU FINISHED ALL OF IT.
NOW THAT YOU'VE HAD THE MEDICINE, YOU'LL FEEL BETTER SOON.
UM...
ARE YOU TIRED, PRINCESS?
IF YOU'D LIKE TO HEAD HOME, I'LL BE FINE NOW.
WRIGGLE

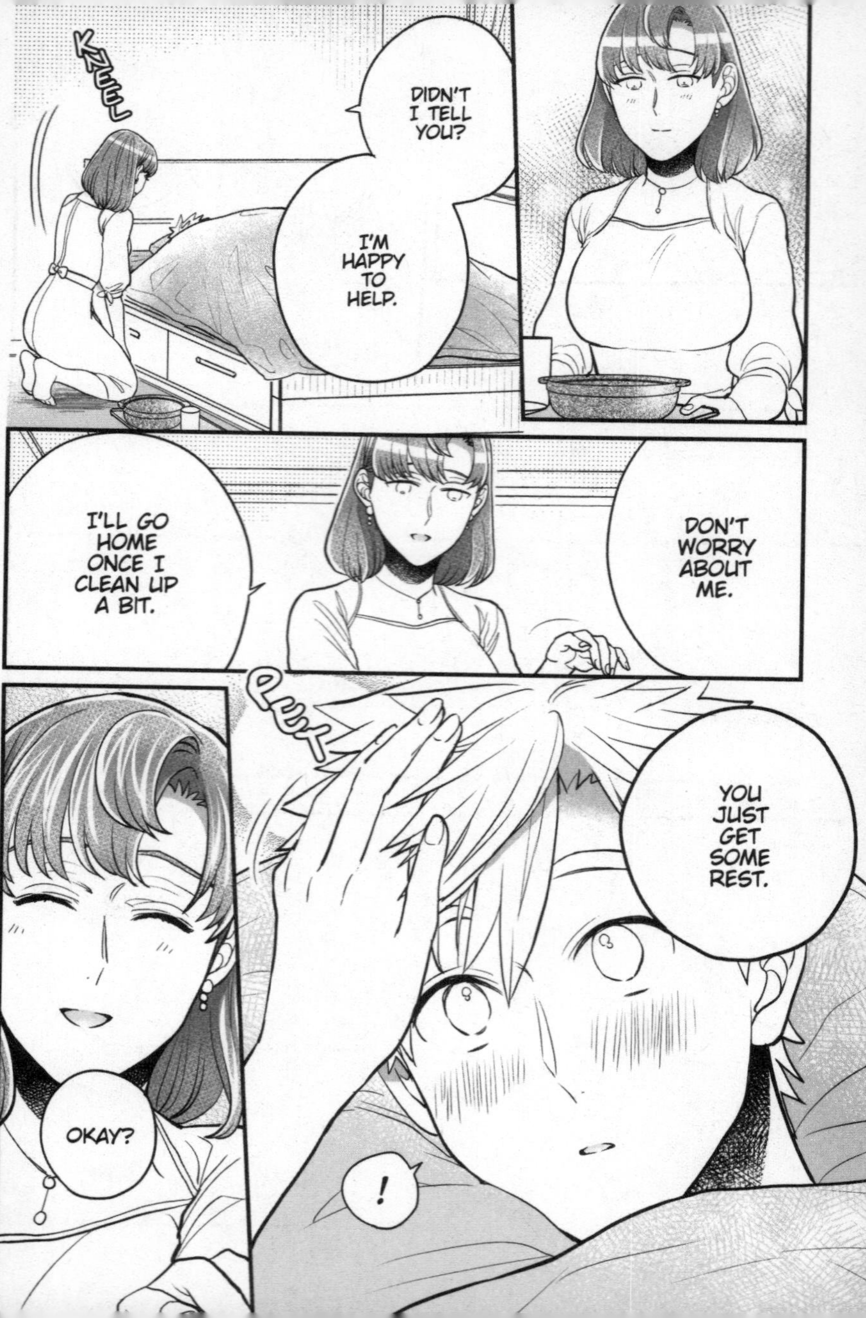
DIDN'T I TELL YOU?
I'M HAPPY TO HELP.
KNEEL
DON'T WORRY ABOUT ME.
I'LL GO HOME ONCE I CLEAN UP A BIT.
PAT
YOU JUST GET SOME REST.
!
OKAY?

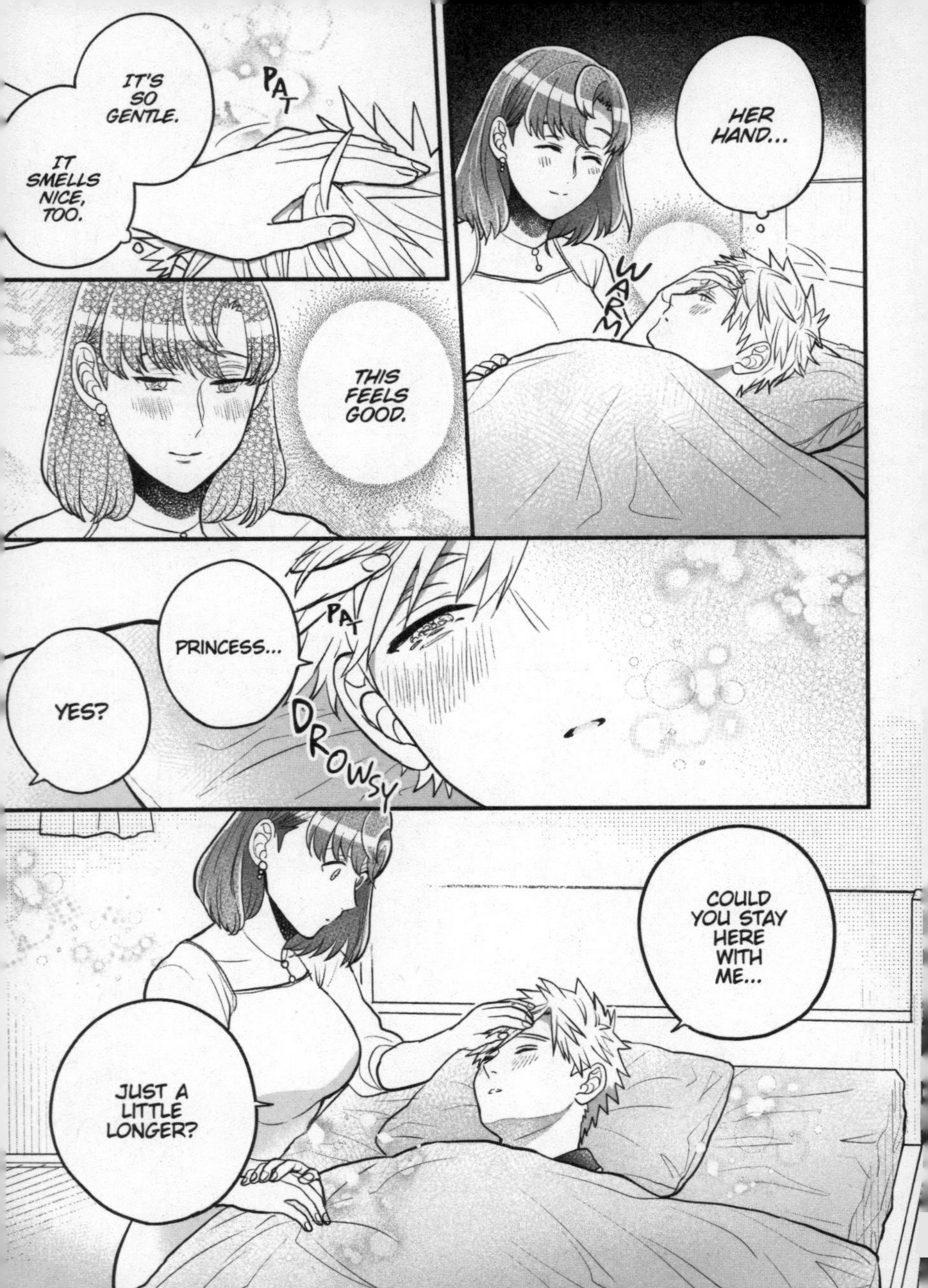
IT'S SO GENTLE.
IT SMELLS NICE, TOO.
PAT
HER HAND...
WARM
THIS FEELS GOOD.
PRINCESS...
YES?
PAT
DROWSY
COULD YOU STAY HERE WITH ME...
JUST A LITTLE LONGER?

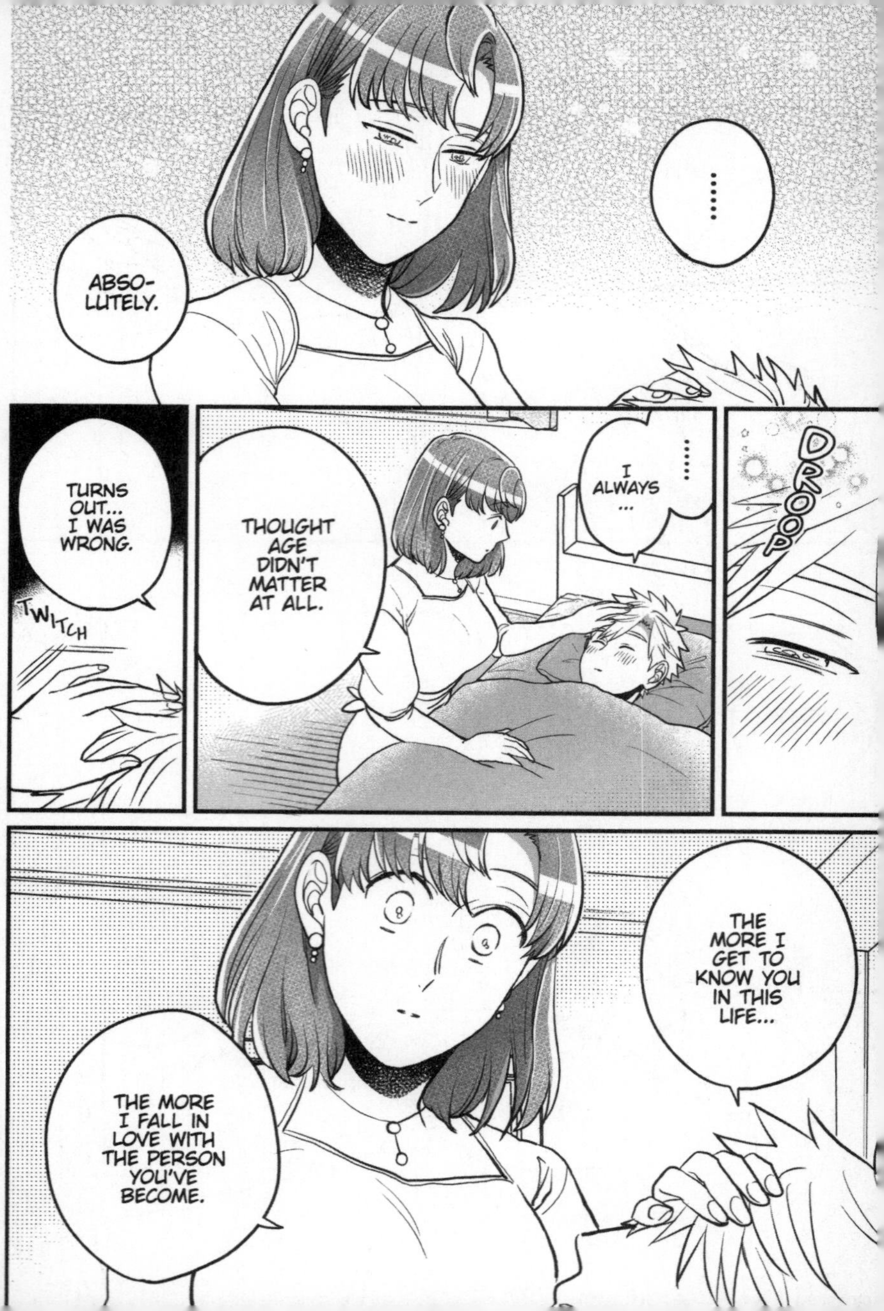

......
ABSO-LUTELY.
DROOP
......
I ALWAYS ...
THOUGHT AGE DIDN'T MATTER AT ALL.
TURNS OUT... I WAS WRONG.
TWITCH
THE MORE I GET TO KNOW YOU IN THIS LIFE...
THE MORE I FALL IN LOVE WITH THE PERSON YOU'VE BECOME.

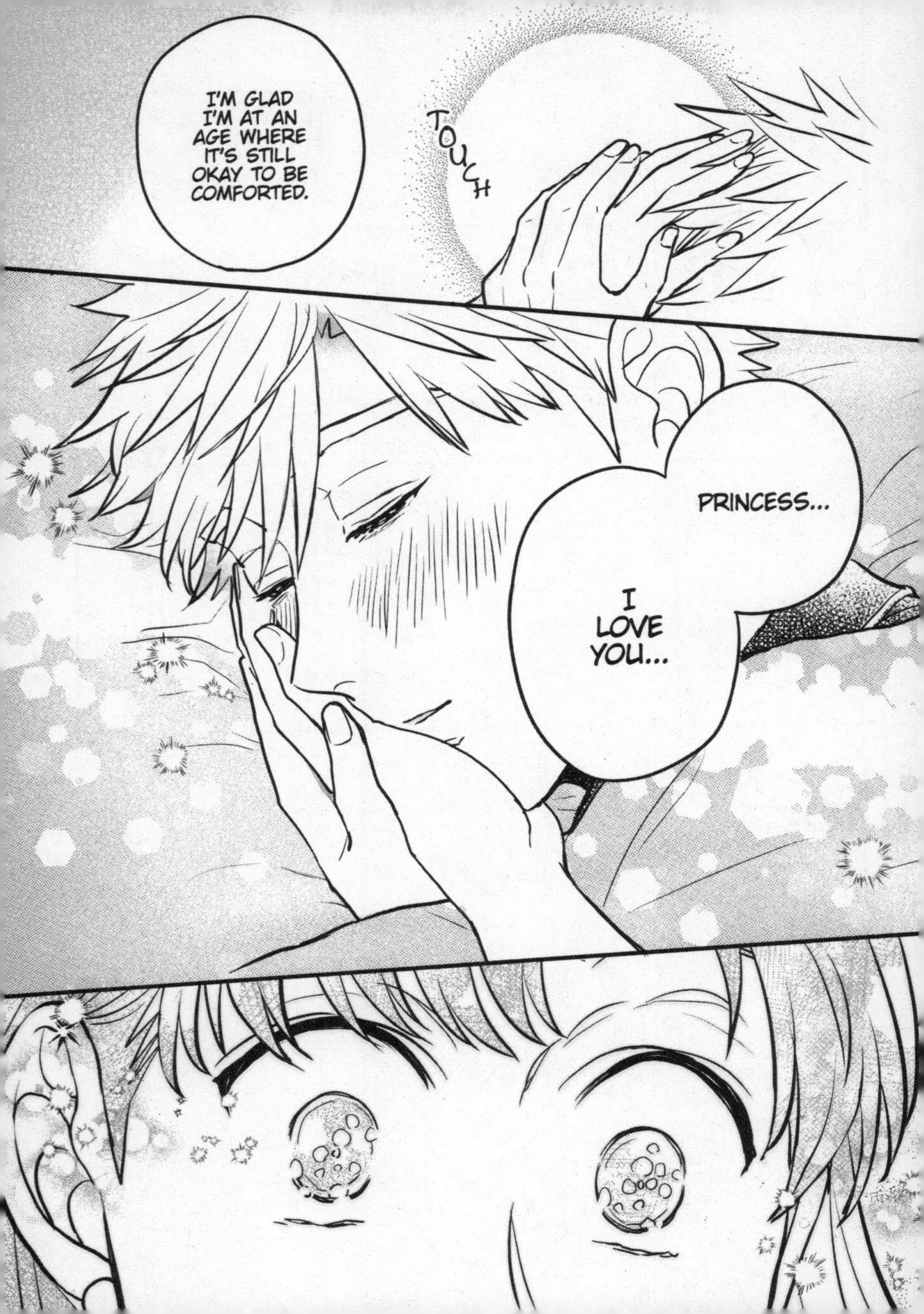

I'M GLAD I'M AT AN AGE WHERE IT'S STILL OKAY TO BE COMFORTED.
TOUCH
PRINCESS...
I LOVE YOU...

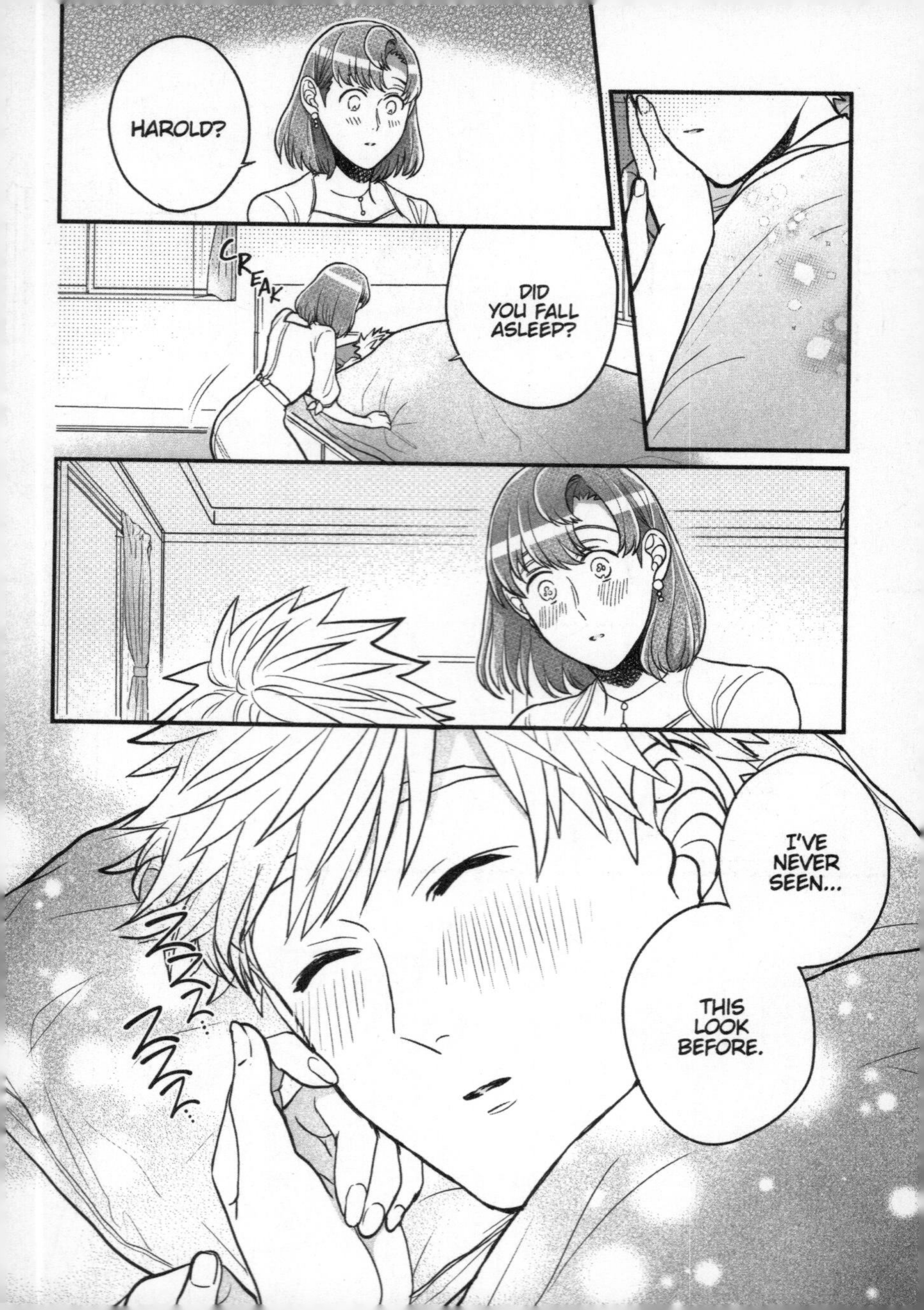
HAROLD?
CREAK
DID YOU FALL ASLEEP?
I'VE NEVER SEEN...
THIS LOOK BEFORE.
ZZZZ...
ZZZ...

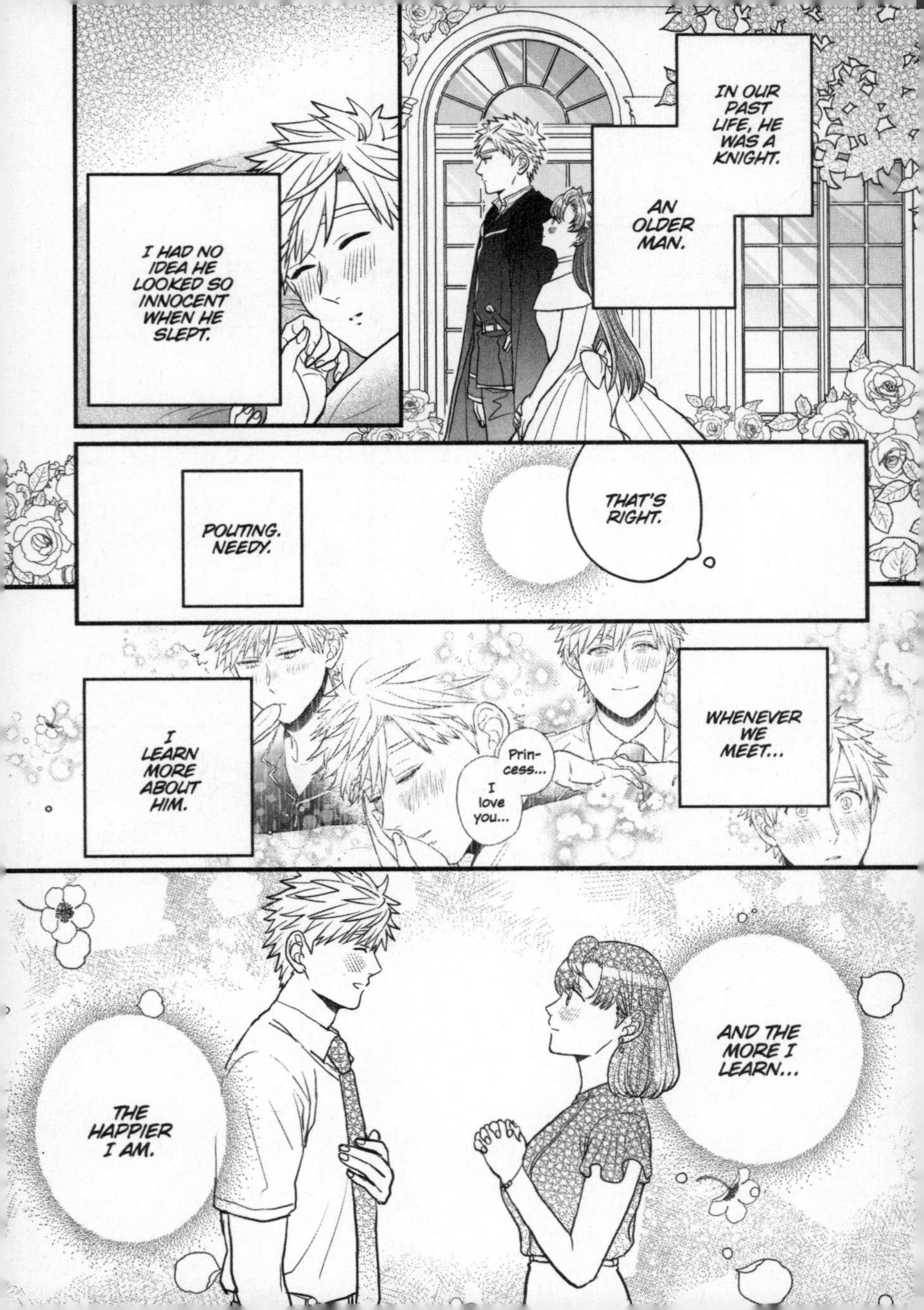
IN OUR PAST LIFE, HE WAS A KNIGHT.
AN OLDER MAN.
I HAD NO IDEA HE LOOKED SO INNOCENT WHEN HE SLEPT.
THAT'S RIGHT.
POUTING. NEEDY.
WHENEVER WE MEET...
Prin-cess...
I love you...
I LEARN MORE ABOUT HIM.
AND THE MORE I LEARN...
THE HAPPIER I AM.

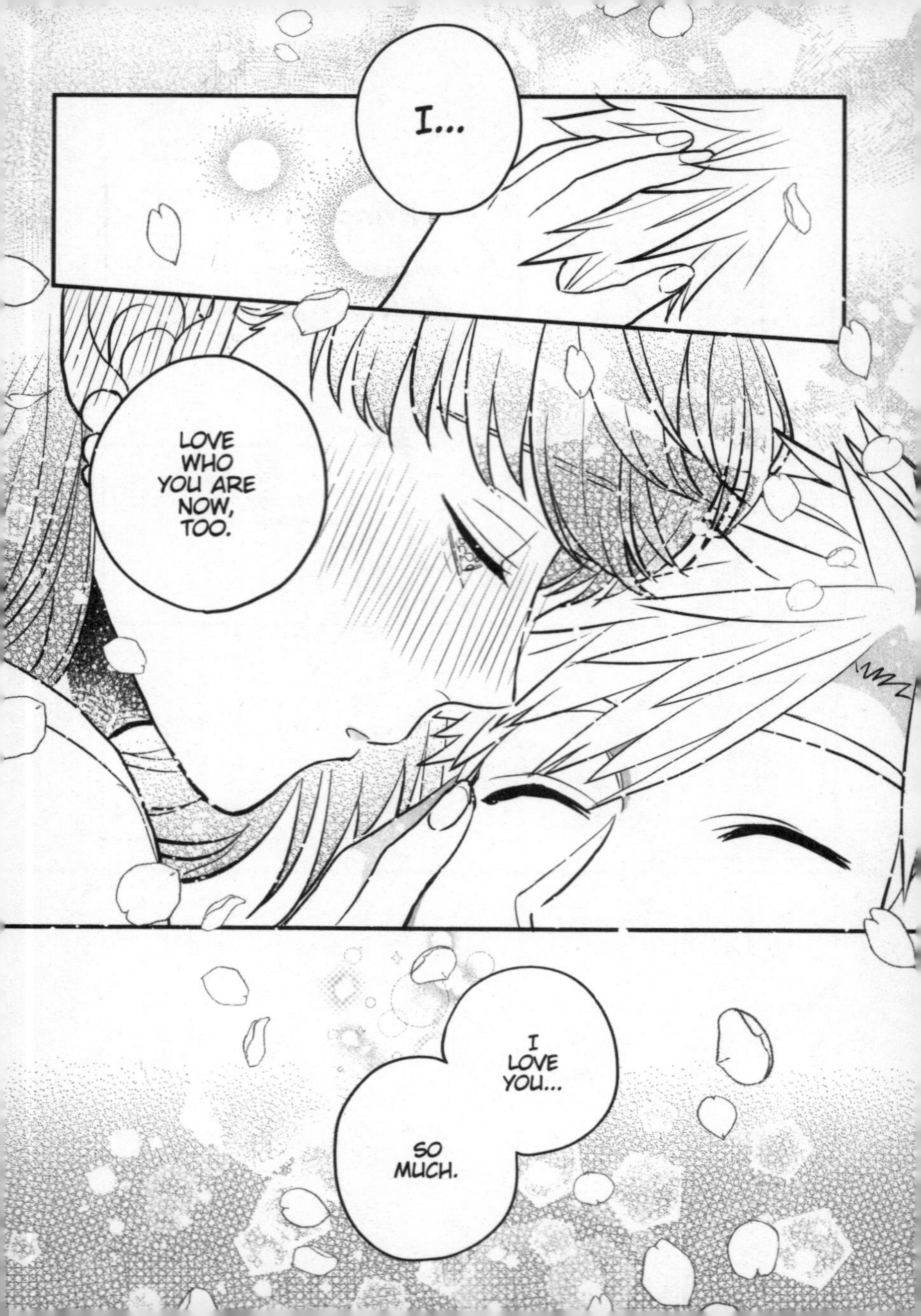
I...
LOVE WHO YOU ARE NOW, TOO.
I LOVE YOU...
SO MUCH.

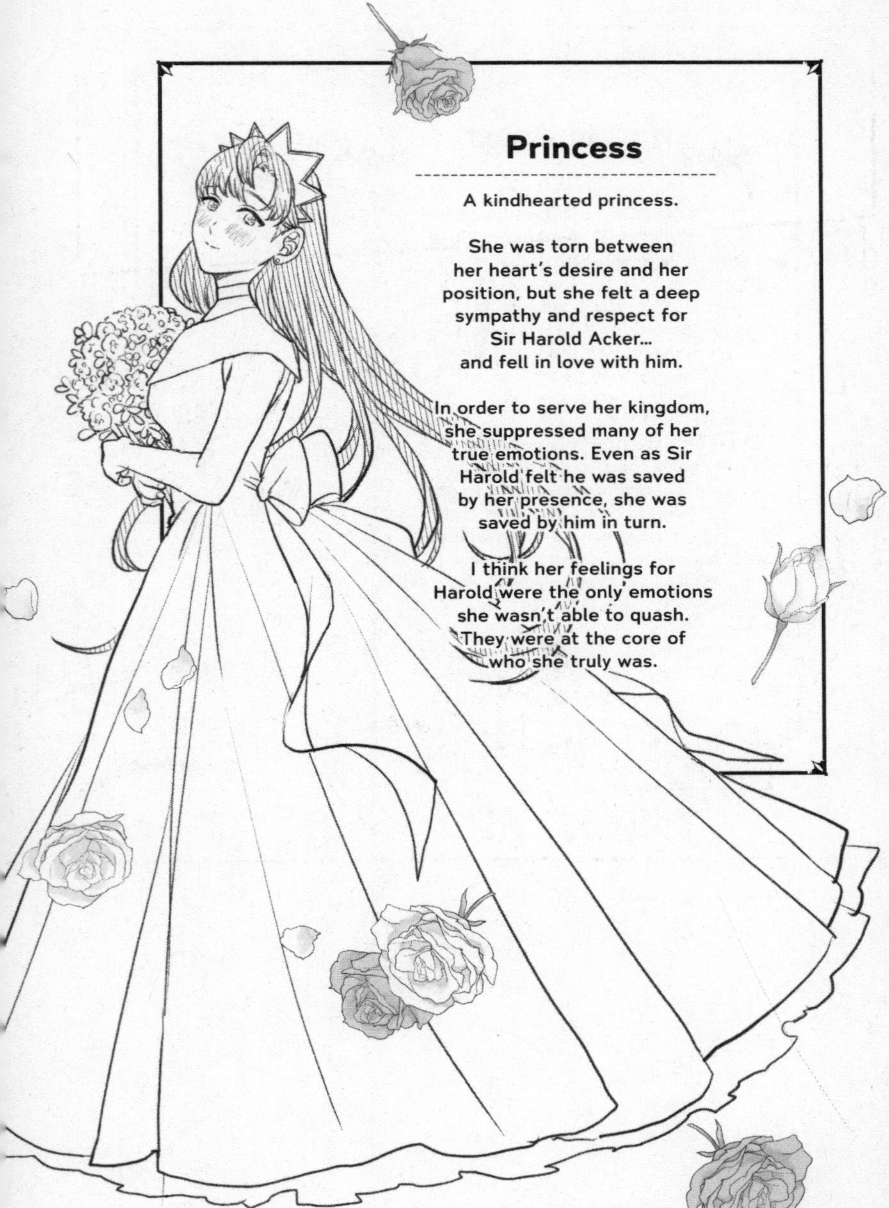

Princess

A kindhearted princess.

She was torn between her heart's desire and her position, but she felt a deep sympathy and respect for Sir Harold Acker... and fell in love with him.

In order to serve her kingdom, she suppressed many of her true emotions. Even as Sir Harold felt he was saved by her presence, she was saved by him in turn.

I think her feelings for Harold were the only emotions she wasn't able to quash. They were at the core of who she truly was.

Harold Acker

A gentle knight who, despite the difference in their social stations, fell in love with the princess.

In order to survive on the battlefield, he sustained himself with the belief that everything he did was for the princess's sake.

As a result, his love for her is more complex than ordinary love, encompassing fealty and reverence as well. In his last life, Harold was keenly aware of his own status and class, and so he was very reserved in how he showed his affection.

It's possible that Haru is so open with his affection now because he feels guilty over being unable to tell her how much he loved her in his past life.

Sometimes I think he's a more fitting main character than the princess.

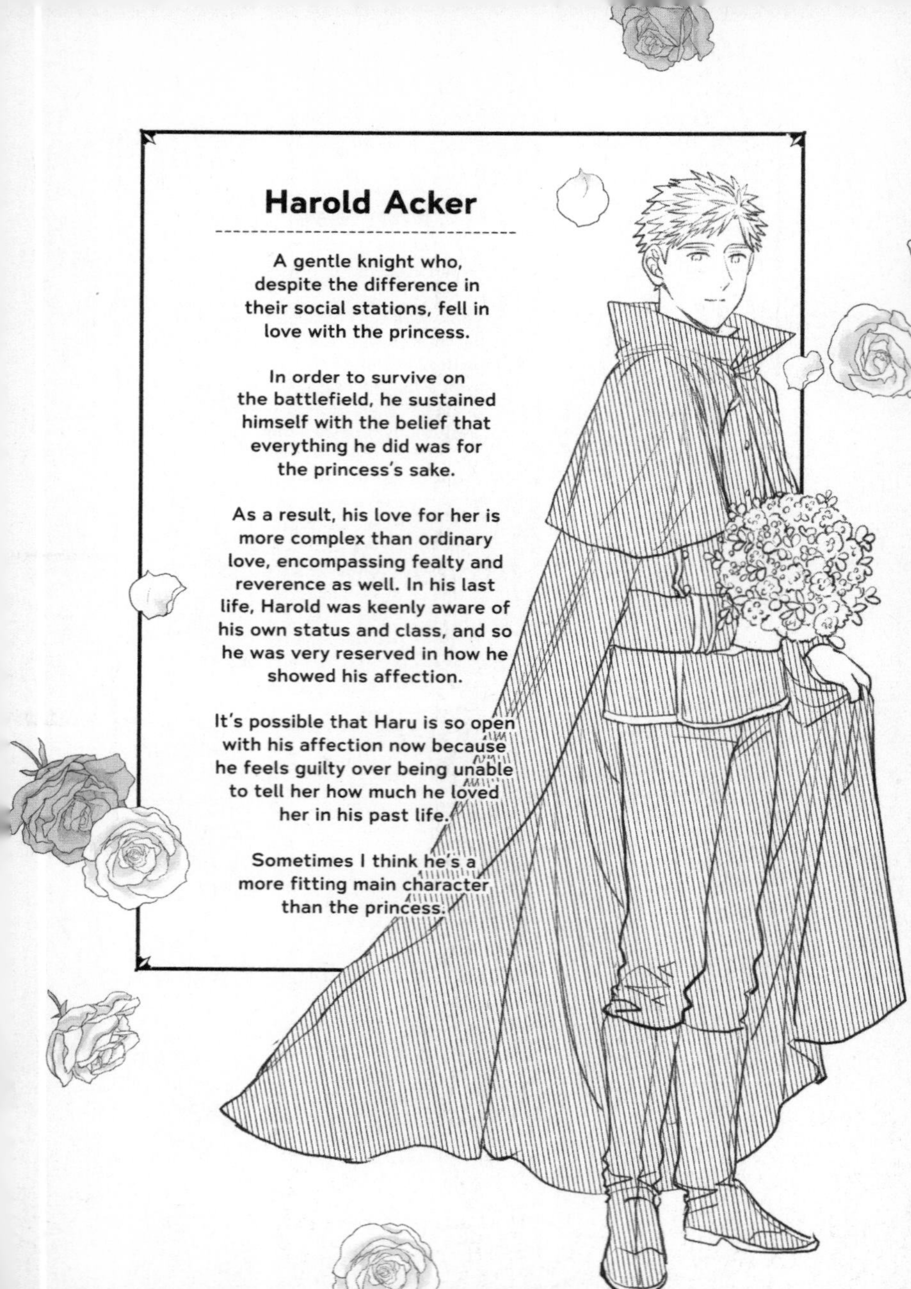

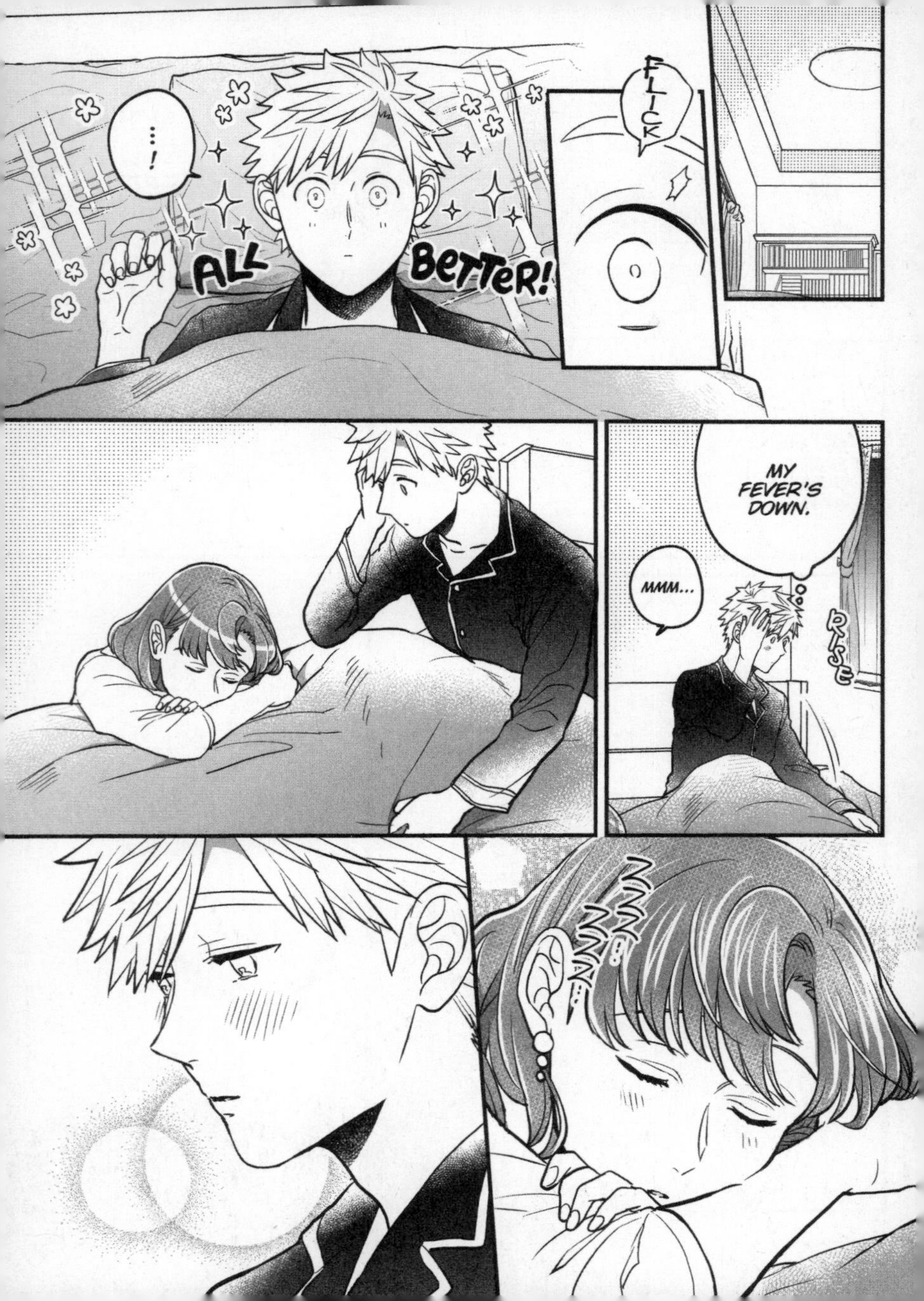
FLICK
...!
ALL BETTER!
MY FEVER'S DOWN.
MMM...
RISE
ZZZ...
ZZZZ...

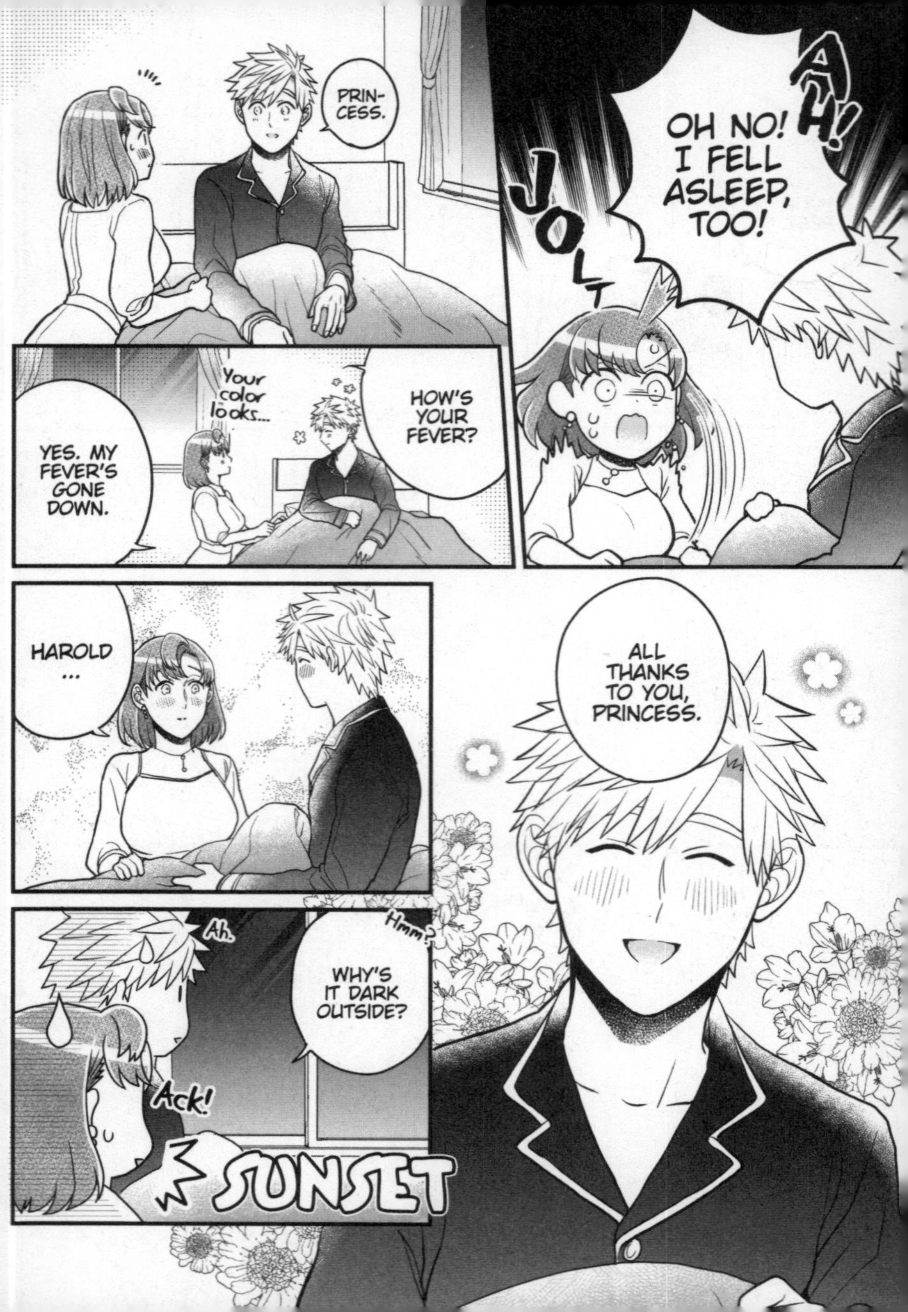

AH!
OH NO! I FELL ASLEEP, TOO!
JOLT
PRIN-CESS.
HOW'S YOUR FEVER?
Your color looks...
YES. MY FEVER'S GONE DOWN.
ALL THANKS TO YOU, PRINCESS.
HAROLD ...
Hmm?
WHY'S IT DARK OUTSIDE?
Ah.
Ack!
SUNSET

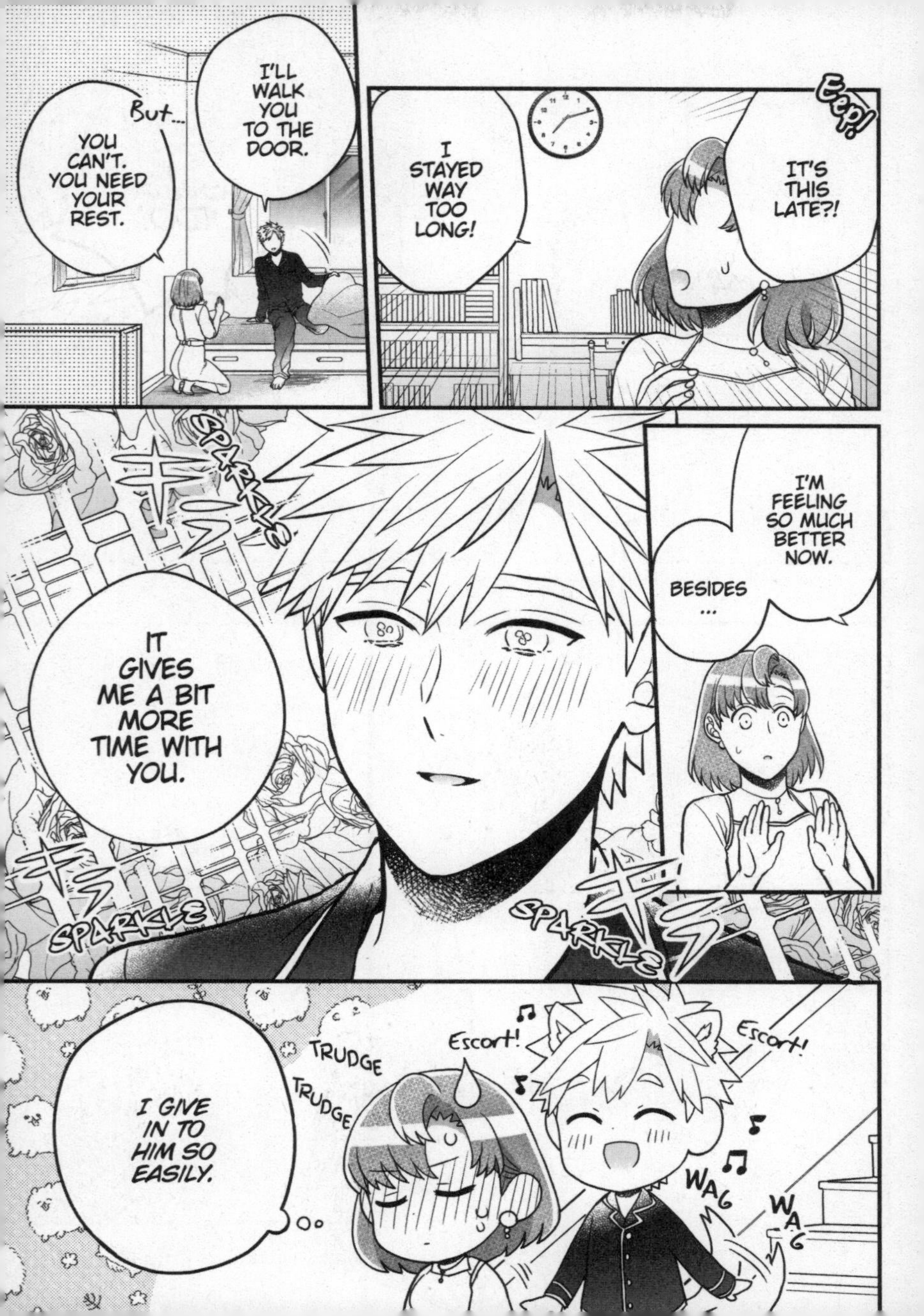
Eep!
IT'S THIS LATE?!
I STAYED WAY TOO LONG!
I'LL WALK YOU TO THE DOOR.
But...
YOU CAN'T. YOU NEED YOUR REST.
I'M FEELING SO MUCH BETTER NOW.
BESIDES...
IT GIVES ME A BIT MORE TIME WITH YOU.
SPARKLE
SPARKLE
SPARKLE
Escort!
Escort!
TRUDGE
TRUDGE
I GIVE IN TO HIM SO EASILY.
WAG
WAG

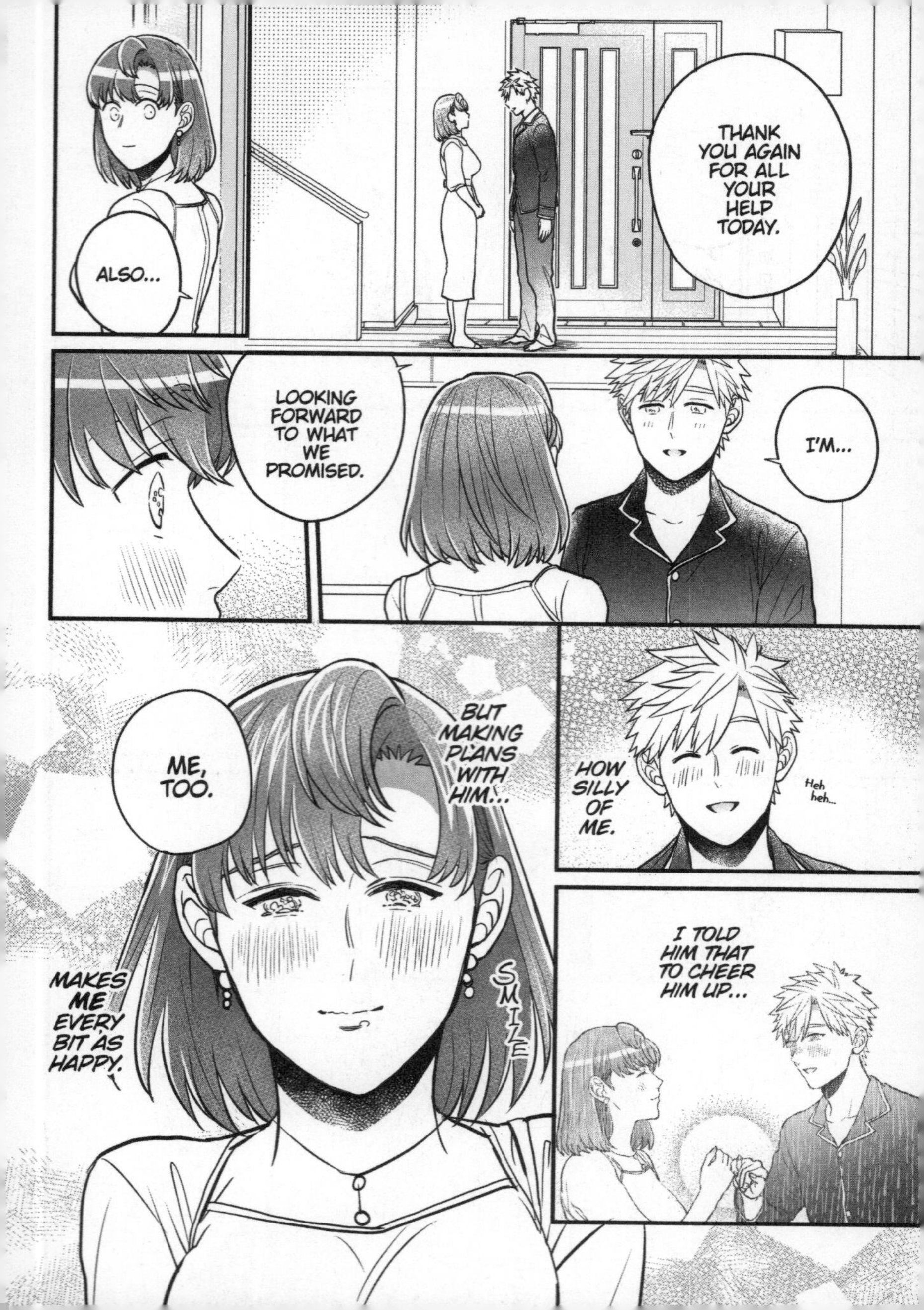
THANK YOU AGAIN FOR ALL YOUR HELP TODAY.
ALSO...
I'M...
LOOKING FORWARD TO WHAT WE PROMISED.
HOW SILLY OF ME.
Heh heh...
BUT MAKING PLANS WITH HIM...
ME, TOO.
I TOLD HIM THAT TO CHEER HIM UP...
MAKES ME EVERY BIT AS HAPPY.
SMILE

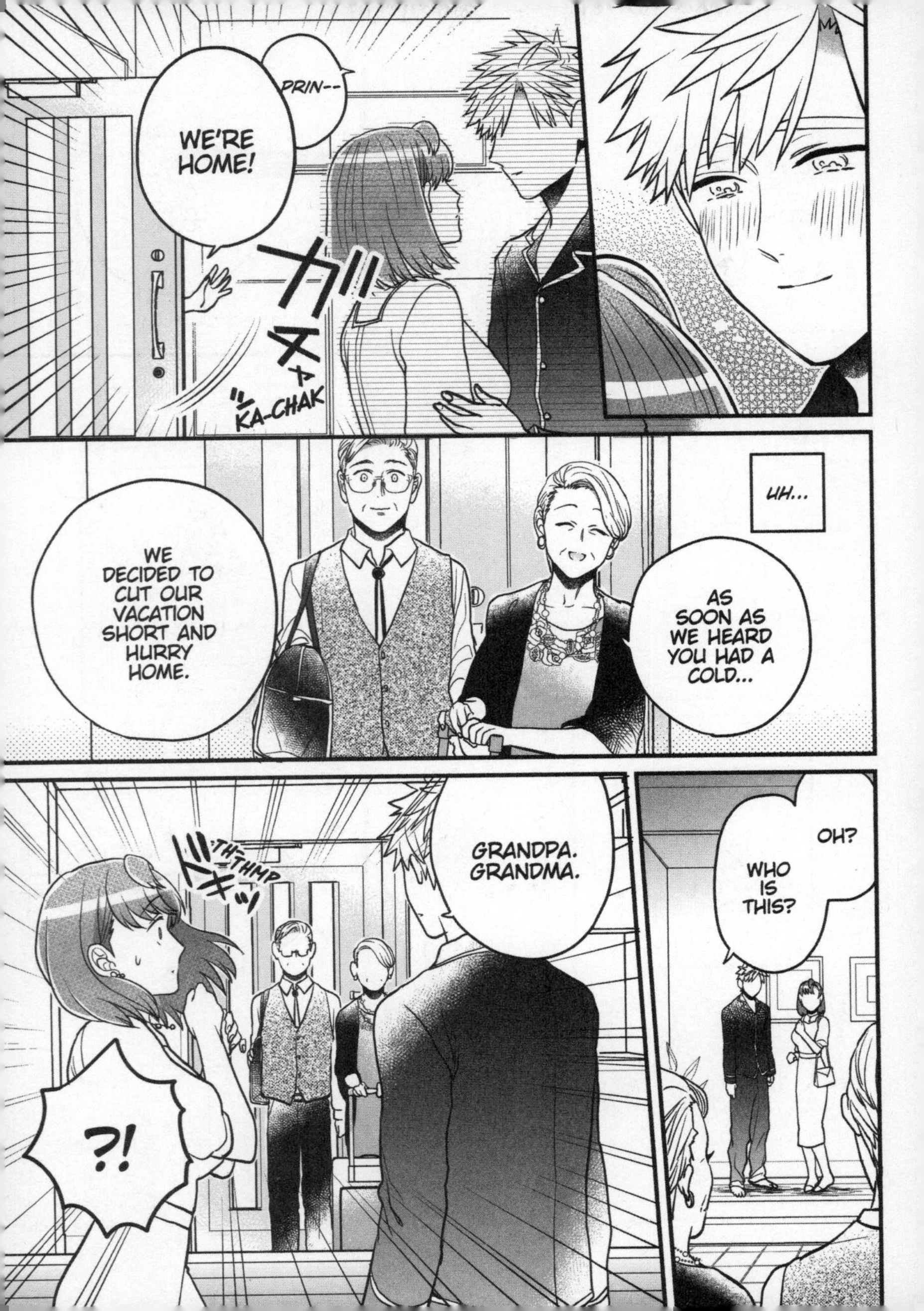
PRIN--
WE'RE HOME!
KA-CHAK
UH...
AS SOON AS WE HEARD YOU HAD A COLD...
WE DECIDED TO CUT OUR VACATION SHORT AND HURRY HOME.
OH?
WHO IS THIS?
GRANDPA. GRANDMA.
TH-THUMP
?!

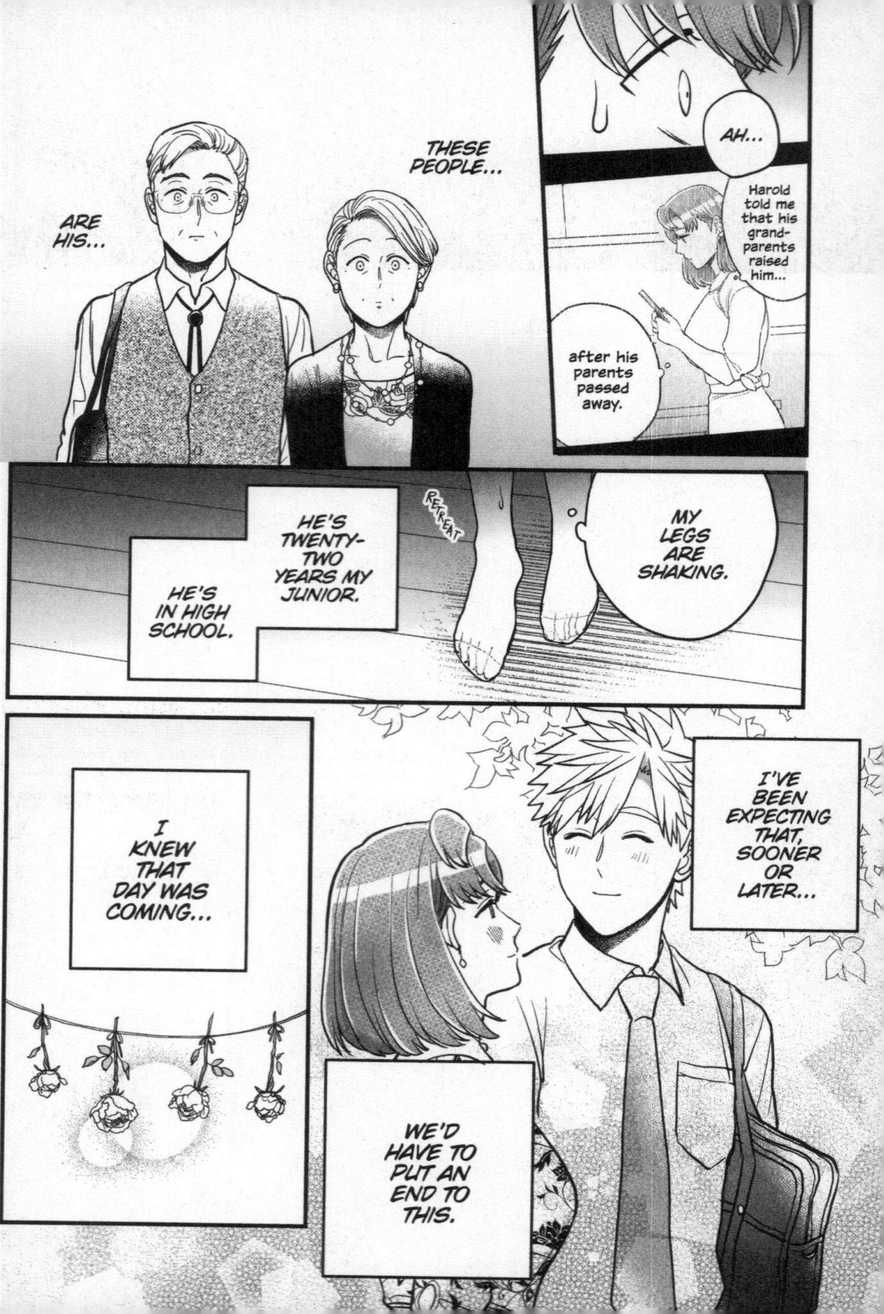
AH...
Harold told me that his grand-parents raised him...
after his parents passed away.
THESE PEOPLE...
ARE HIS...
MY LEGS ARE SHAKING.
RETREAT
HE'S TWENTY-TWO YEARS MY JUNIOR.
HE'S IN HIGH SCHOOL.
I'VE BEEN EXPECTING THAT, SOONER OR LATER...
I KNEW THAT DAY WAS COMING...
WE'D HAVE TO PUT AN END TO THIS.

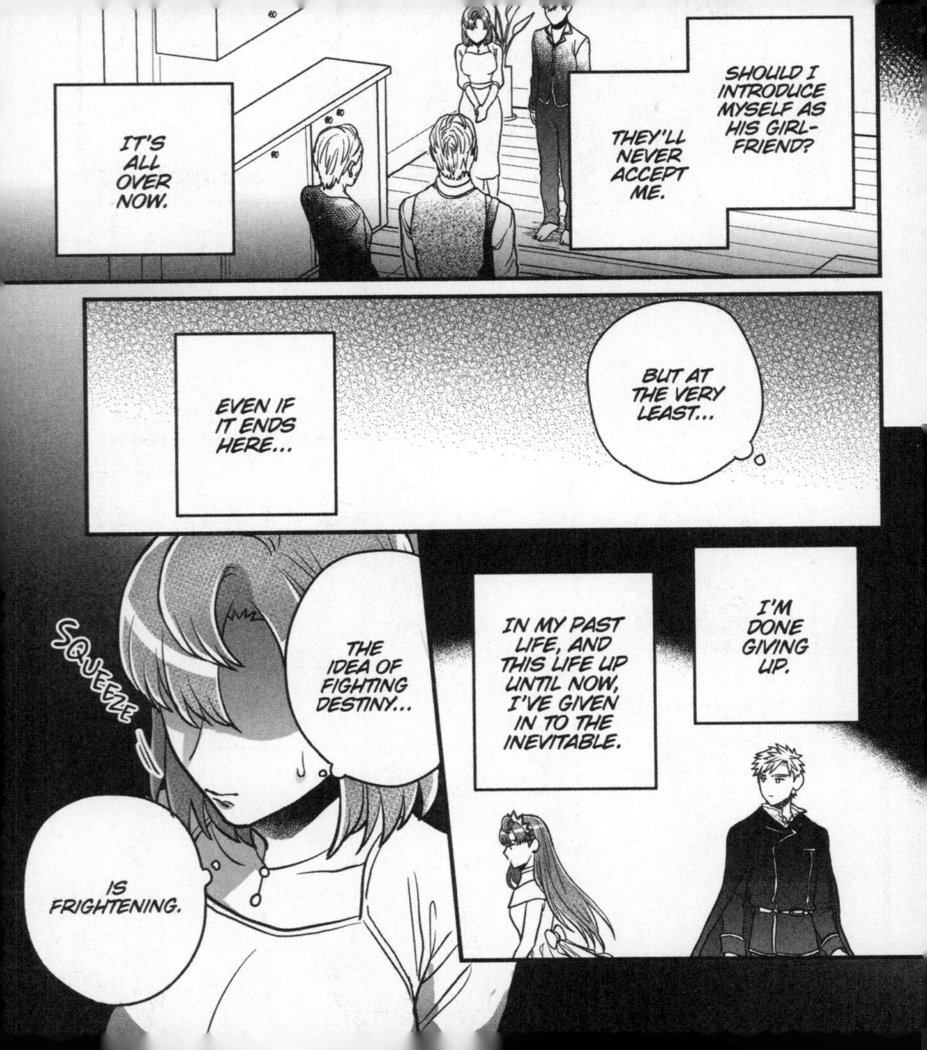
SHOULD I INTRODUCE MYSELF AS HIS GIRL-FRIEND?
THEY'LL NEVER ACCEPT ME.
IT'S ALL OVER NOW.
BUT AT THE VERY LEAST...
EVEN IF IT ENDS HERE...
I'M DONE GIVING UP.
IN MY PAST LIFE, AND THIS LIFE UP UNTIL NOW, I'VE GIVEN IN TO THE INEVITABLE.
THE IDEA OF FIGHTING DESTINY...
IS FRIGHTENING.
SQUEEZE

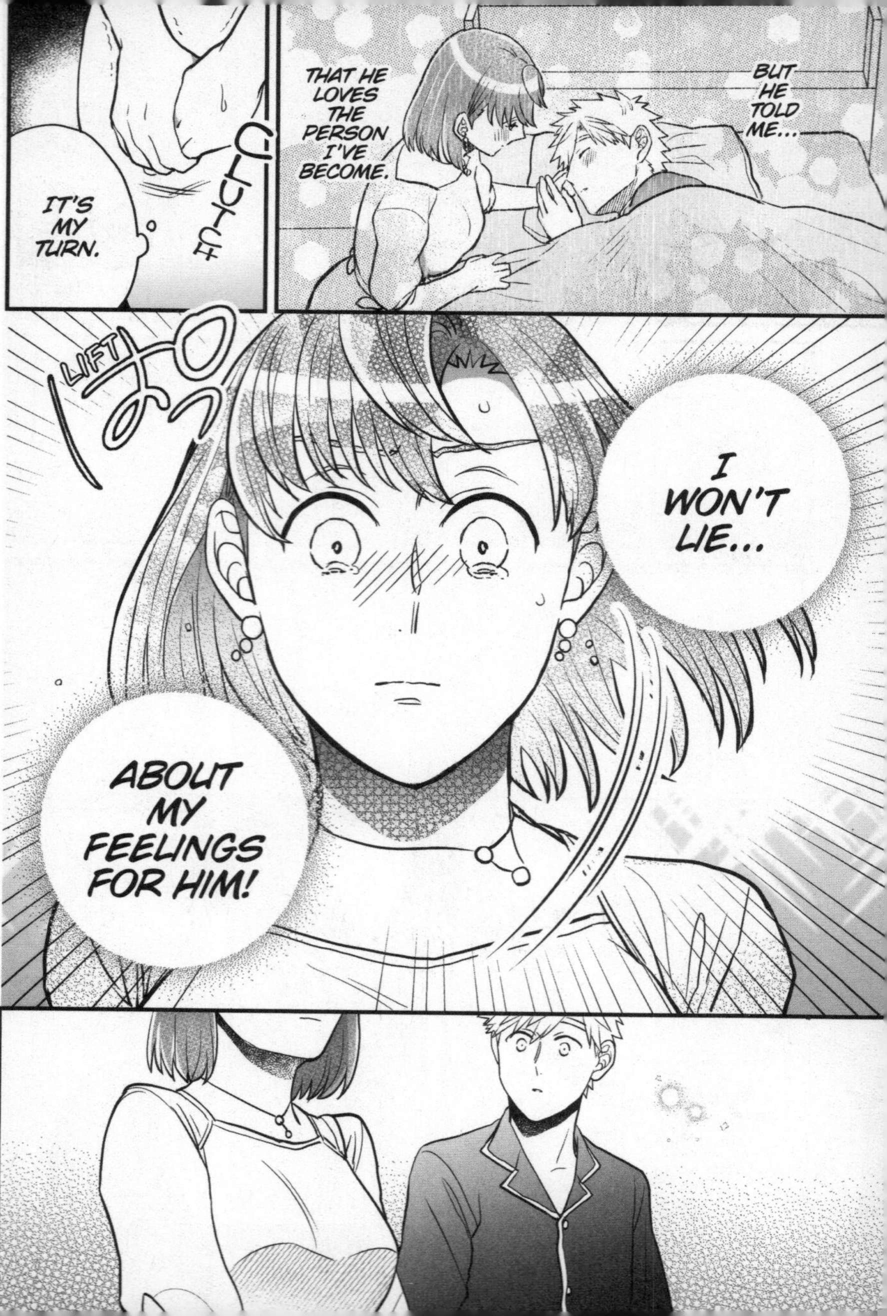
BUT HE TOLD ME...
THAT HE LOVES THE PERSON I'VE BECOME.
CLUTCH
IT'S MY TURN.
LIFT
I WON'T LIE...
ABOUT MY FEELINGS FOR HIM!

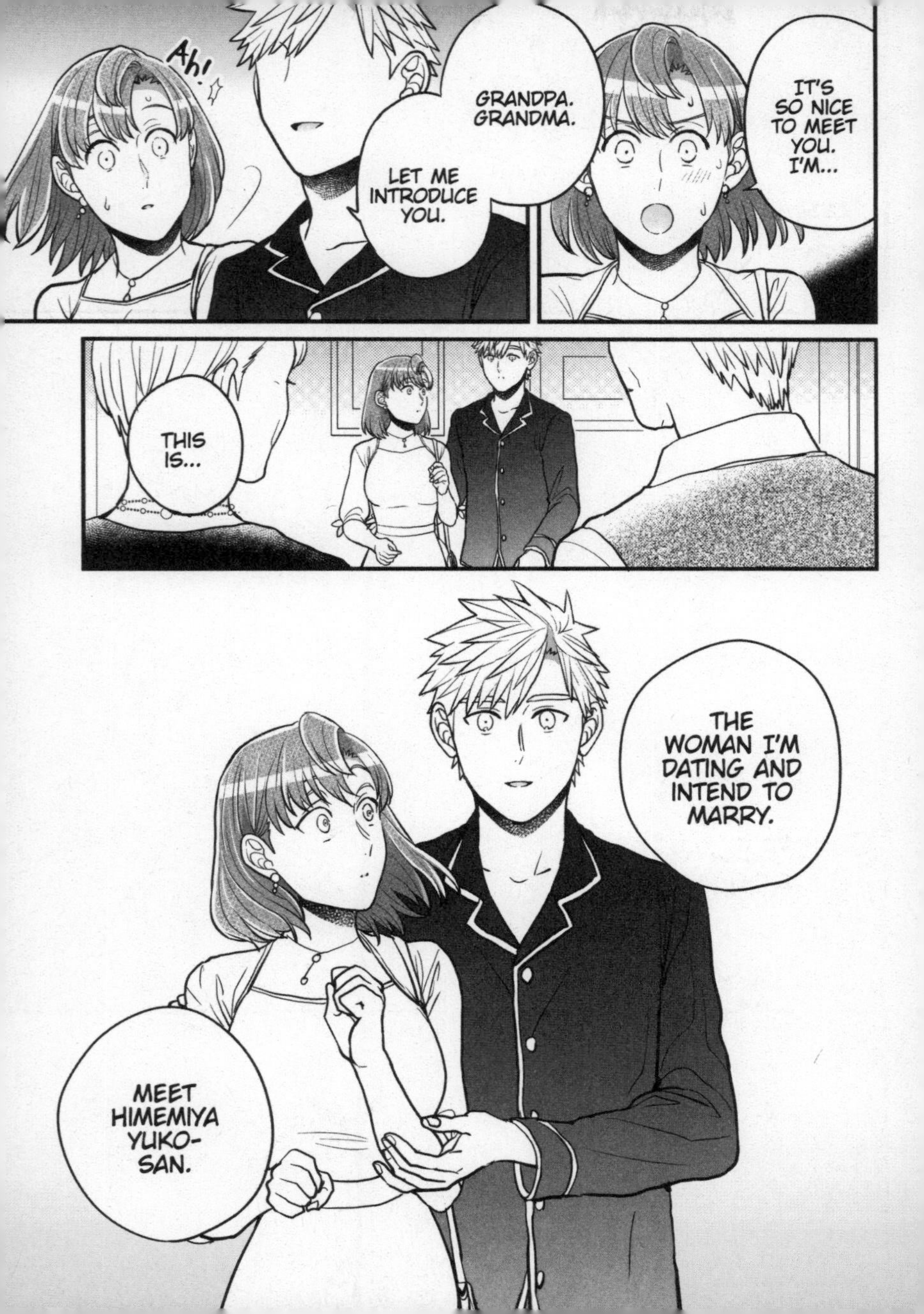
IT'S SO NICE TO MEET YOU. I'M...
GRANDPA. GRANDMA.
LET ME INTRODUCE YOU.
Ah!
THIS IS...
THE WOMAN I'M DATING AND INTEND TO MARRY.
MEET HIMEMIYA YUKO-SAN.

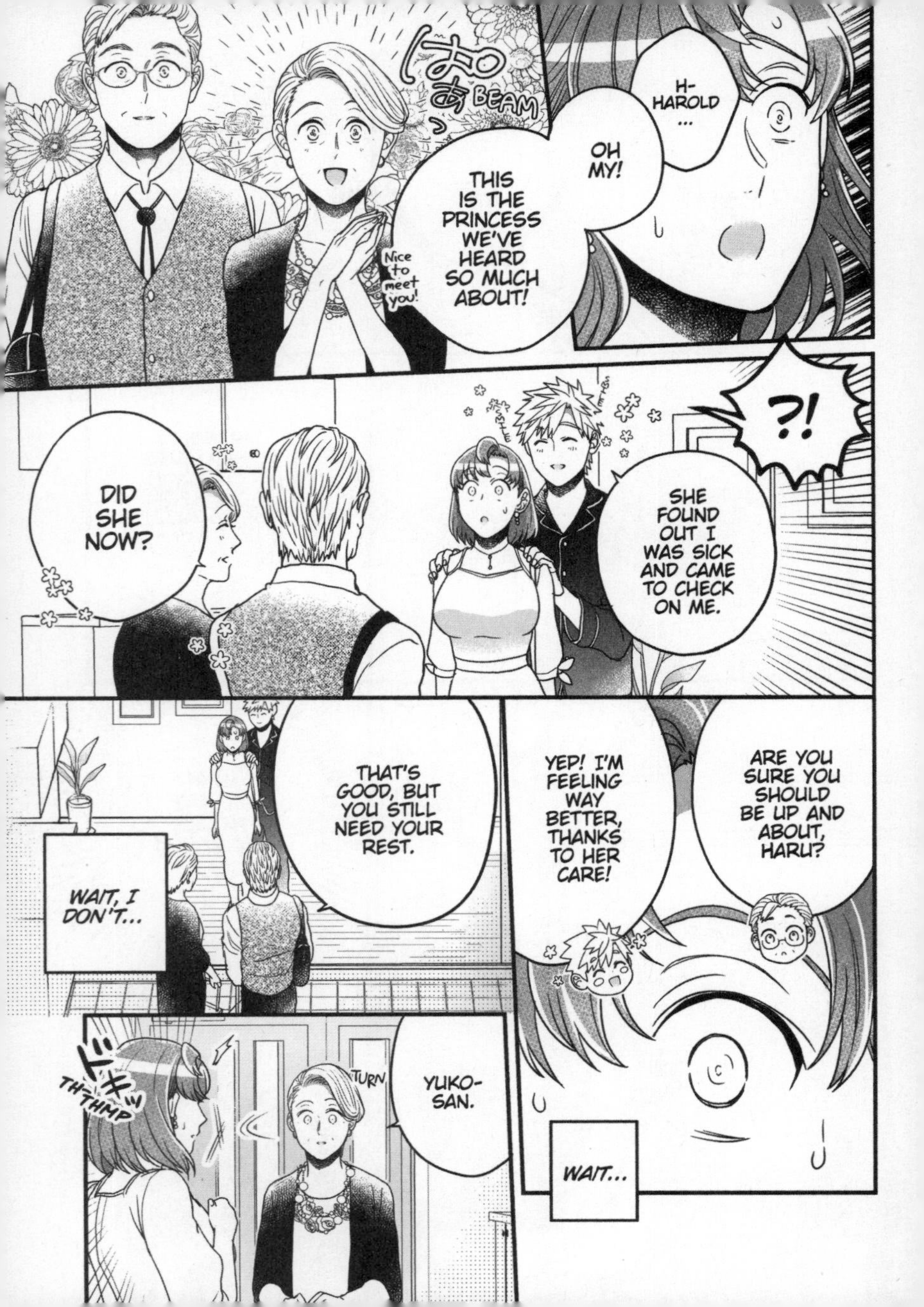
H-HAROLD...
BEAM
OH MY!
THIS IS THE PRINCESS WE'VE HEARD SO MUCH ABOUT!
Nice to meet you!
?!
SHE FOUND OUT I WAS SICK AND CAME TO CHECK ON ME.
DID SHE NOW?
ARE YOU SURE YOU SHOULD BE UP AND ABOUT, HARU?
YEP! I'M FEELING WAY BETTER, THANKS TO HER CARE!
WAIT...
THAT'S GOOD, BUT YOU STILL NEED YOUR REST.
WAIT, I DON'T...
YUKO-SAN.
TURN
TH-THMP

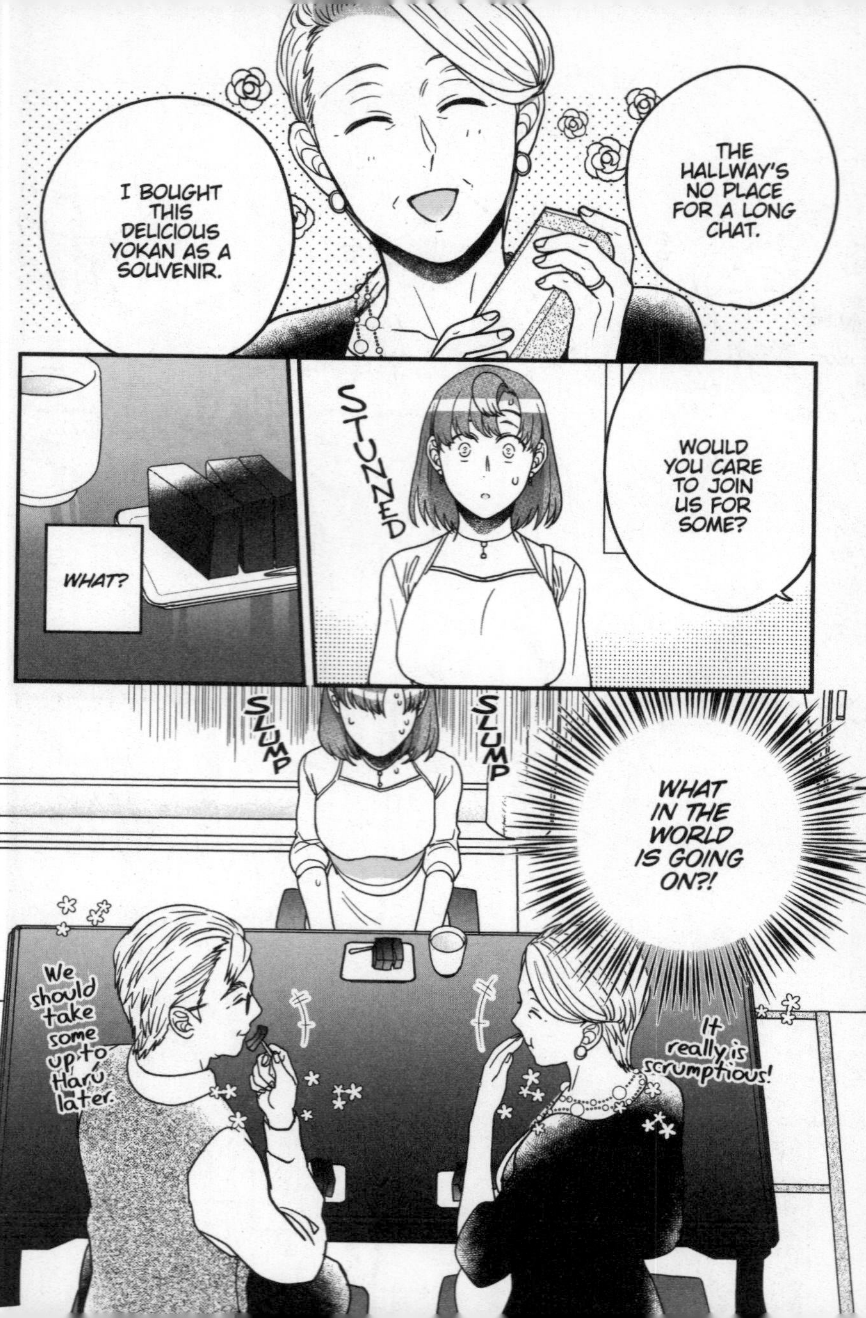
THE HALLWAY'S NO PLACE FOR A LONG CHAT.
I BOUGHT THIS DELICIOUS YOKAN AS A SOUVENIR.
WOULD YOU CARE TO JOIN US FOR SOME?
STUNNED
WHAT?
SLUMP
SLUMP
WHAT IN THE WORLD IS GOING ON?!
It really is scrumptious!
We should take some up to Haru later.

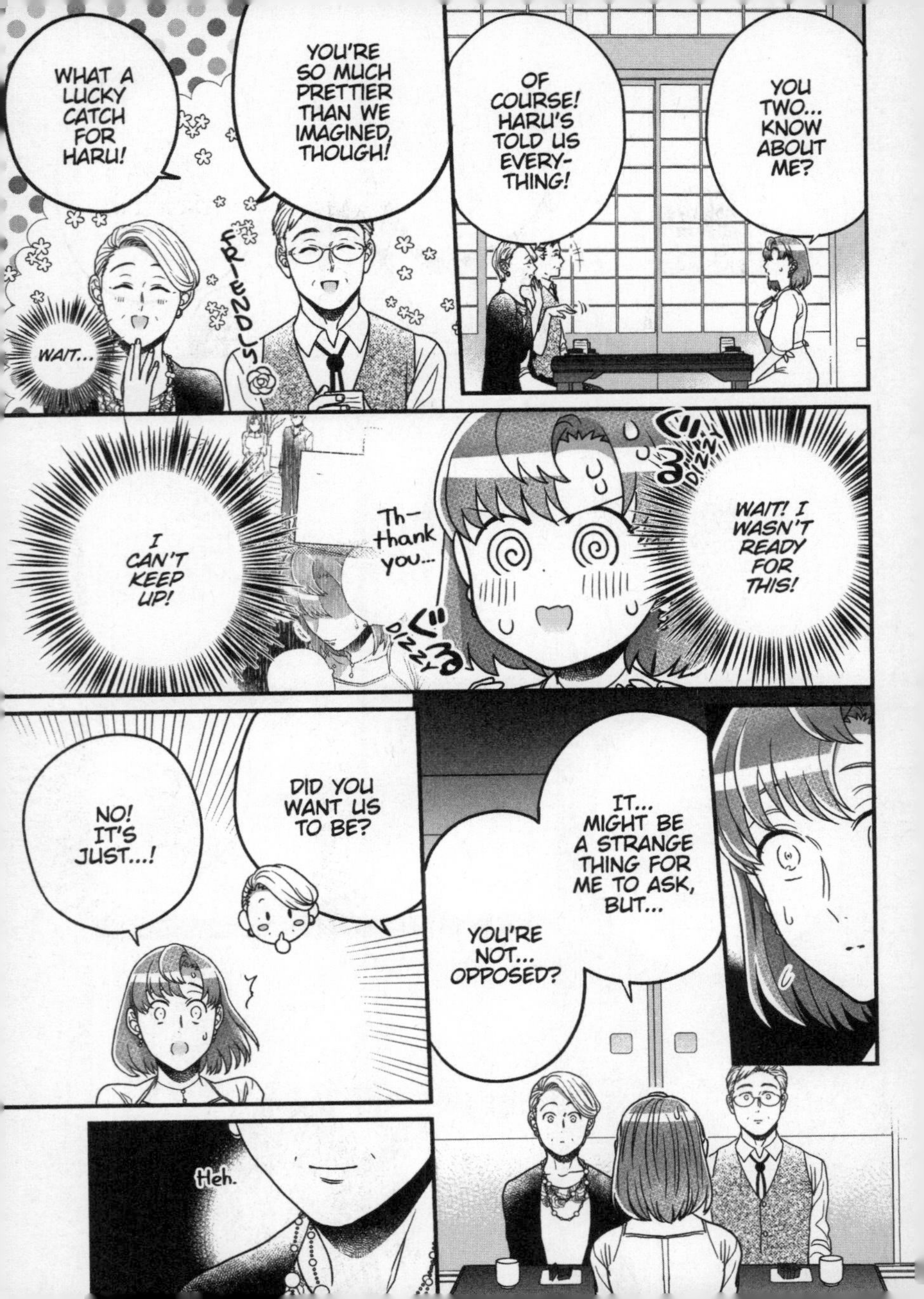
YOU TWO... KNOW ABOUT ME?
OF COURSE! HARU'S TOLD US EVERYTHING!
YOU'RE SO MUCH PRETTIER THAN WE IMAGINED THOUGH!
WHAT A LUCKY CATCH FOR HARU!
WAIT...
WAIT! I WASN'T READY FOR THIS!
DIZZY
Th-thank you...
DIZZY
I CAN'T KEEP UP!
IT... MIGHT BE A STRANGE THING FOR ME TO ASK, BUT...
YOU'RE NOT... OPPOSED?
DID YOU WANT US TO BE?
NO! IT'S JUST...!
Heh.

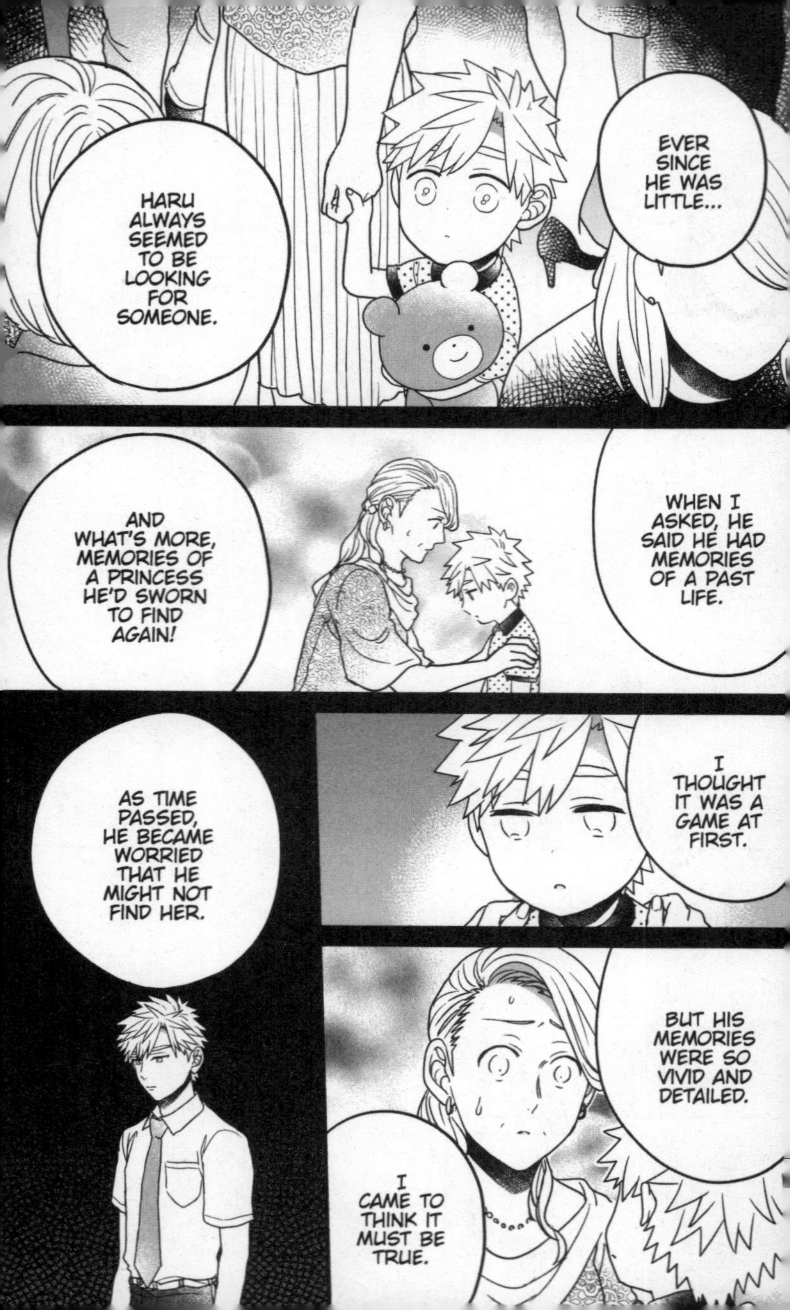
EVER SINCE HE WAS LITTLE...
HARU ALWAYS SEEMED TO BE LOOKING FOR SOMEONE.
WHEN I ASKED, HE SAID HE HAD MEMORIES OF A PAST LIFE.
AND WHAT'S MORE, MEMORIES OF A PRINCESS HE'D SWORN TO FIND AGAIN!
I THOUGHT IT WAS A GAME AT FIRST.
BUT HIS MEMORIES WERE SO VIVID AND DETAILED.
I CAME TO THINK IT MUST BE TRUE.
AS TIME PASSED, HE BECAME WORRIED THAT HE MIGHT NOT FIND HER.

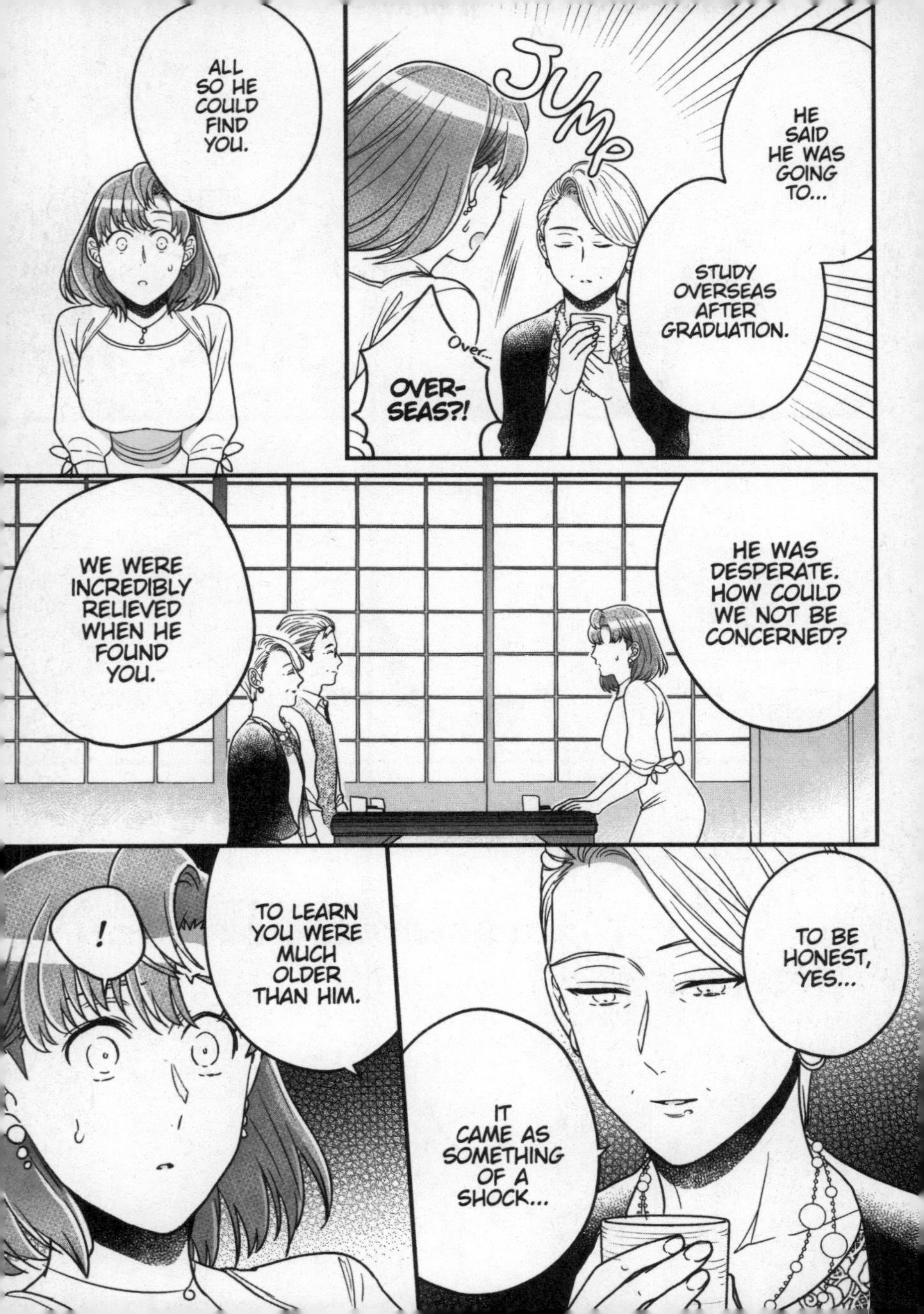
HE SAID HE WAS GOING TO...
JUMP
STUDY OVERSEAS AFTER GRADUATION.
Over...
OVER-SEAS?!
ALL SO HE COULD FIND YOU.
HE WAS DESPERATE. HOW COULD WE NOT BE CONCERNED?
WE WERE INCREDIBLY RELIEVED WHEN HE FOUND YOU.
TO BE HONEST, YES...
IT CAME AS SOMETHING OF A SHOCK...
TO LEARN YOU WERE MUCH OLDER THAN HIM.
!

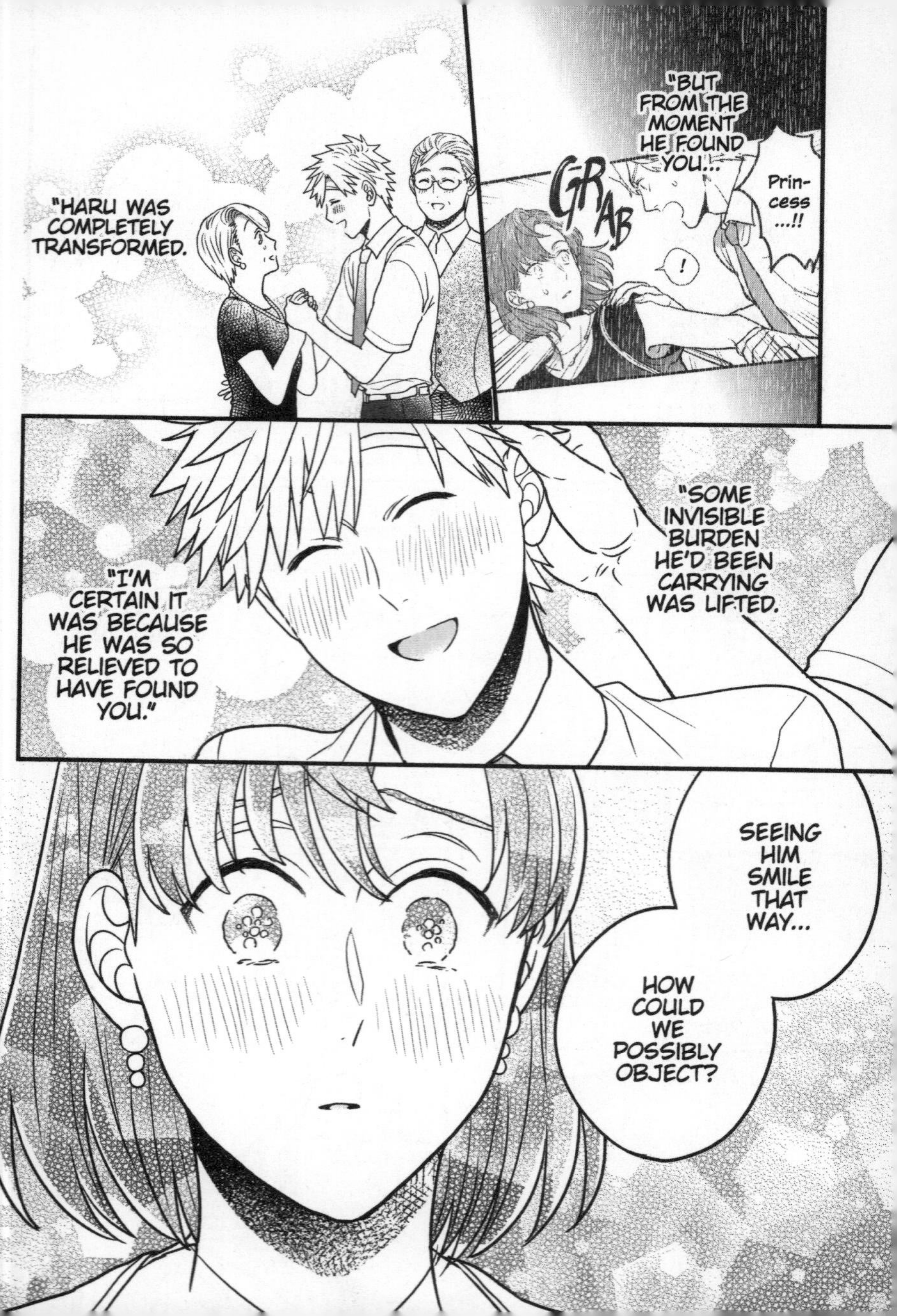
"BUT FROM THE MOMENT HE FOUND YOU...
GRAB
Prin-cess ...!!
!
"HARU WAS COMPLETELY TRANSFORMED.
"SOME INVISIBLE BURDEN HE'D BEEN CARRYING WAS LIFTED.
"I'M CERTAIN IT WAS BECAUSE HE WAS SO RELIEVED TO HAVE FOUND YOU."
SEEING HIM SMILE THAT WAY...
HOW COULD WE POSSIBLY OBJECT?

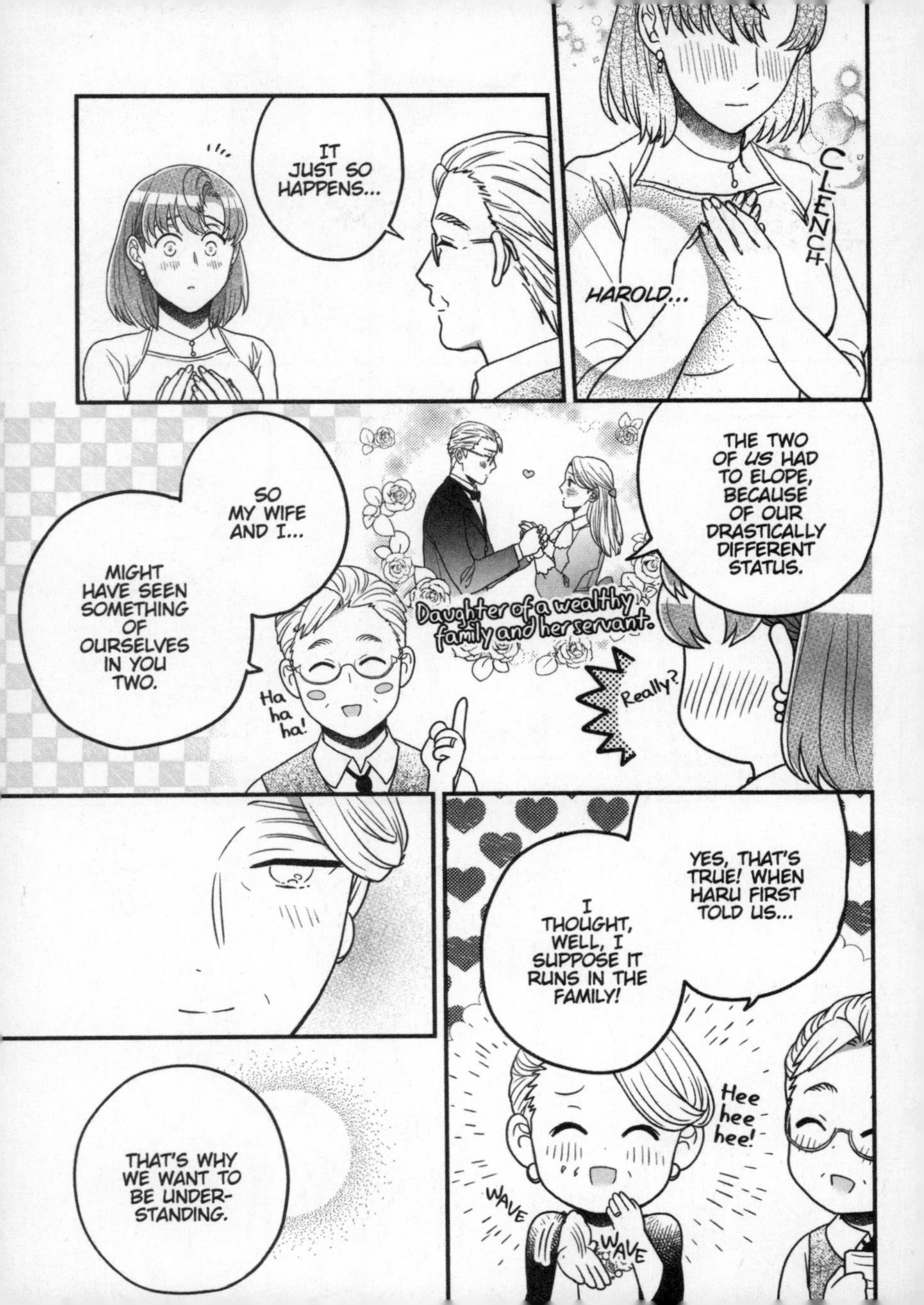
IT JUST SO HAPPENS...
HAROLD...
CLENCH
THE TWO OF US HAD TO ELOPE, BECAUSE OF OUR DRASTICALLY DIFFERENT STATUS.
SO MY WIFE AND I...
MIGHT HAVE SEEN SOMETHING OF OURSELVES IN YOU TWO.
Daughter of a wealthy family and her servant.
Really?
Ha ha ha!
YES, THAT'S TRUE! WHEN HARU FIRST TOLD US...
I THOUGHT, WELL, I SUPPOSE IT RUNS IN THE FAMILY!
THAT'S WHY WE WANT TO BE UNDER-STANDING.
Hee hee hee!
WAVE
WAVE

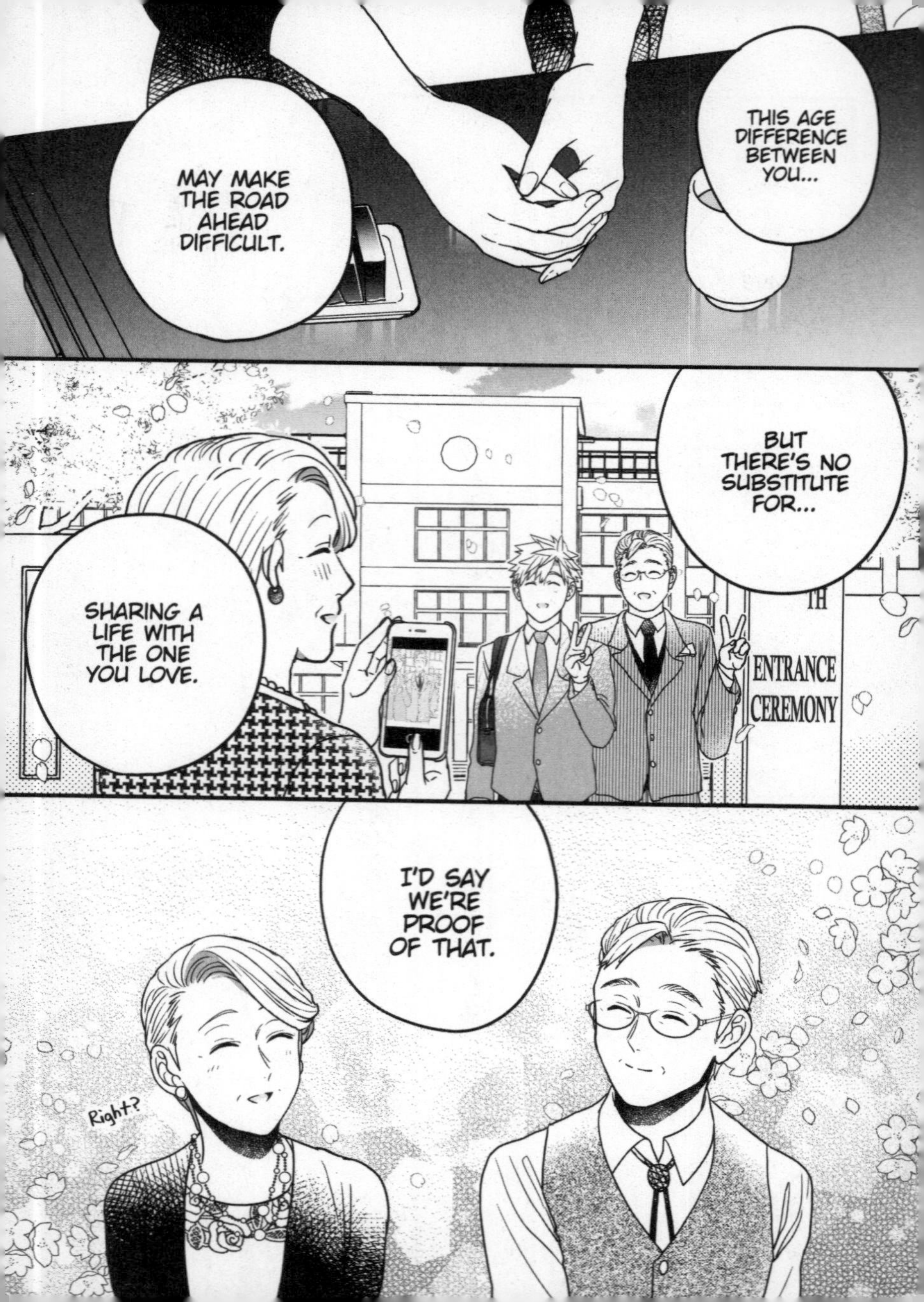
THIS AGE DIFFERENCE BETWEEN YOU...
MAY MAKE THE ROAD AHEAD DIFFICULT.
BUT THERE'S NO SUBSTITUTE FOR...
SHARING A LIFE WITH THE ONE YOU LOVE.
TH
ENTRANCE CEREMONY
I'D SAY WE'RE PROOF OF THAT.
Right?

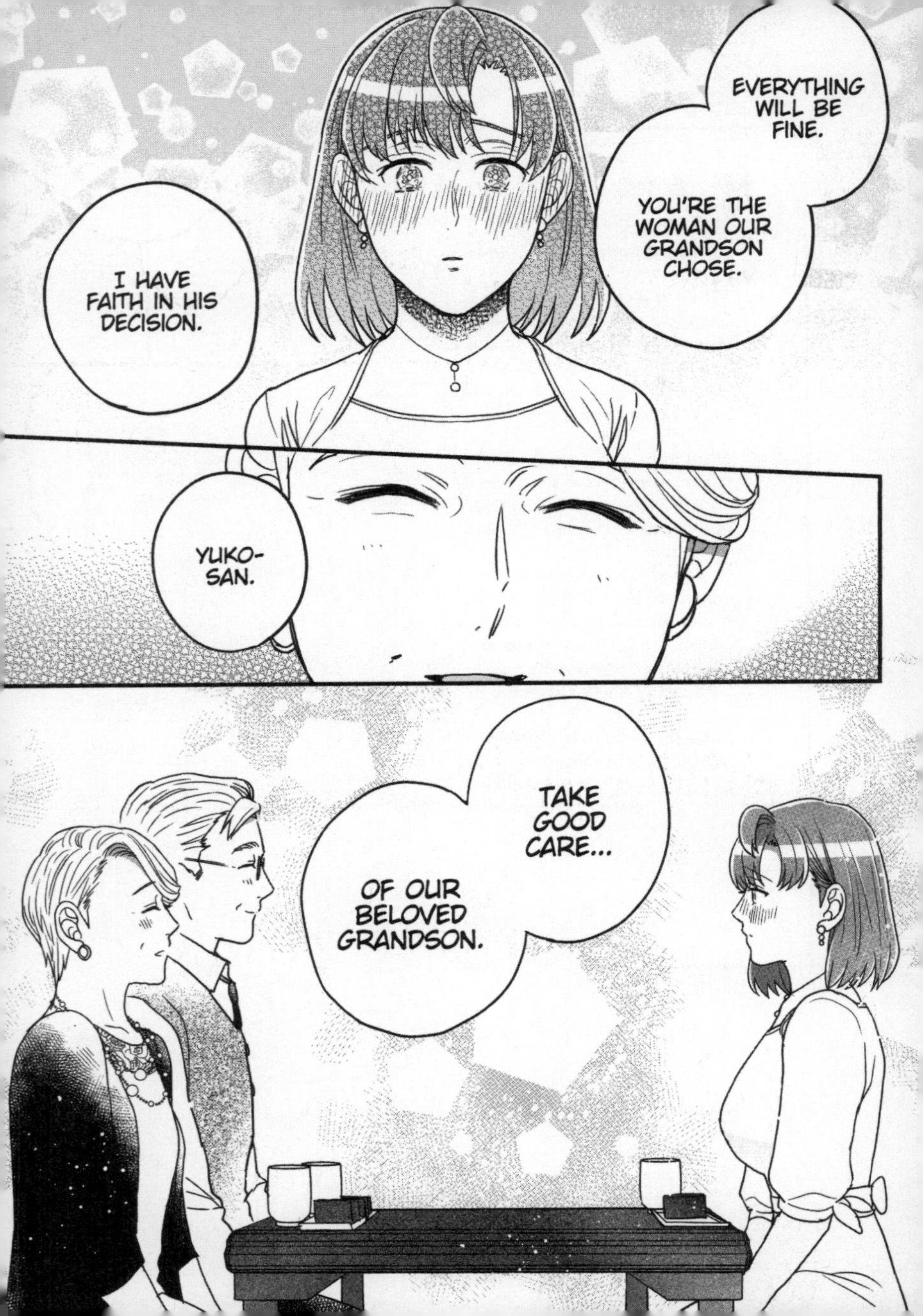
EVERYTHING WILL BE FINE.
YOU'RE THE WOMAN OUR GRANDSON CHOSE.
I HAVE FAITH IN HIS DECISION.
YUKO-SAN.
TAKE GOOD CARE...
OF OUR BELOVED GRANDSON.

Mr. & Mrs. Shirosaki

Haru's grandpa and grandma.

They're a couple of lovebirds. Grandma was the daughter of a wealthy family and Grandpa was a family servant. However, they fell in love, eloped, and are now happily married.

Haru gets along great with his grandparents, and the three of them often go out together. Grandma's been heard to say, "There's nothing better than being out in public with a handsome man on each arm." Hopefully she can be a positive influence on Yuko-san, who's concerned about being seen. (In fact, I think she will be!)

By the way, Haru's love of chicken stew and bitter foods is completely thanks to these two.

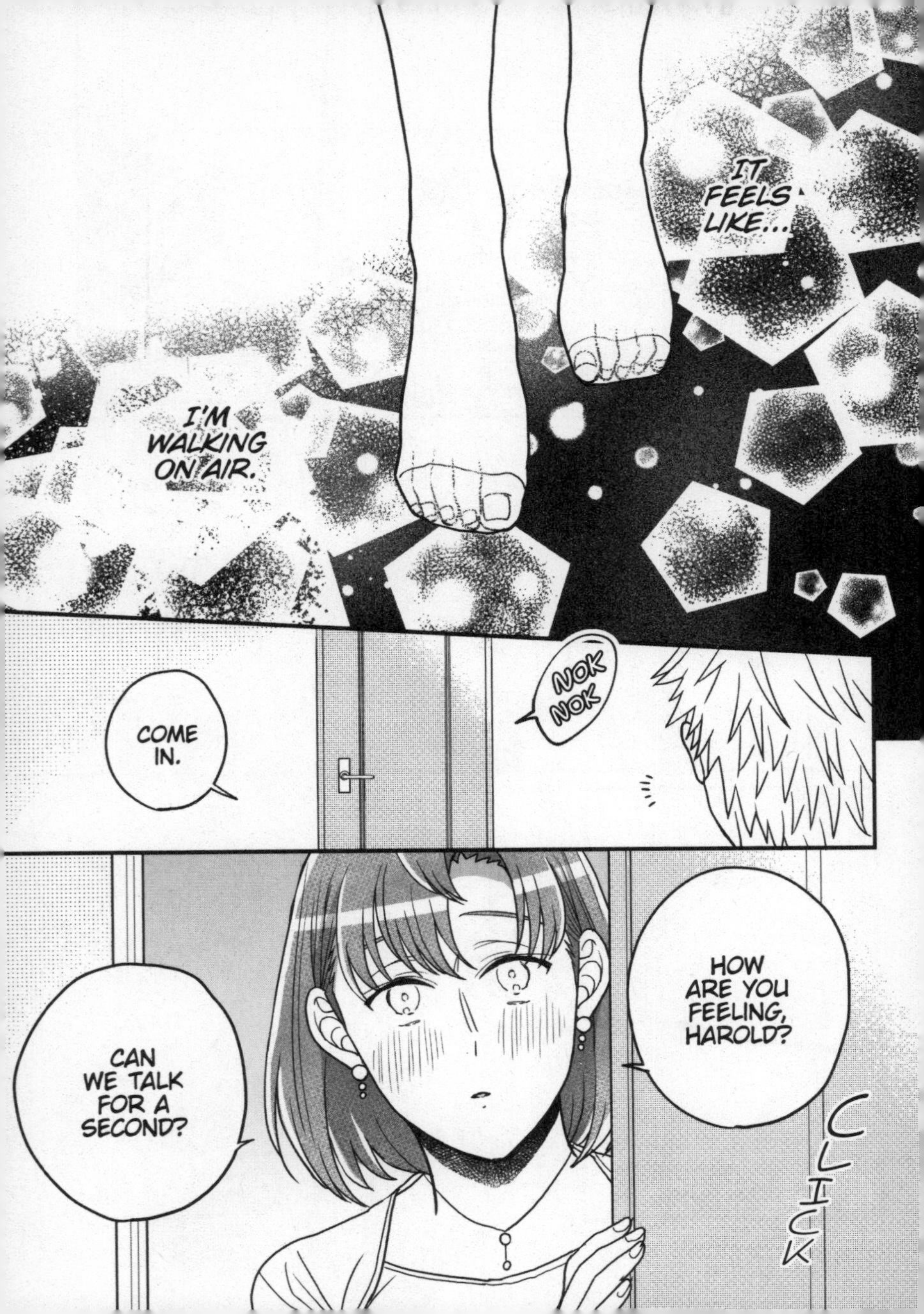
IT FEELS LIKE...
I'M WALKING ON AIR.
NOK NOK
COME IN.
HOW ARE YOU FEELING, HAROLD?
CAN WE TALK FOR A SECOND?
CLICK

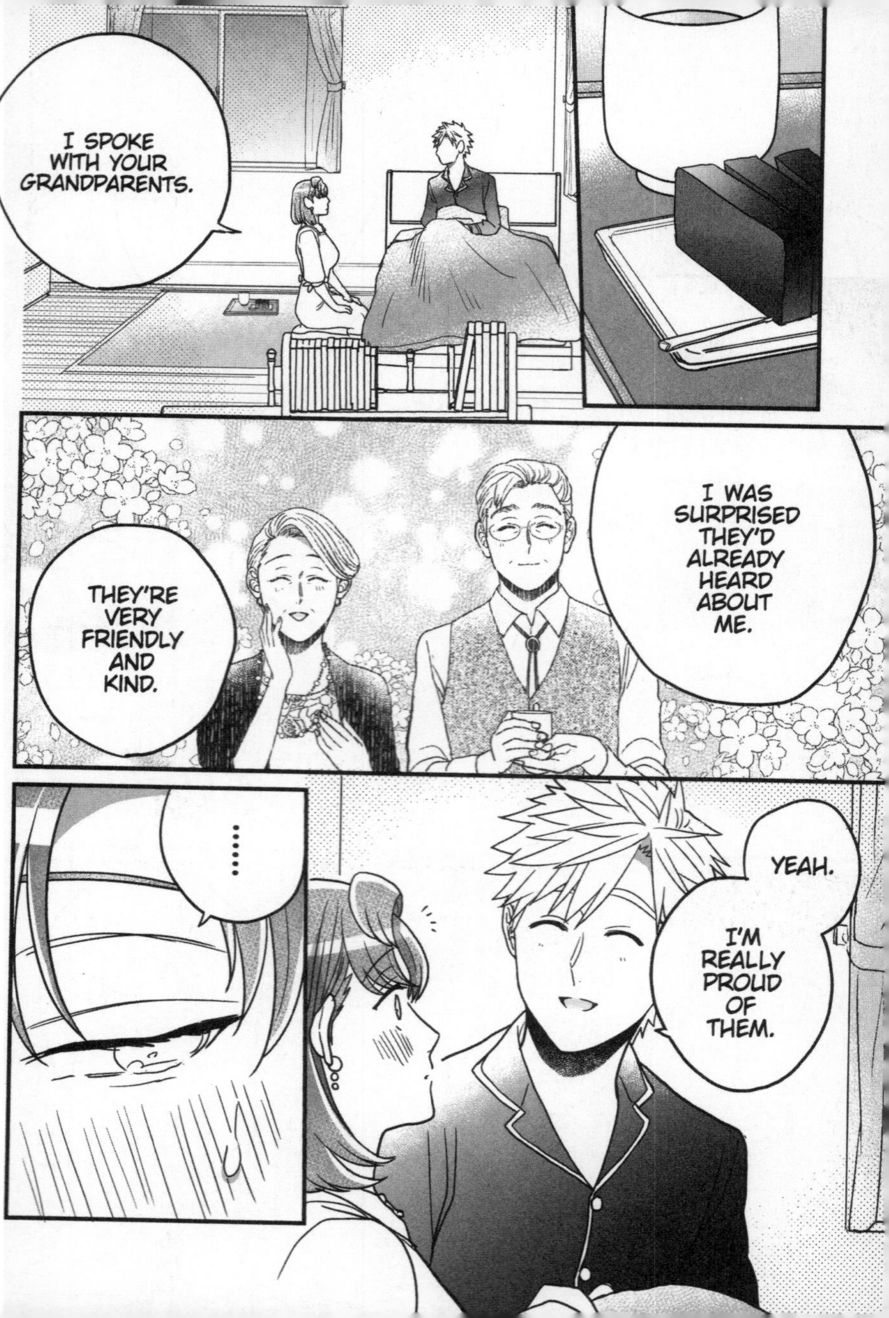
I SPOKE WITH YOUR GRANDPARENTS.
I WAS SURPRISED THEY'D ALREADY HEARD ABOUT ME.
THEY'RE VERY FRIENDLY AND KIND.
YEAH.
I'M REALLY PROUD OF THEM.
......

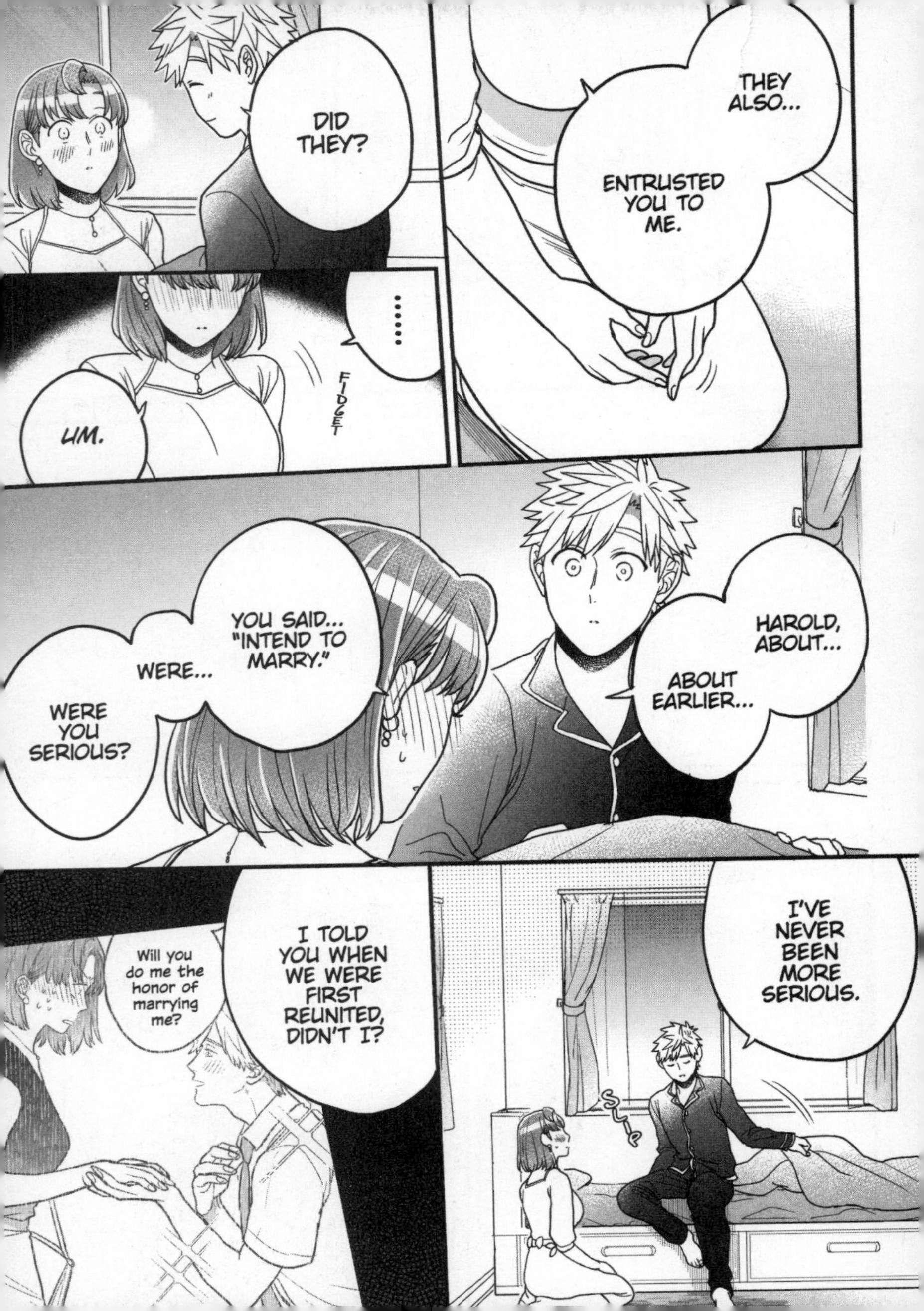

THEY ALSO...
ENTRUSTED YOU TO ME.
DID THEY?
......
FIDGET
UM.
HAROLD, ABOUT...
ABOUT EARLIER...
YOU SAID... "INTEND TO MARRY."
WERE...
WERE YOU SERIOUS?
I'VE NEVER BEEN MORE SERIOUS.
SLIP
I TOLD YOU WHEN WE WERE FIRST REUNITED, DIDN'T I?
Will you do me the honor of marrying me?

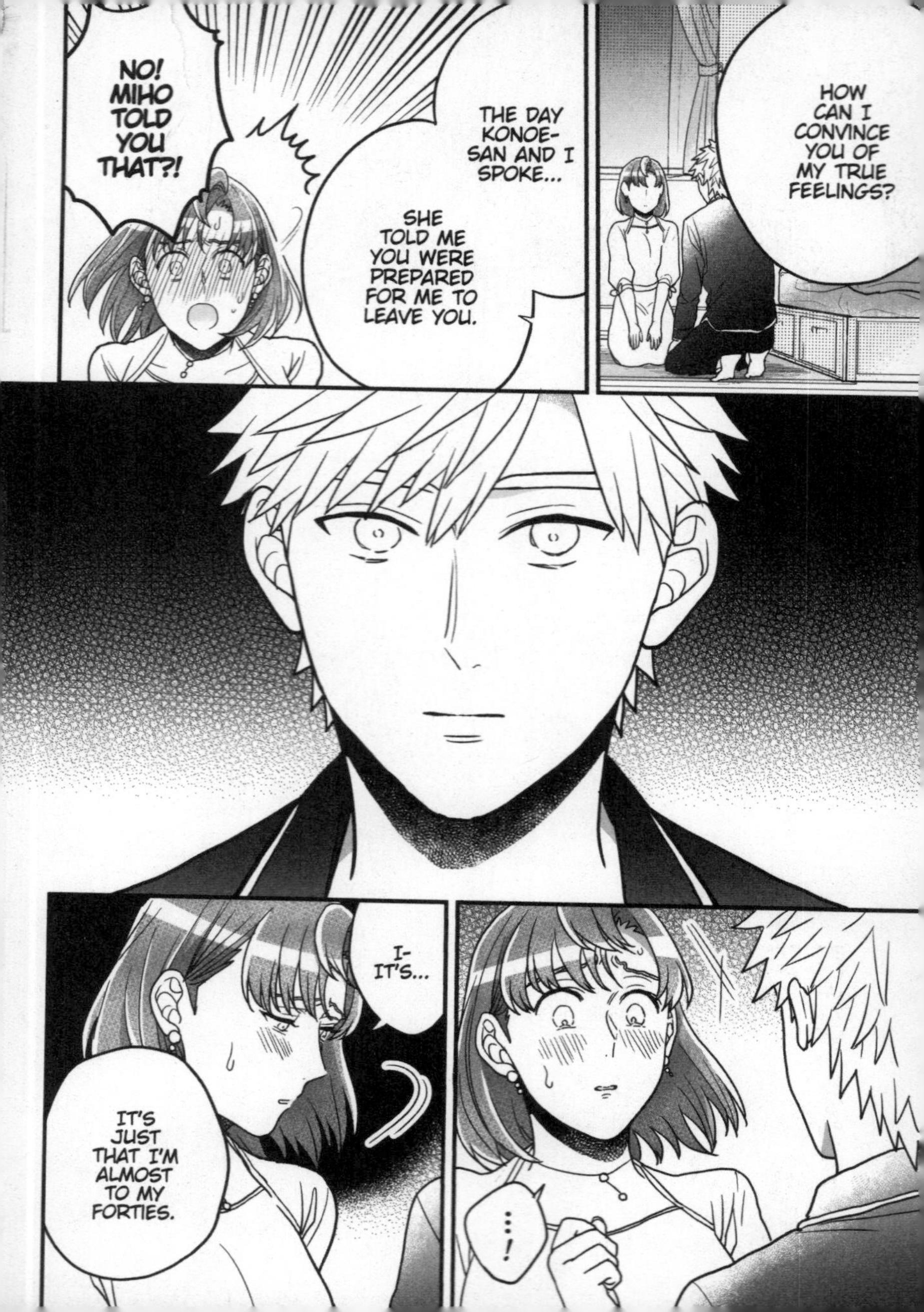
HOW CAN I CONVINCE YOU OF MY TRUE FEELINGS?
THE DAY KONOE-SAN AND I SPOKE...
SHE TOLD ME YOU WERE PREPARED FOR ME TO LEAVE YOU.
NO! MIHO TOLD YOU THAT?!
...!
I- IT'S...
IT'S JUST THAT I'M ALMOST TO MY FORTIES.

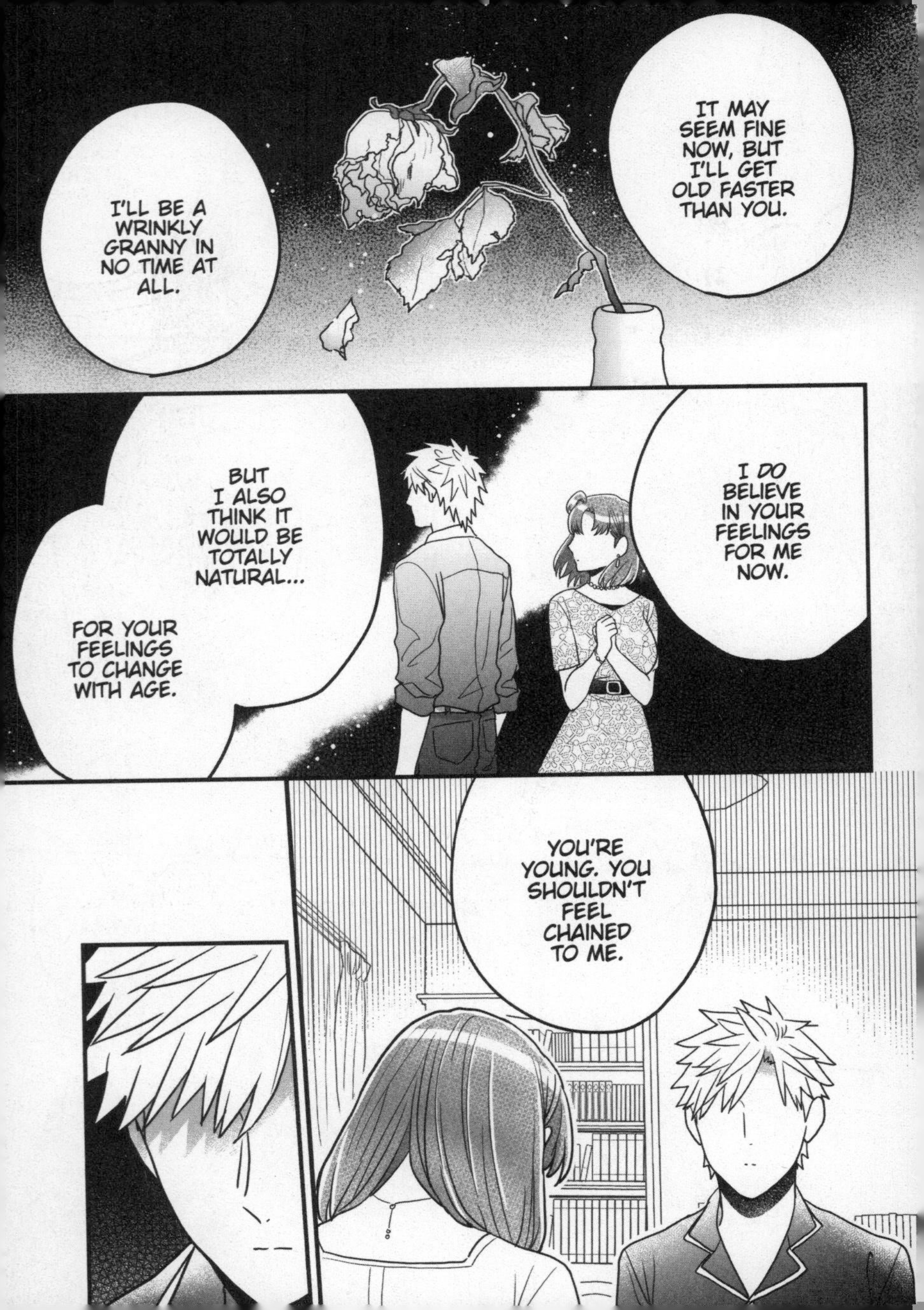

IT MAY SEEM FINE NOW, BUT I'LL GET OLD FASTER THAN YOU.
I'LL BE A WRINKLY GRANNY IN NO TIME AT ALL.
I DO BELIEVE IN YOUR FEELINGS FOR ME NOW.
BUT I ALSO THINK IT WOULD BE TOTALLY NATURAL...
FOR YOUR FEELINGS TO CHANGE WITH AGE.
YOU'RE YOUNG. YOU SHOULDN'T FEEL CHAINED TO ME.
...

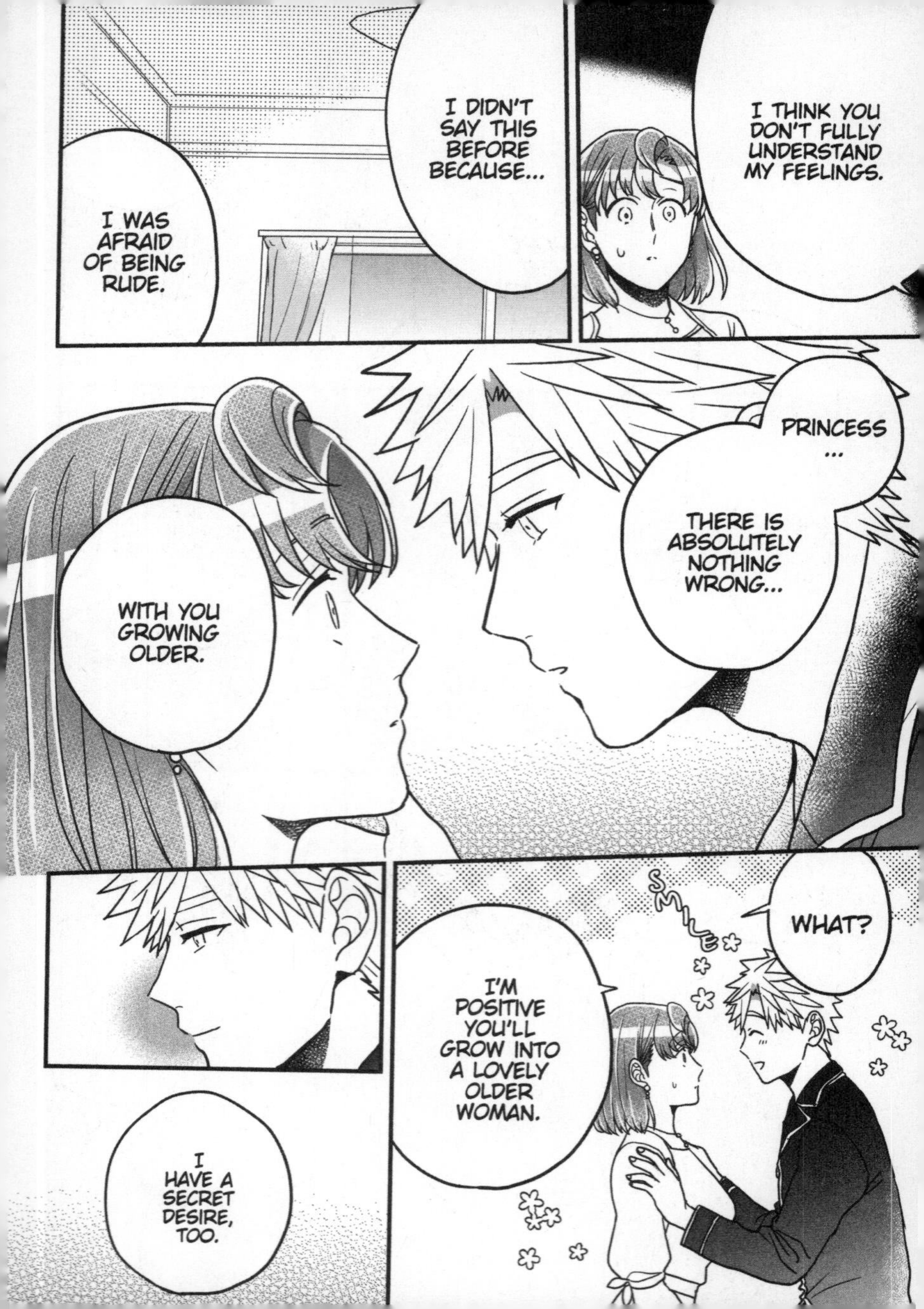
I THINK YOU DON'T FULLY UNDERSTAND MY FEELINGS.
I DIDN'T SAY THIS BEFORE BECAUSE...
I WAS AFRAID OF BEING RUDE.
PRINCESS ...
THERE IS ABSOLUTELY NOTHING WRONG...
WITH YOU GROWING OLDER.
WHAT?
SMILE
I'M POSITIVE YOU'LL GROW INTO A LOVELY OLDER WOMAN.
I HAVE A SECRET DESIRE, TOO.

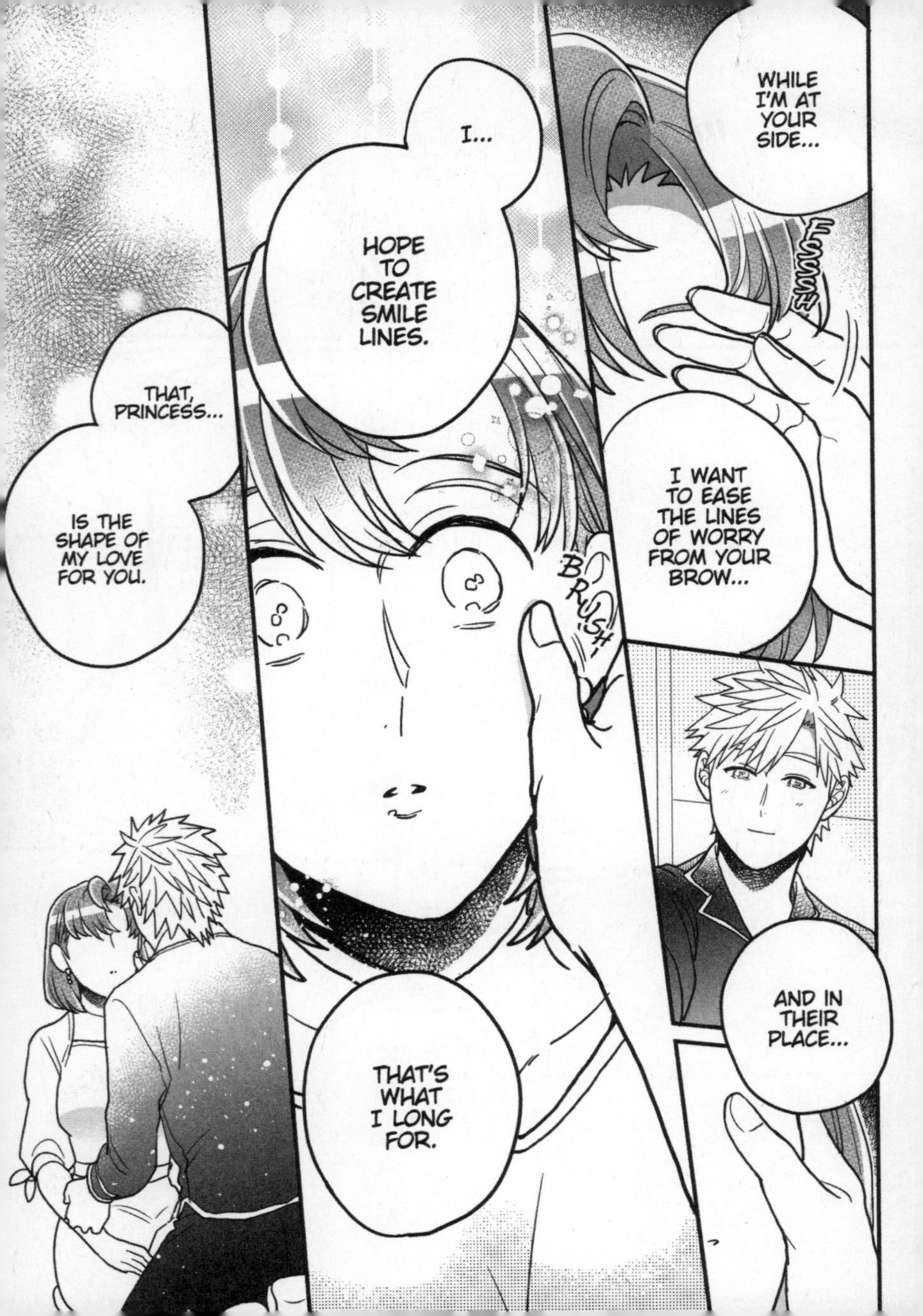
WHILE I'M AT YOUR SIDE...
FSSSH
I WANT TO EASE THE LINES OF WORRY FROM YOUR BROW...
AND IN THEIR PLACE...
I...
HOPE TO CREATE SMILE LINES.
BRUSH
THAT'S WHAT I LONG FOR.
THAT, PRINCESS...
IS THE SHAPE OF MY LOVE FOR YOU.

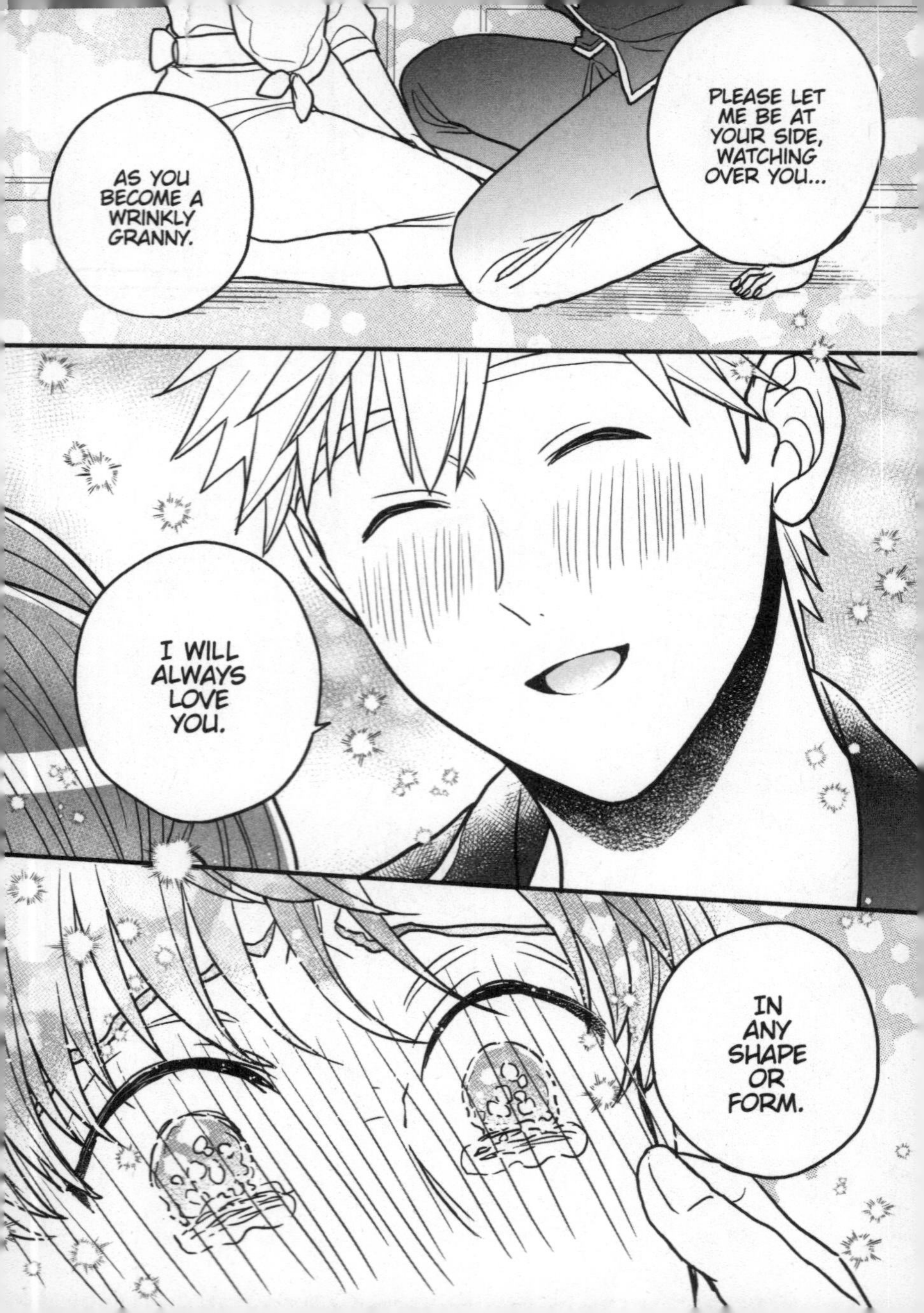
PLEASE LET ME BE AT YOUR SIDE, WATCHING OVER YOU...
AS YOU BECOME A WRINKLY GRANNY.
I WILL ALWAYS LOVE YOU.
IN ANY SHAPE OR FORM.

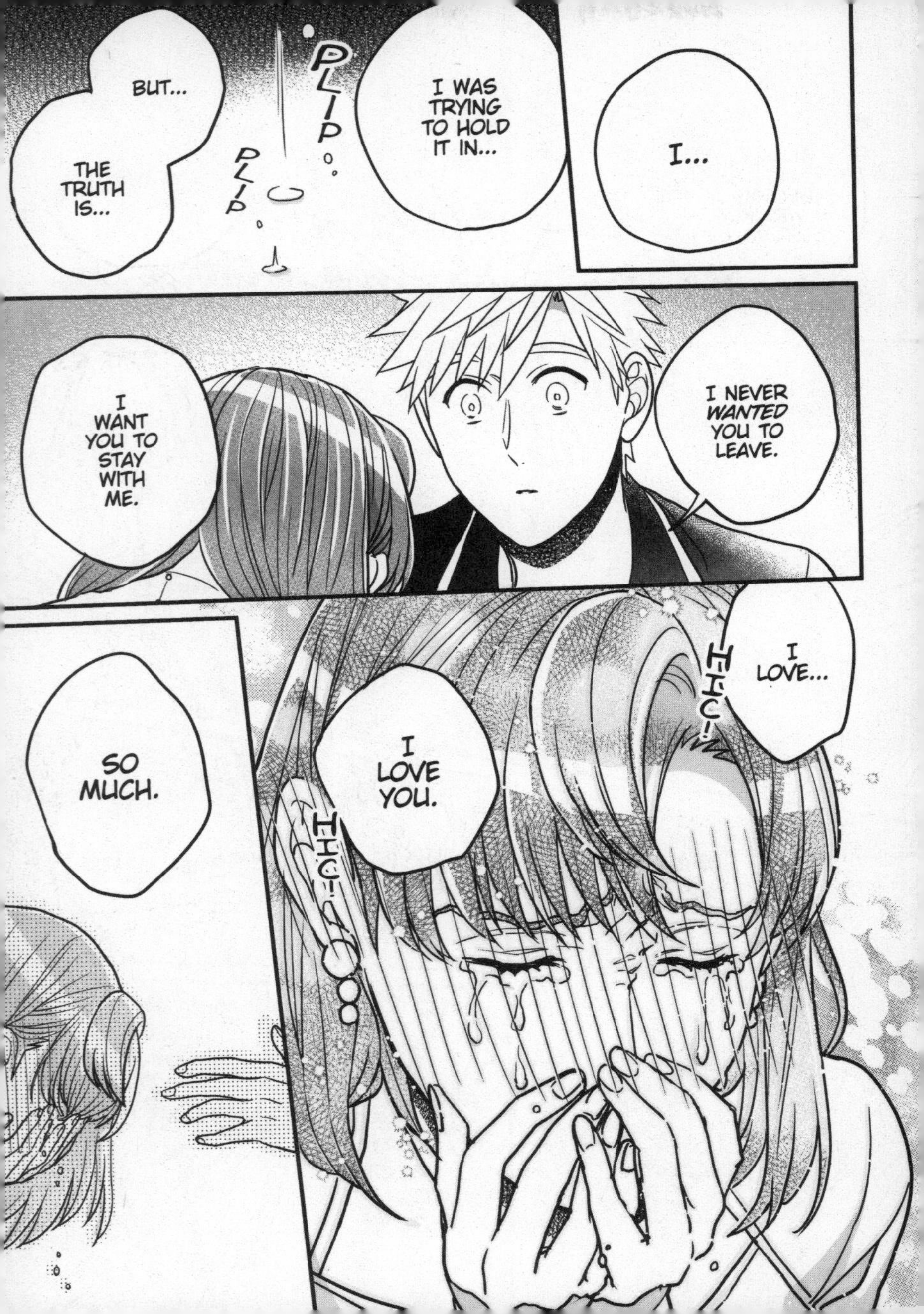
I...
I WAS TRYING TO HOLD IT IN...
PLIP
PLIP
BUT...
THE TRUTH IS...
I NEVER WANTED YOU TO LEAVE.
I WANT YOU TO STAY WITH ME.
I LOVE...
HIC!
I LOVE YOU.
HIC!
SO MUCH.

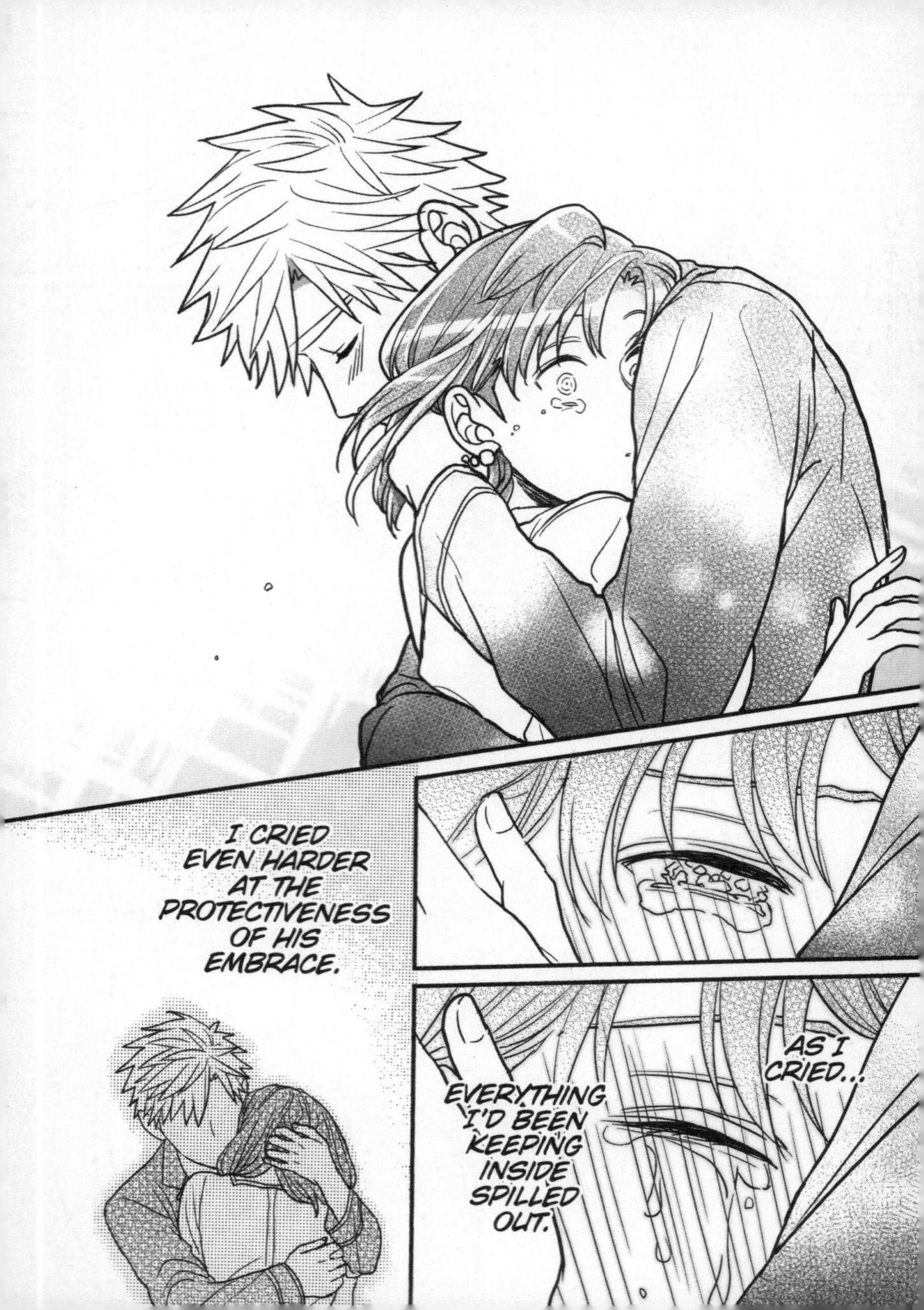

I CRIED EVEN HARDER AT THE PROTECTIVENESS OF HIS EMBRACE.
AS I CRIED...
EVERYTHING I'D BEEN KEEPING INSIDE SPILLED OUT.

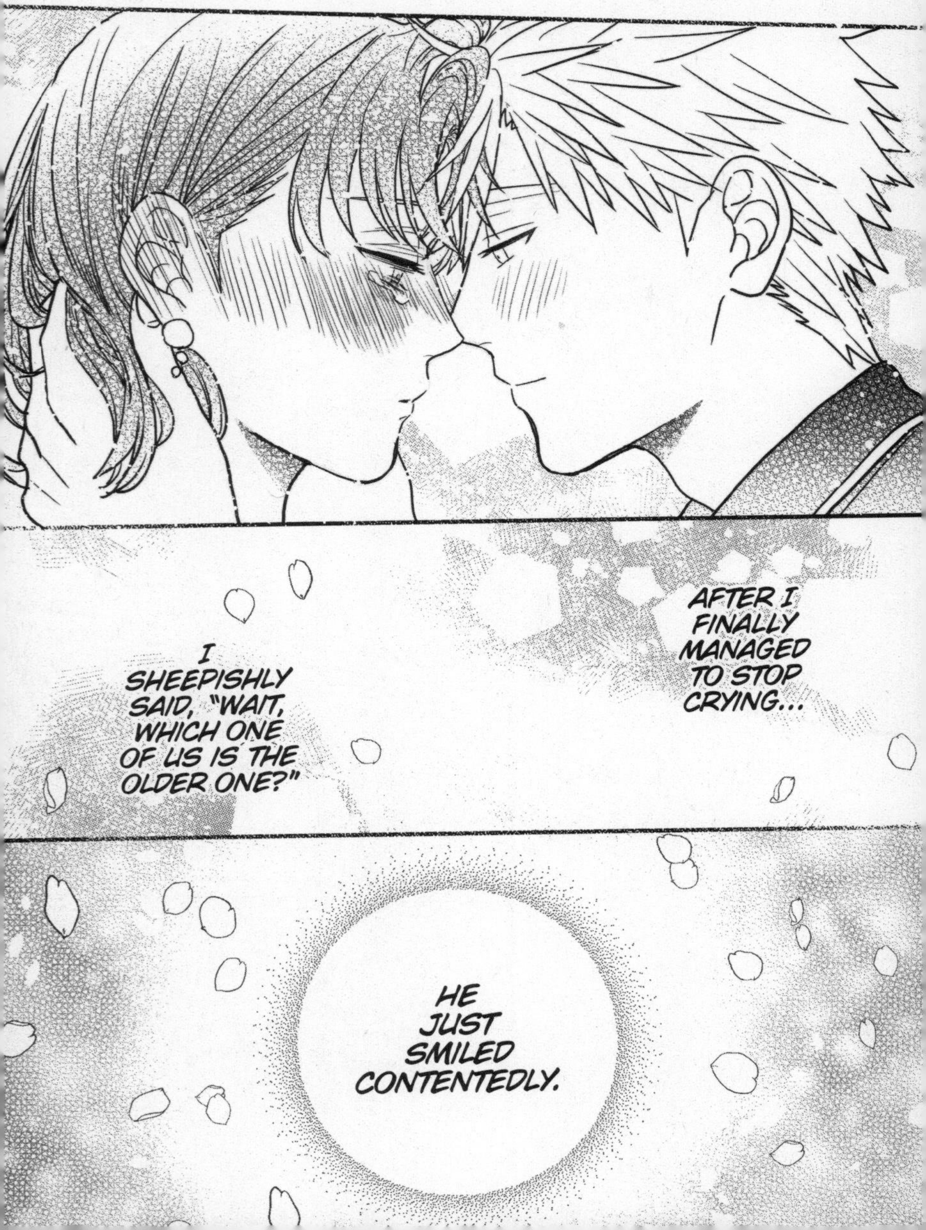
AFTER I FINALLY MANAGED TO STOP CRYING...
I SHEEPISHLY SAID, "WAIT, WHICH ONE OF US IS THE OLDER ONE?"
HE JUST SMILED CONTENTEDLY.

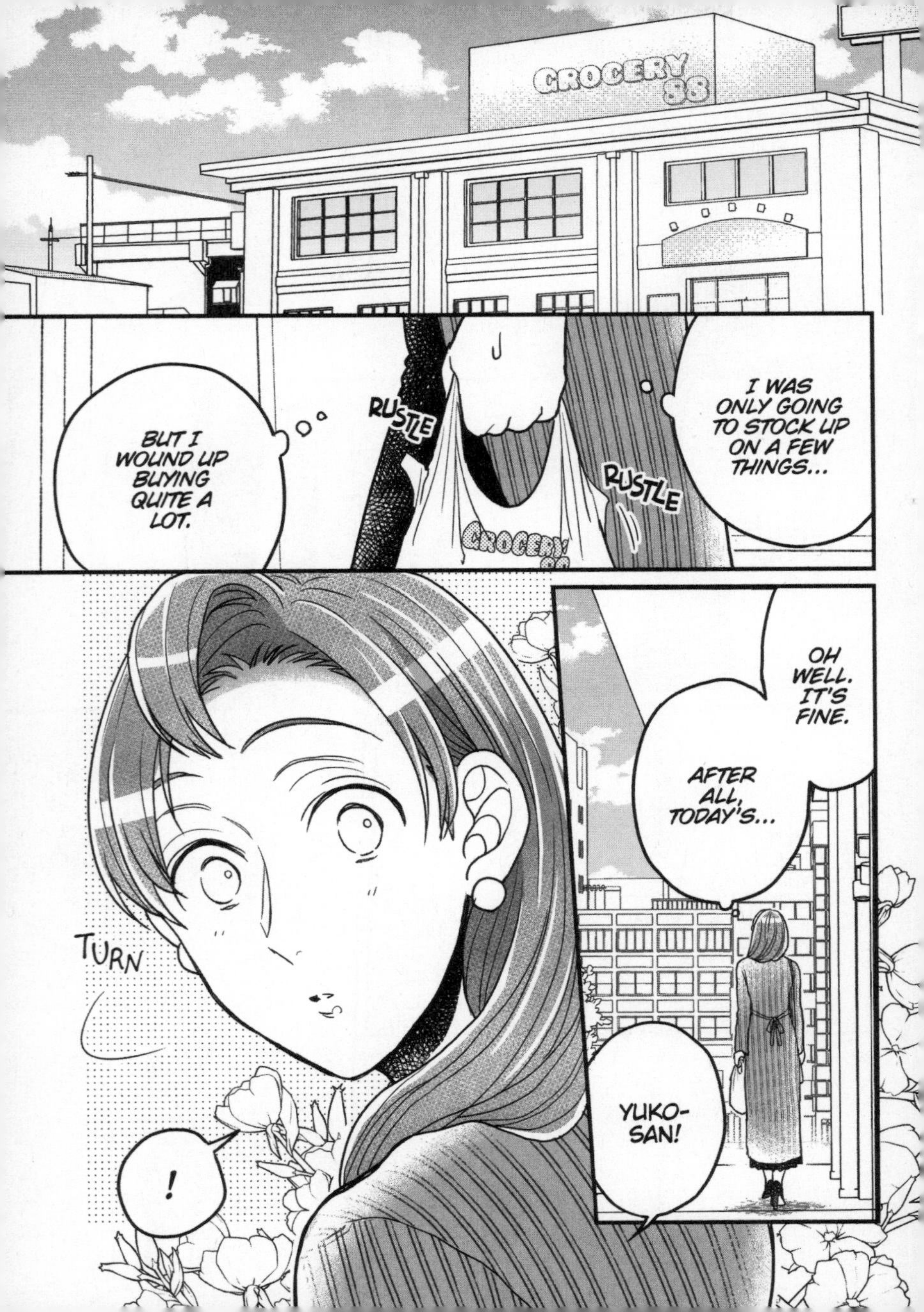
GROCERY 88
I WAS ONLY GOING TO STOCK UP ON A FEW THINGS...
RUSTLE
RUSTLE
BUT I WOUND UP BUYING QUITE A LOT.
OH WELL. IT'S FINE.
AFTER ALL, TODAY'S...
YUKO-SAN!
TURN
!

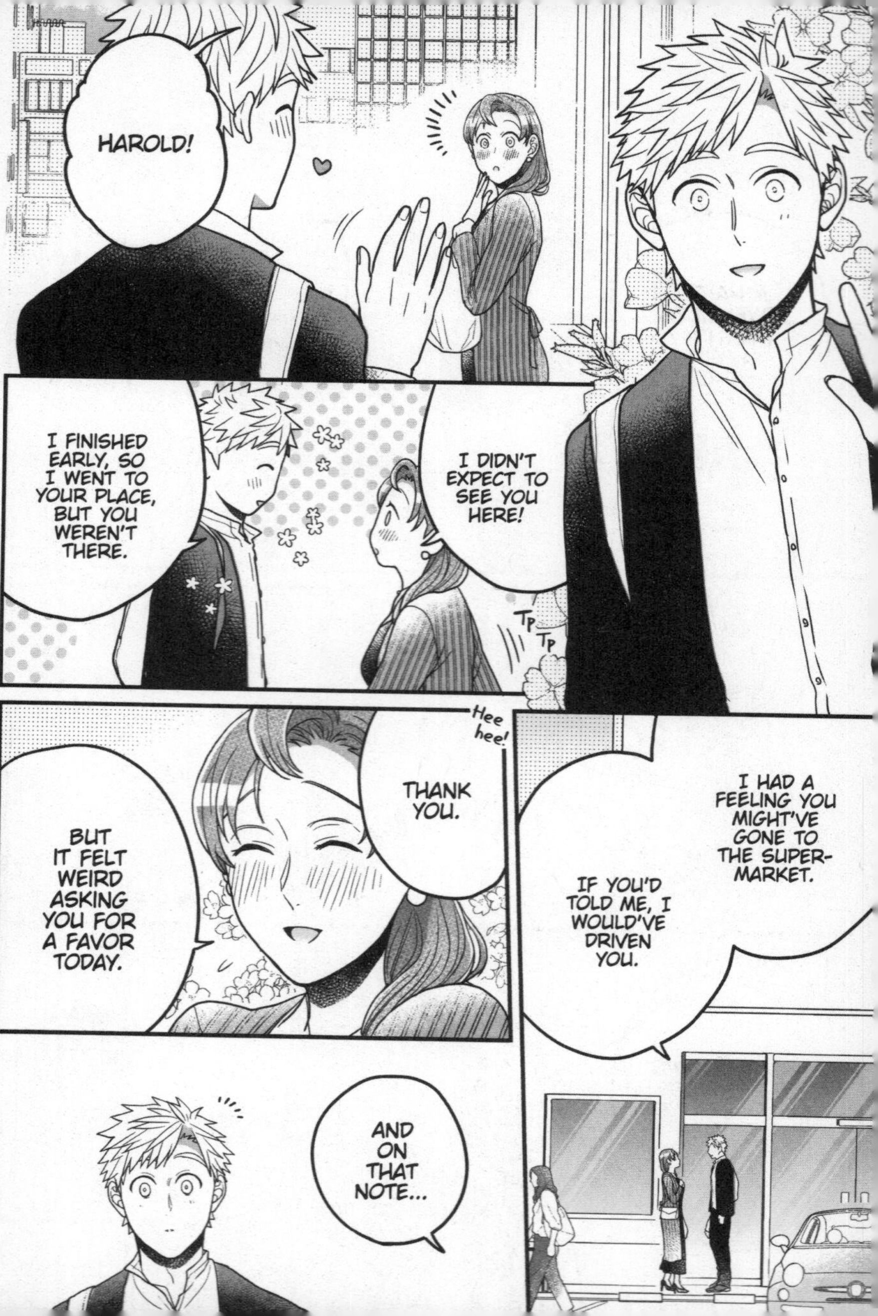
HAROLD!
I DIDN'T EXPECT TO SEE YOU HERE!
I FINISHED EARLY, SO I WENT TO YOUR PLACE, BUT YOU WEREN'T THERE.
TP TP
I HAD A FEELING YOU MIGHT'VE GONE TO THE SUPER-MARKET.
IF YOU'D TOLD ME, I WOULD'VE DRIVEN YOU.
THANK YOU.
Hee hee!
BUT IT FELT WEIRD ASKING YOU FOR A FAVOR TODAY.
AND ON THAT NOTE...

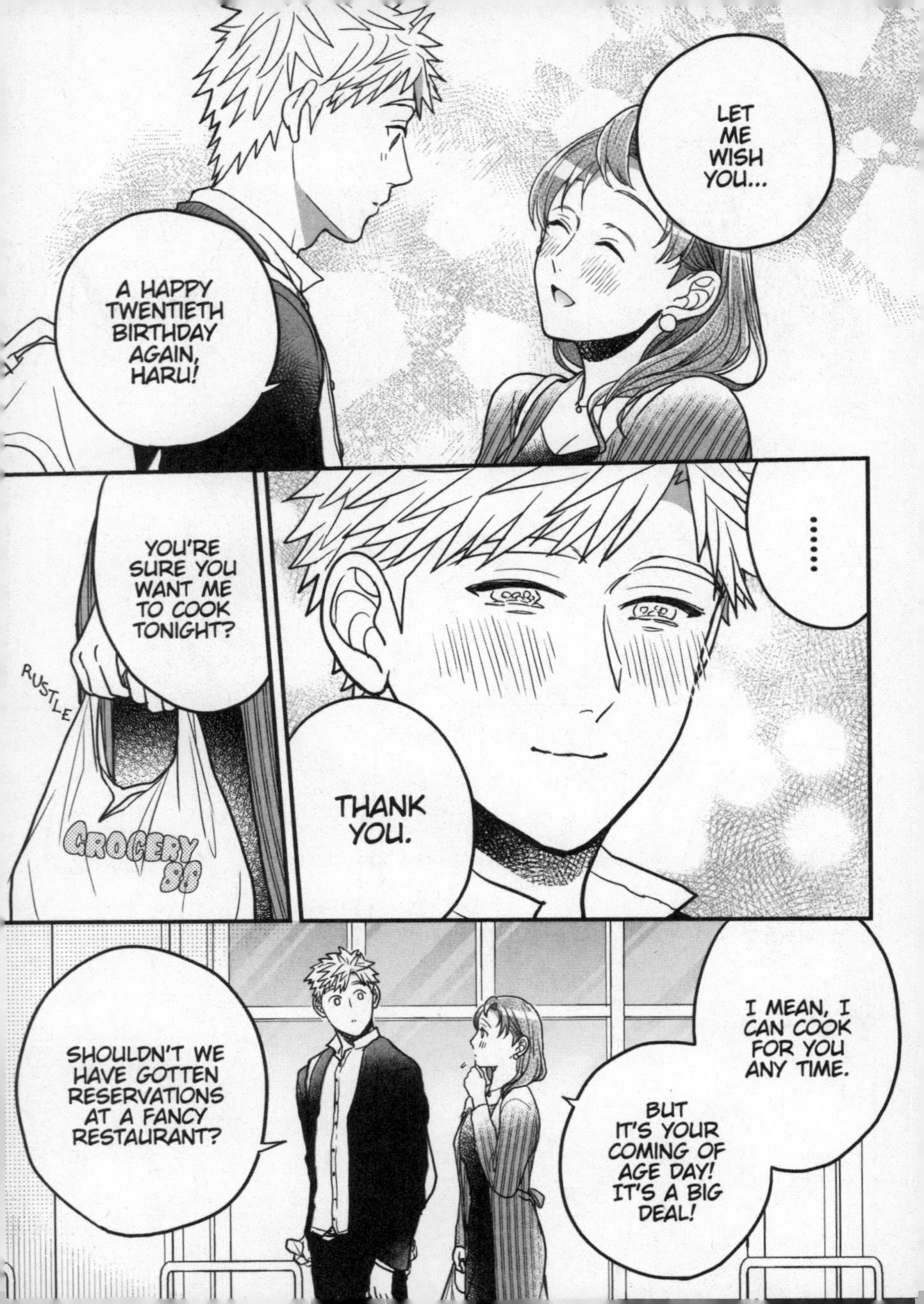
LET ME WISH YOU...
A HAPPY TWENTIETH BIRTHDAY AGAIN, HARU!
......
YOU'RE SURE YOU WANT ME TO COOK TONIGHT?
RUSTLE
GROCERY 88
THANK YOU.
I MEAN, I CAN COOK FOR YOU ANY TIME.
BUT IT'S YOUR COMING OF AGE DAY! IT'S A BIG DEAL!
SHOULDN'T WE HAVE GOTTEN RESERVATIONS AT A FANCY RESTAURANT?

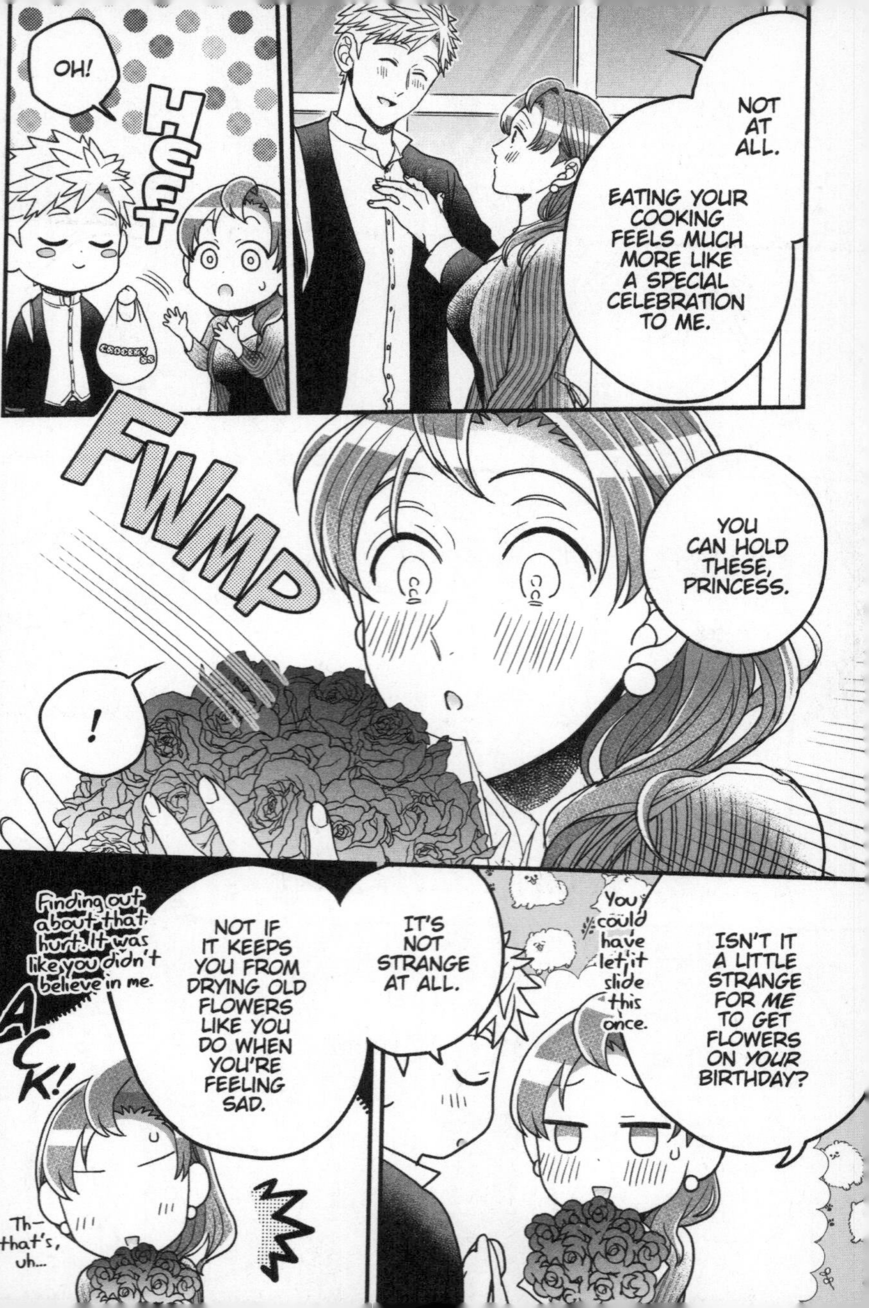
NOT AT ALL.
EATING YOUR COOKING FEELS MUCH MORE LIKE A SPECIAL CELEBRATION TO ME.
OH!
HEFT
YOU CAN HOLD THESE, PRINCESS.
FWMP
!
ISN'T IT A LITTLE STRANGE FOR *ME* TO GET FLOWERS ON *YOUR* BIRTHDAY?
You could have let it slide this once.
IT'S NOT STRANGE AT ALL.
NOT IF IT KEEPS YOU FROM DRYING OLD FLOWERS LIKE YOU DO WHEN YOU'RE FEELING SAD.
ACK!
Finding out about that hurt. It was like you didn't believe in me.
Th-that's, uh...

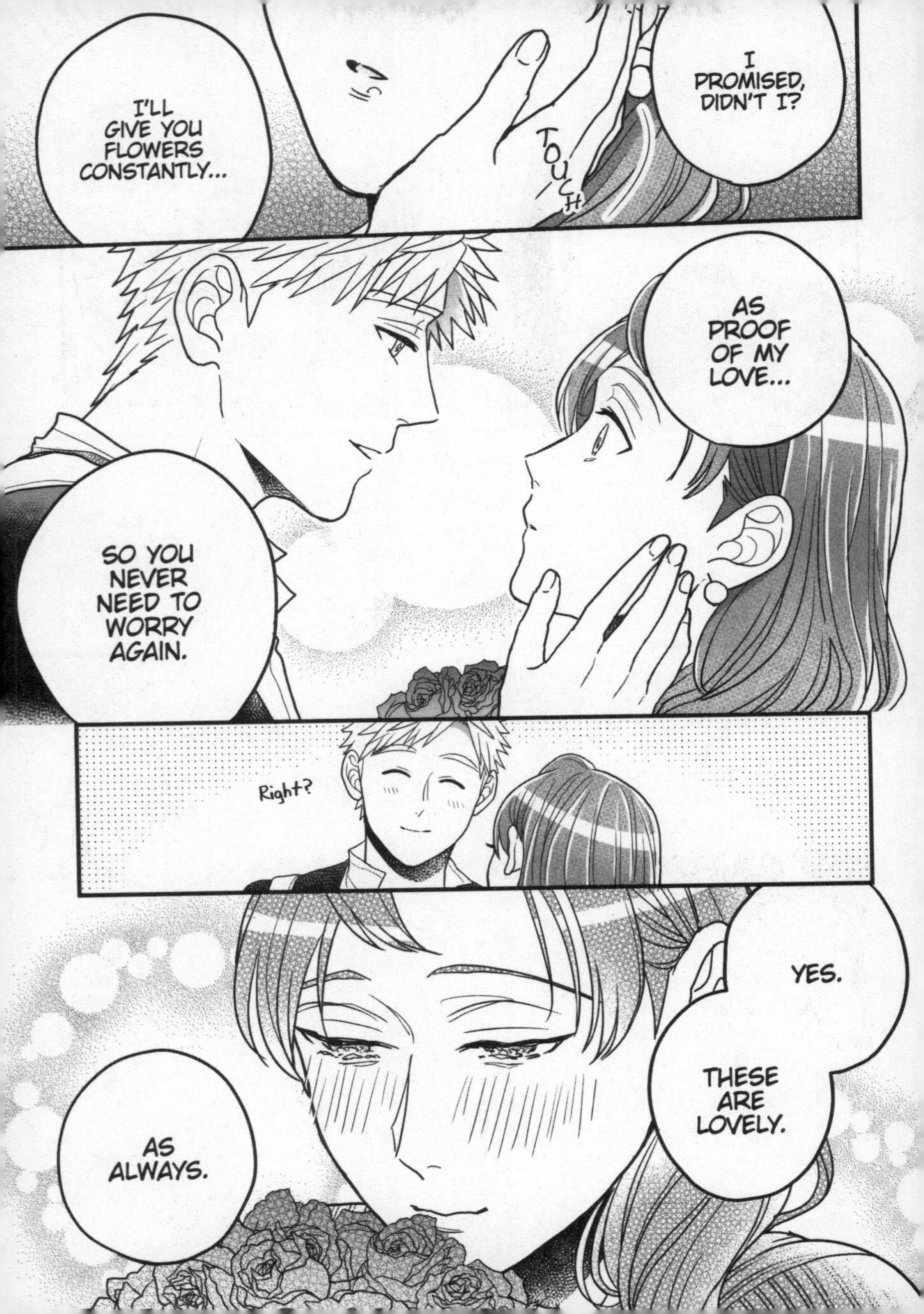
I PROMISED, DIDN'T I?
TOUCH
I'LL GIVE YOU FLOWERS CONSTANTLY...
AS PROOF OF MY LOVE...
SO YOU NEVER NEED TO WORRY AGAIN.
Right?
YES.
THESE ARE LOVELY.
AS ALWAYS.

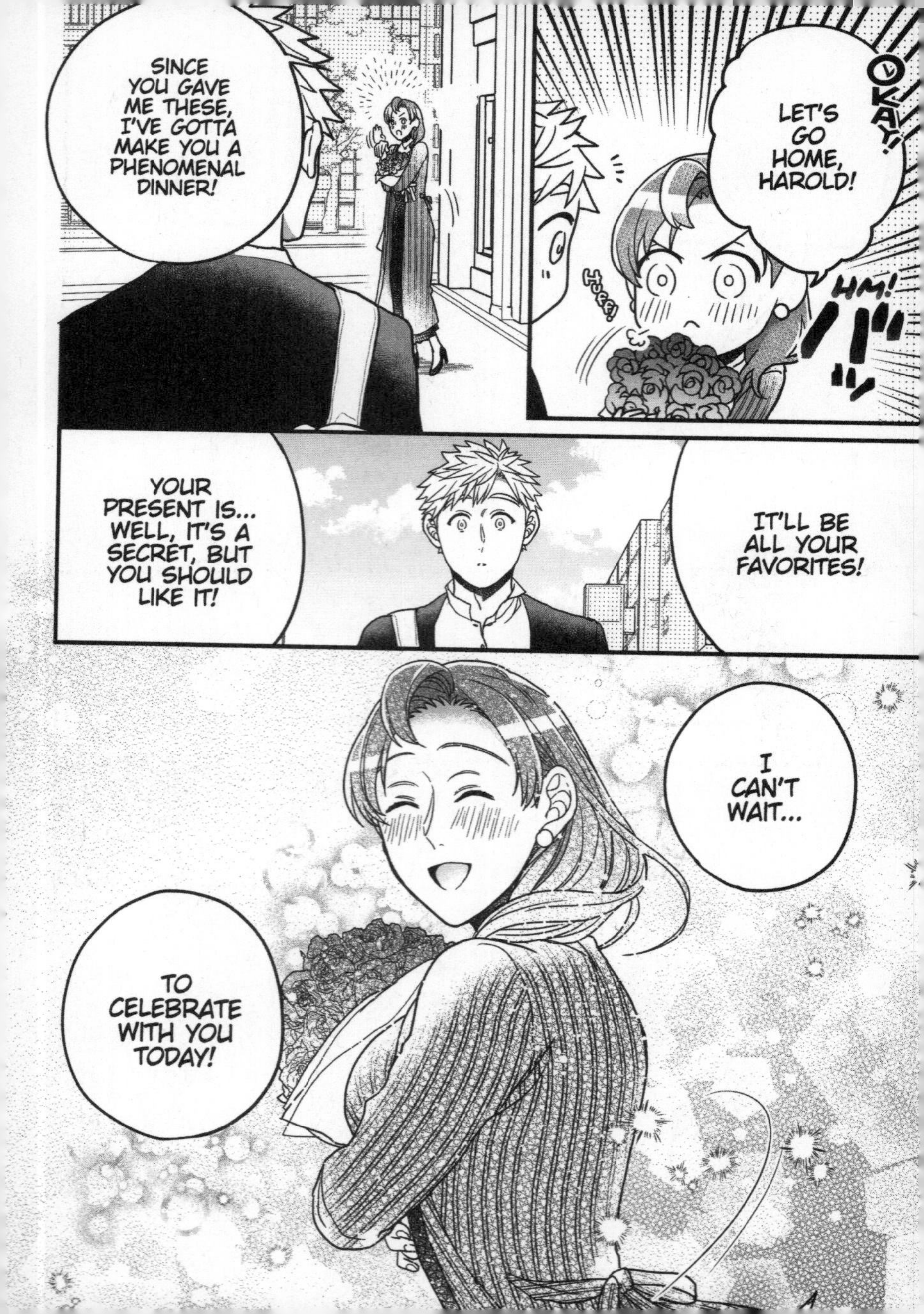
OKAY!
LET'S GO HOME, HAROLD!
HM!
HUFF!
SINCE YOU GAVE ME THESE, I'VE GOTTA MAKE YOU A PHENOMENAL DINNER!
IT'LL BE ALL YOUR FAVORITES!
YOUR PRESENT IS... WELL, IT'S A SECRET, BUT YOU SHOULD LIKE IT!
I CAN'T WAIT...
TO CELEBRATE WITH YOU TODAY!

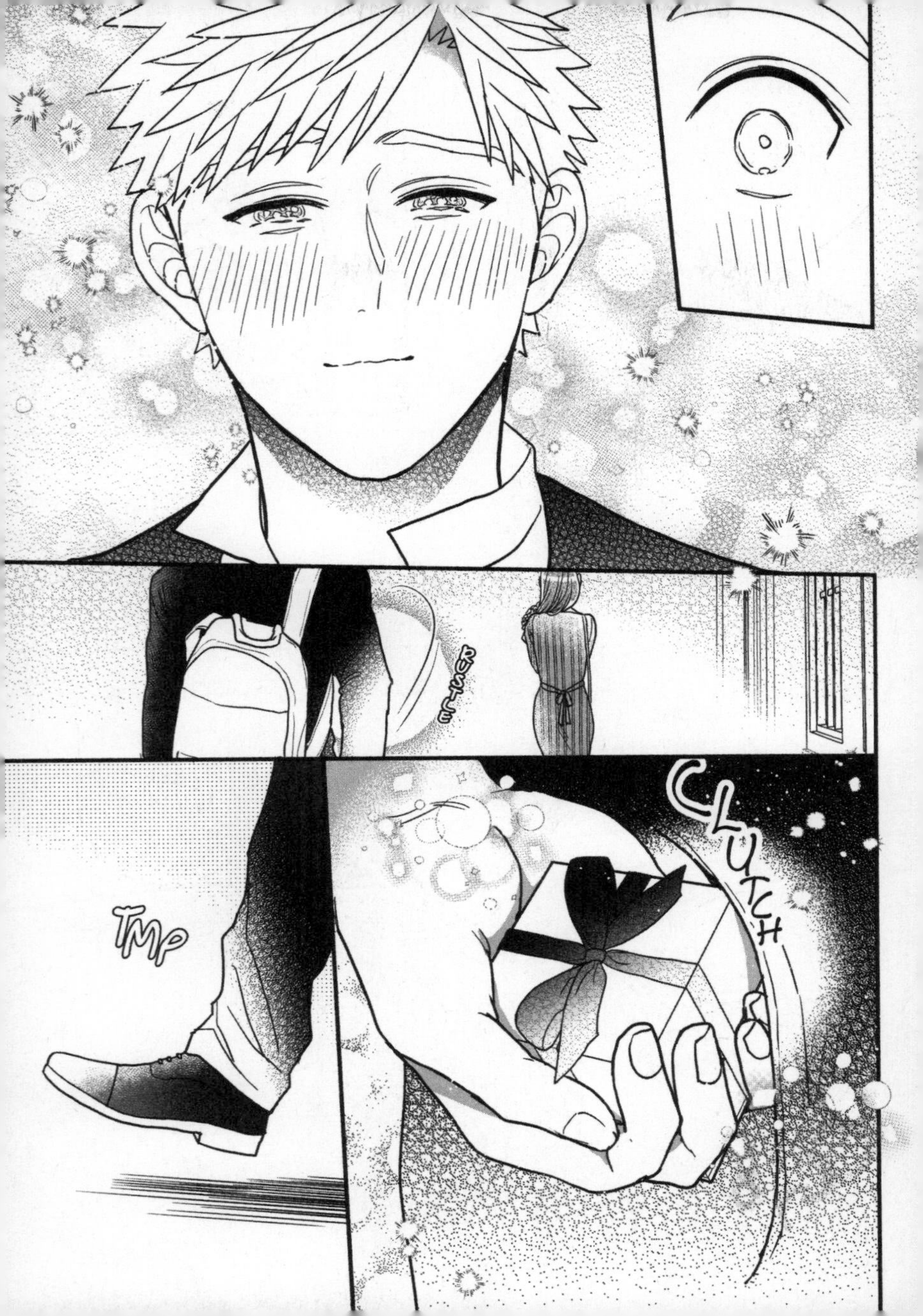
RUSTLE
CLUTCH
TMP

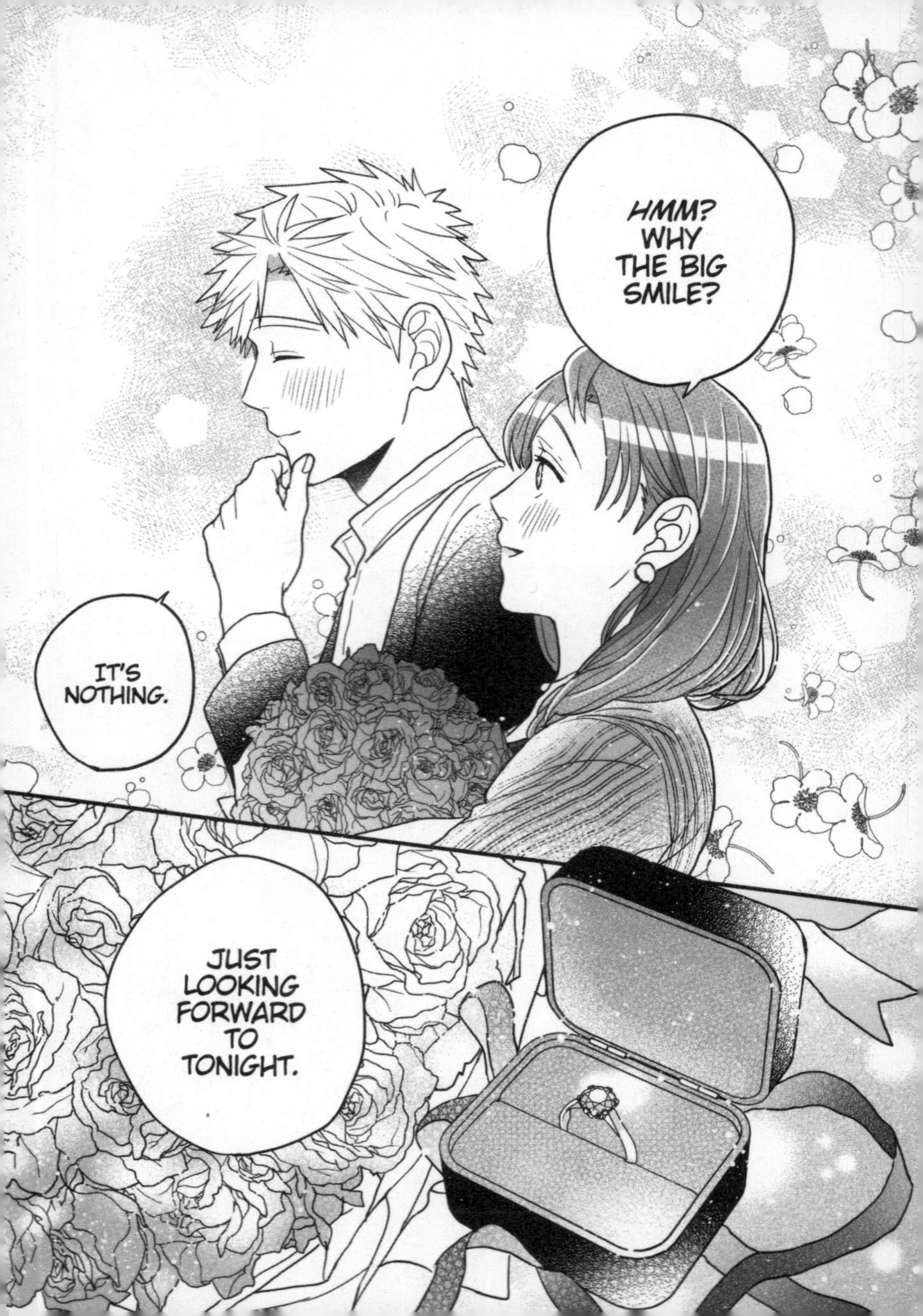
HMM? WHY THE BIG SMILE?
IT'S NOTHING.
JUST LOOKING FORWARD TO TONIGHT.

We Swore to
Meet in the Next Life
and That's When
Things Got
Weird!

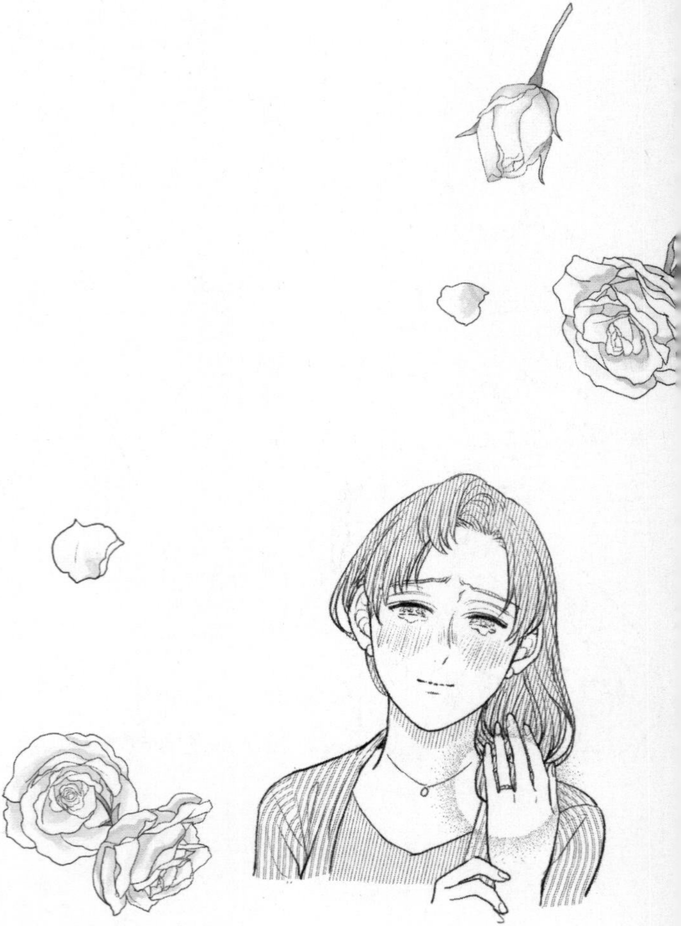

A Memory of the Previous Life

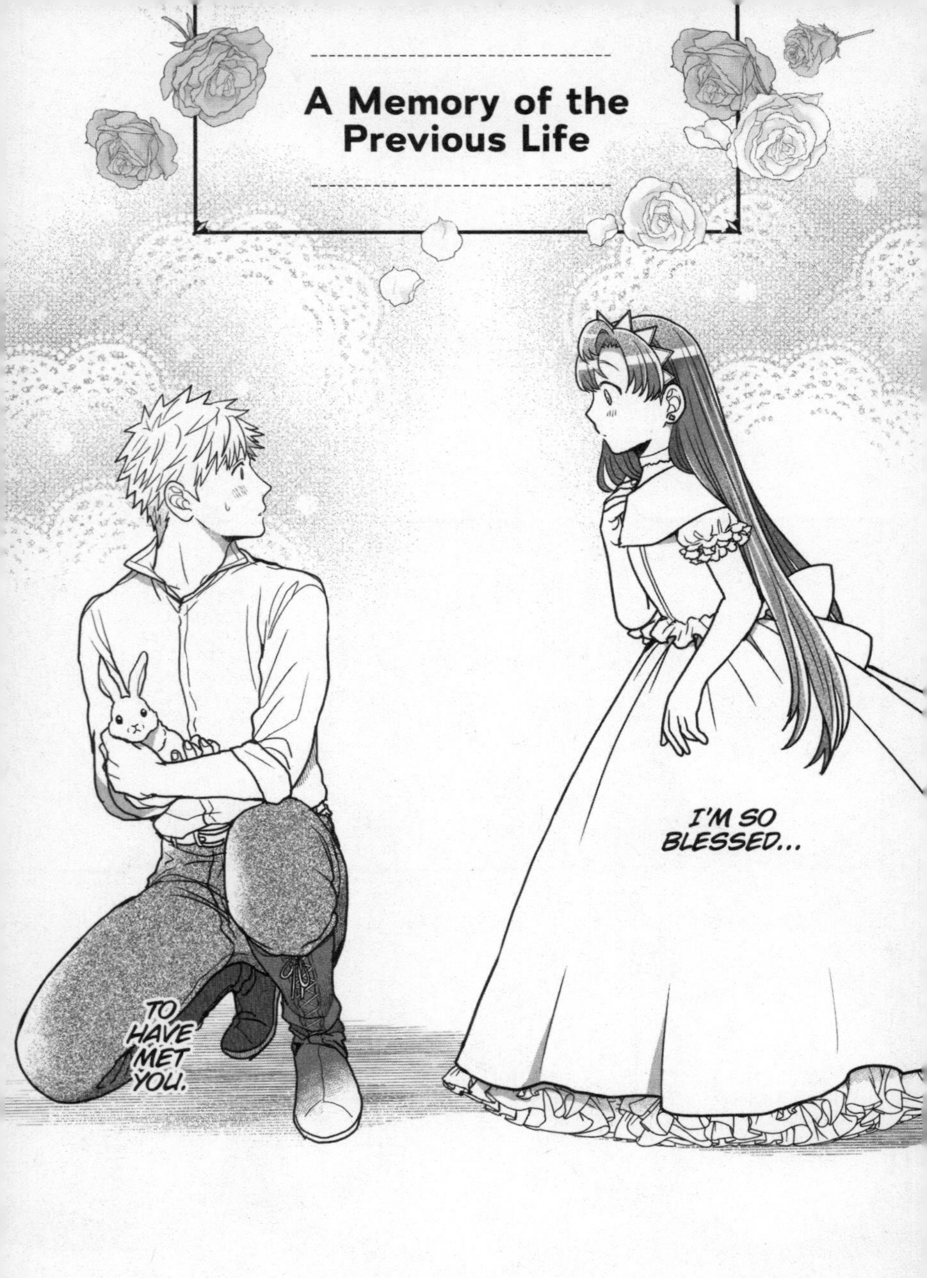
I'M SO BLESSED...
TO HAVE MET YOU.

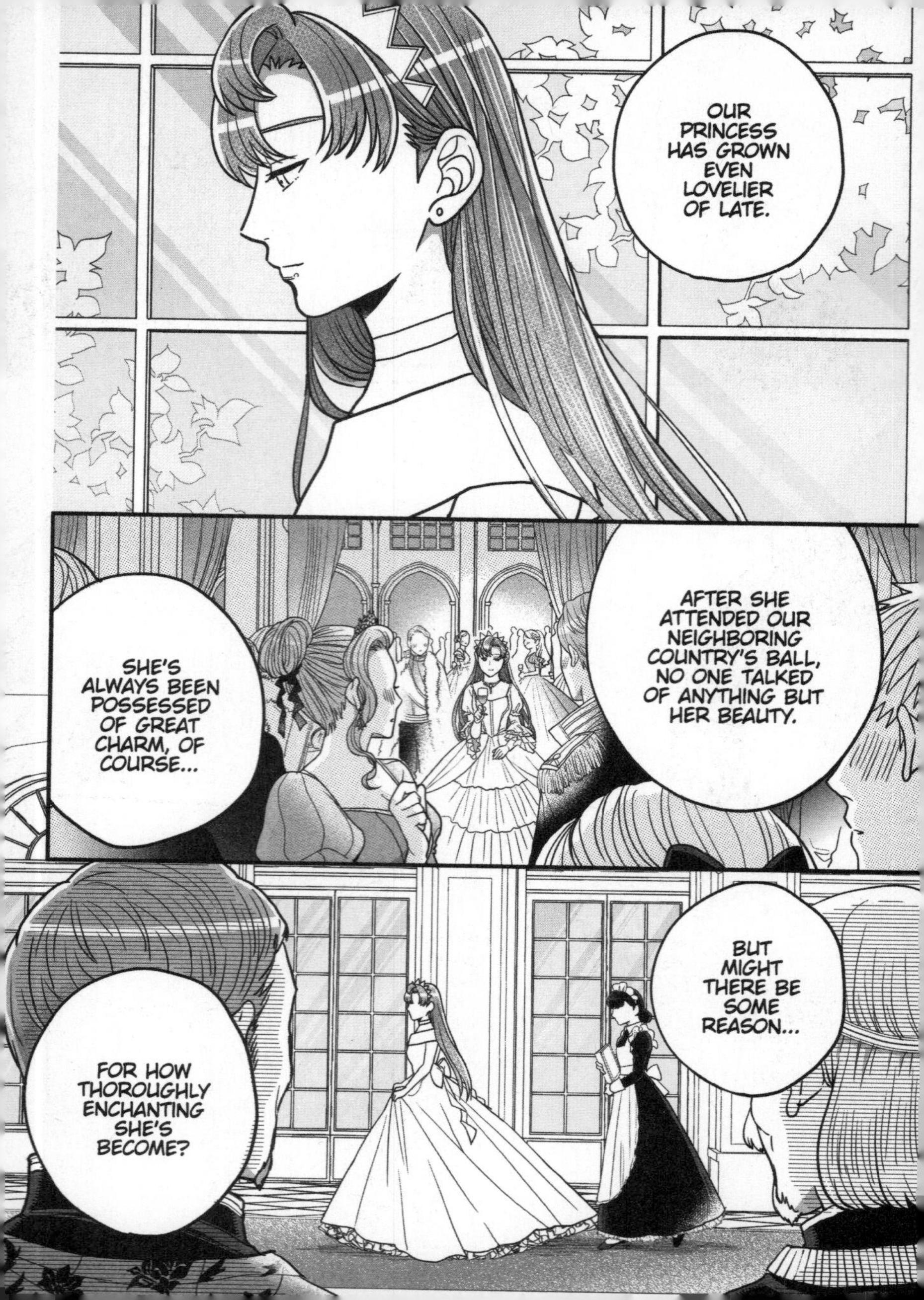
OUR PRINCESS HAS GROWN EVEN LOVELIER OF LATE.
AFTER SHE ATTENDED OUR NEIGHBORING COUNTRY'S BALL, NO ONE TALKED OF ANYTHING BUT HER BEAUTY.
SHE'S ALWAYS BEEN POSSESSED OF GREAT CHARM, OF COURSE...
BUT MIGHT THERE BE SOME REASON...
FOR HOW THOROUGHLY ENCHANTING SHE'S BECOME?

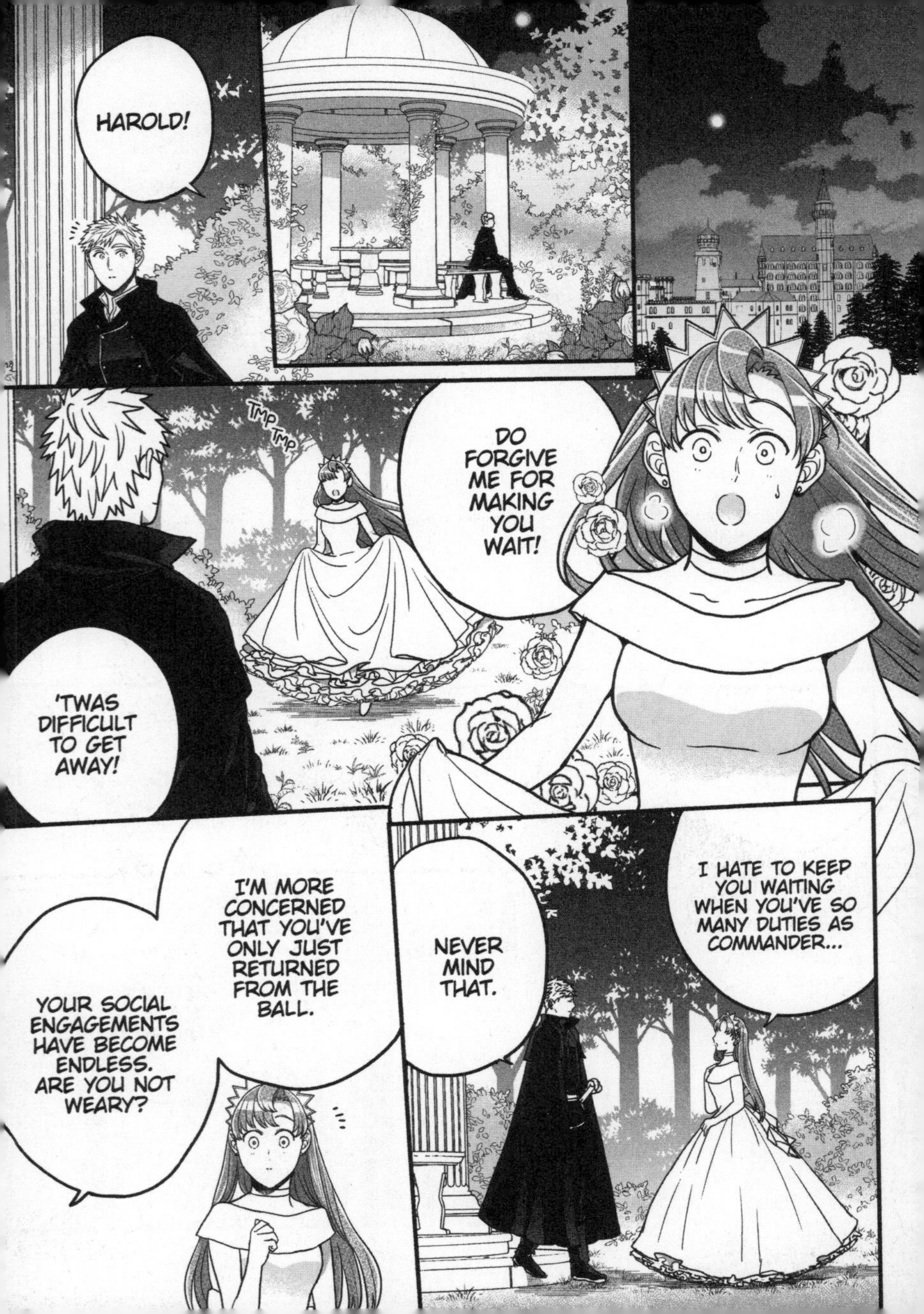
HAROLD!
TMP TMP
DO FORGIVE ME FOR MAKING YOU WAIT!
'TWAS DIFFICULT TO GET AWAY!
I HATE TO KEEP YOU WAITING WHEN YOU'VE SO MANY DUTIES AS COMMANDER...
NEVER MIND THAT.
I'M MORE CONCERNED THAT YOU'VE ONLY JUST RETURNED FROM THE BALL.
YOUR SOCIAL ENGAGEMENTS HAVE BECOME ENDLESS. ARE YOU NOT WEARY?

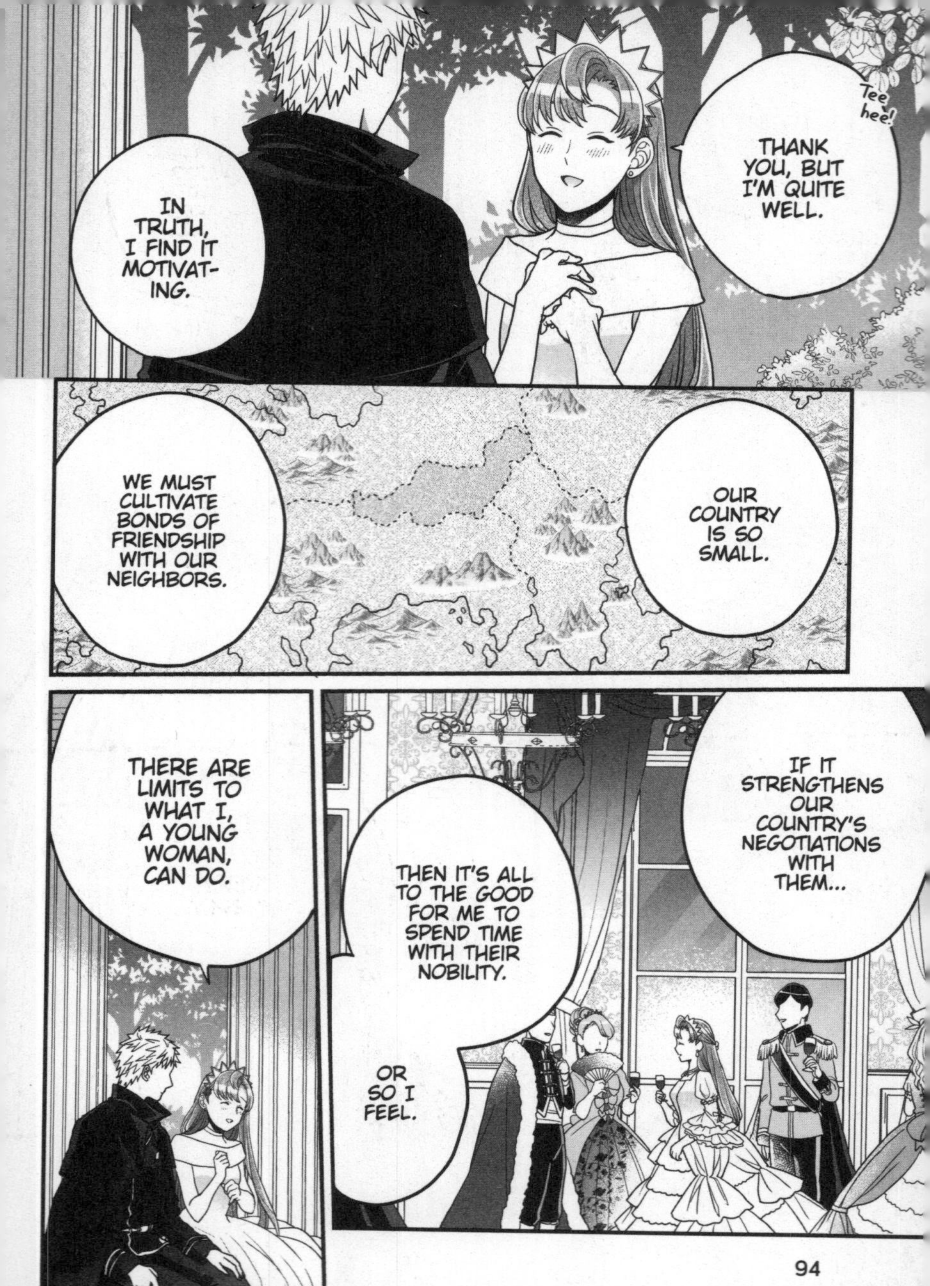
Tee hee!
THANK YOU, BUT I'M QUITE WELL.
IN TRUTH, I FIND IT MOTIVAT-ING.
OUR COUNTRY IS SO SMALL.
WE MUST CULTIVATE BONDS OF FRIENDSHIP WITH OUR NEIGHBORS.
THERE ARE LIMITS TO WHAT I, A YOUNG WOMAN, CAN DO.
IF IT STRENGTHENS OUR COUNTRY'S NEGOTIATIONS WITH THEM...
THEN IT'S ALL TO THE GOOD FOR ME TO SPEND TIME WITH THEIR NOBILITY.
OR SO I FEEL.

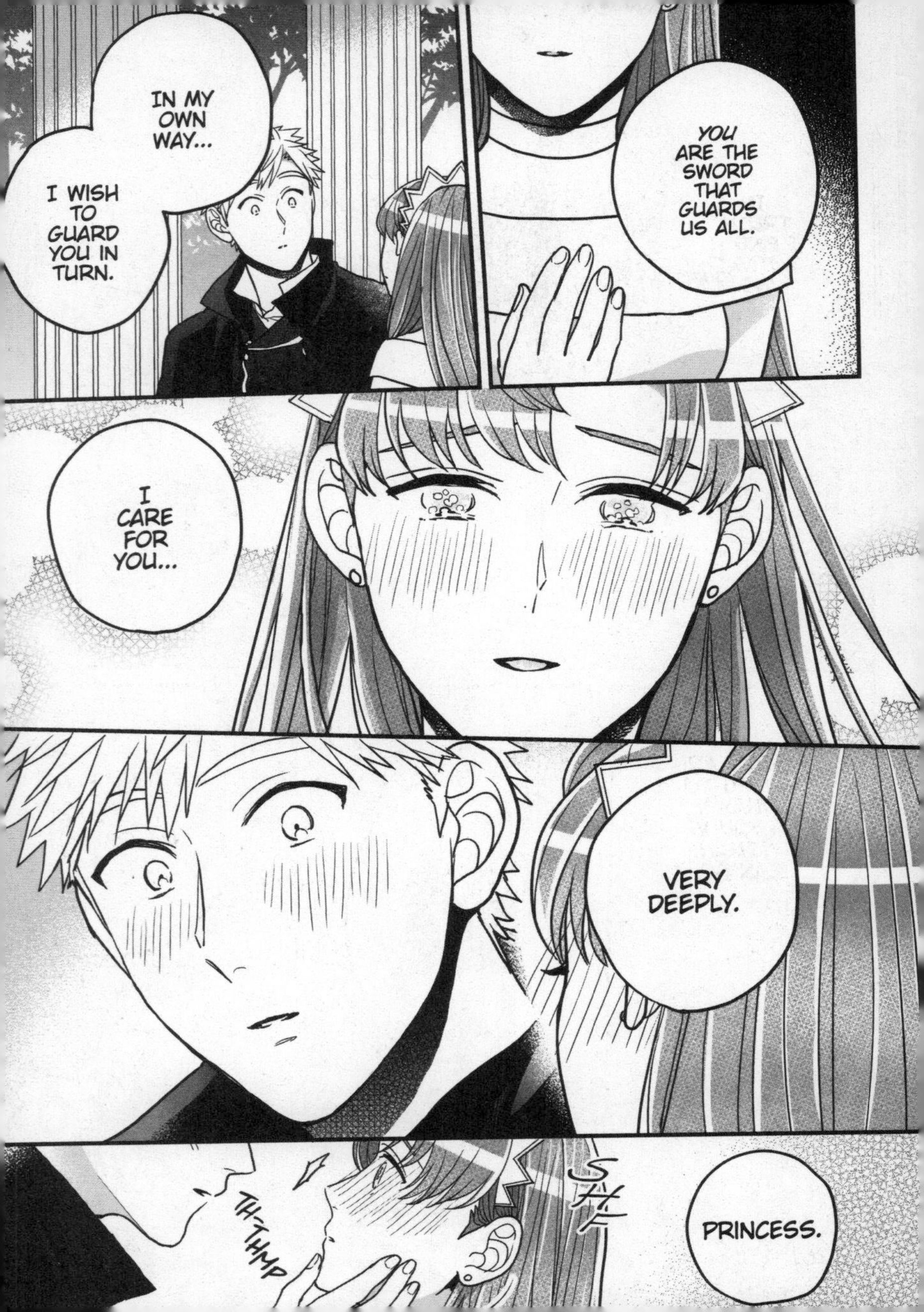
YOU ARE THE SWORD THAT GUARDS US ALL.
IN MY OWN WAY...
I WISH TO GUARD YOU IN TURN.
I CARE FOR YOU...
VERY DEEPLY.
PRINCESS.
SHF
TH-THMP

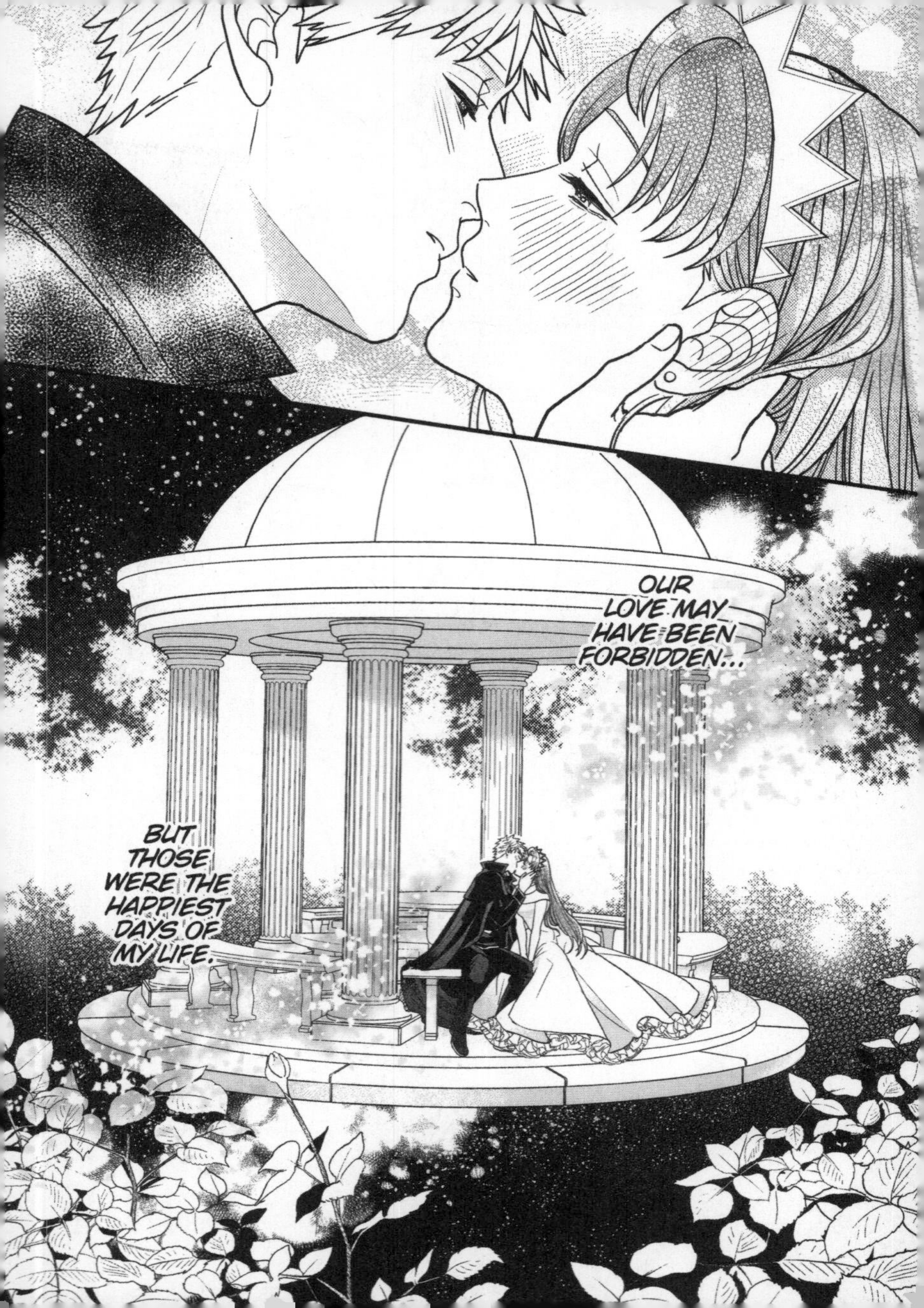
OUR LOVE MAY HAVE BEEN FORBIDDEN...
BUT THOSE WERE THE HAPPIEST DAYS OF MY LIFE.

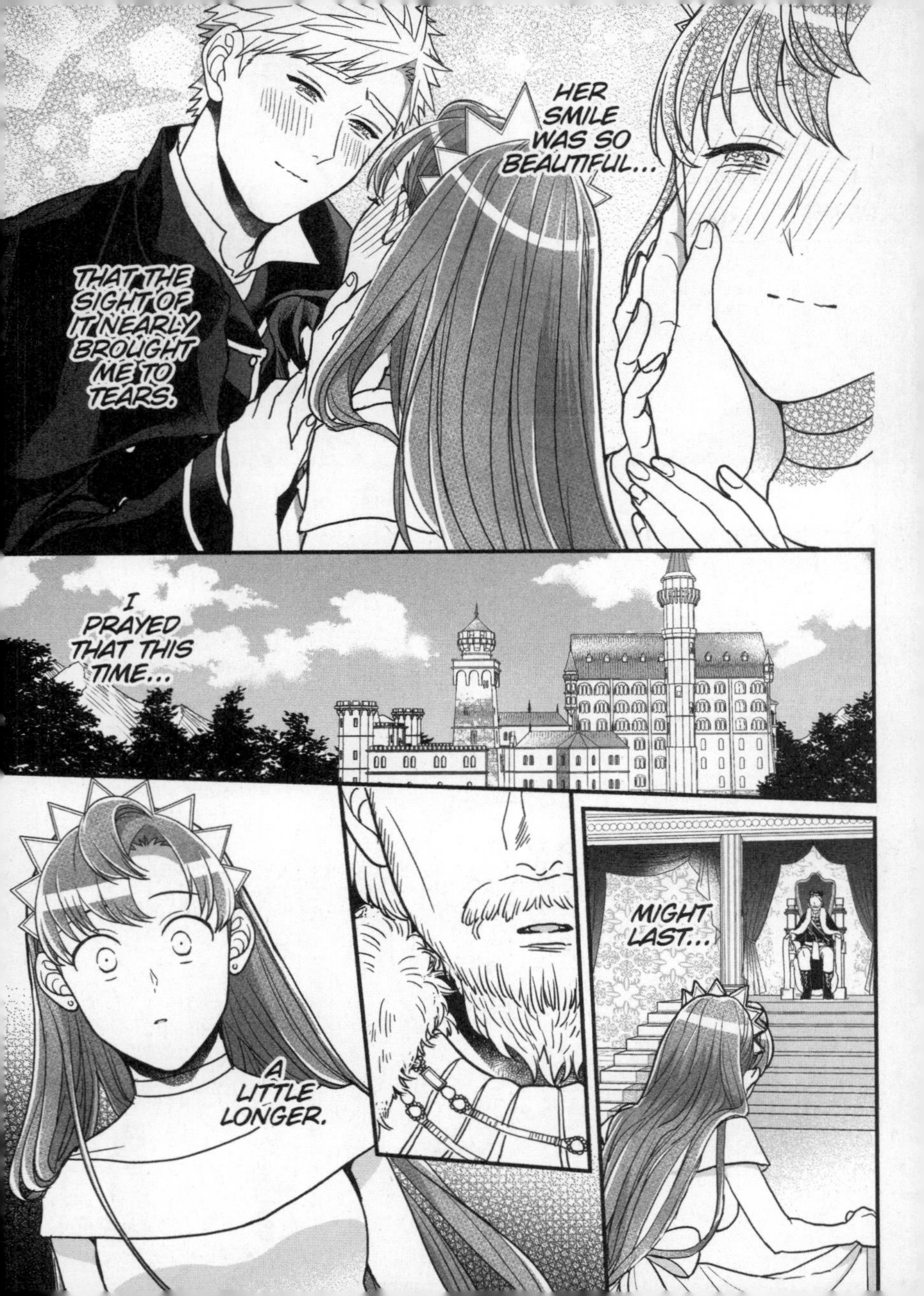
HER SMILE WAS SO BEAUTIFUL...
THAT THE SIGHT OF IT NEARLY BROUGHT ME TO TEARS.
I PRAYED THAT THIS TIME...
MIGHT LAST...
A LITTLE LONGER.

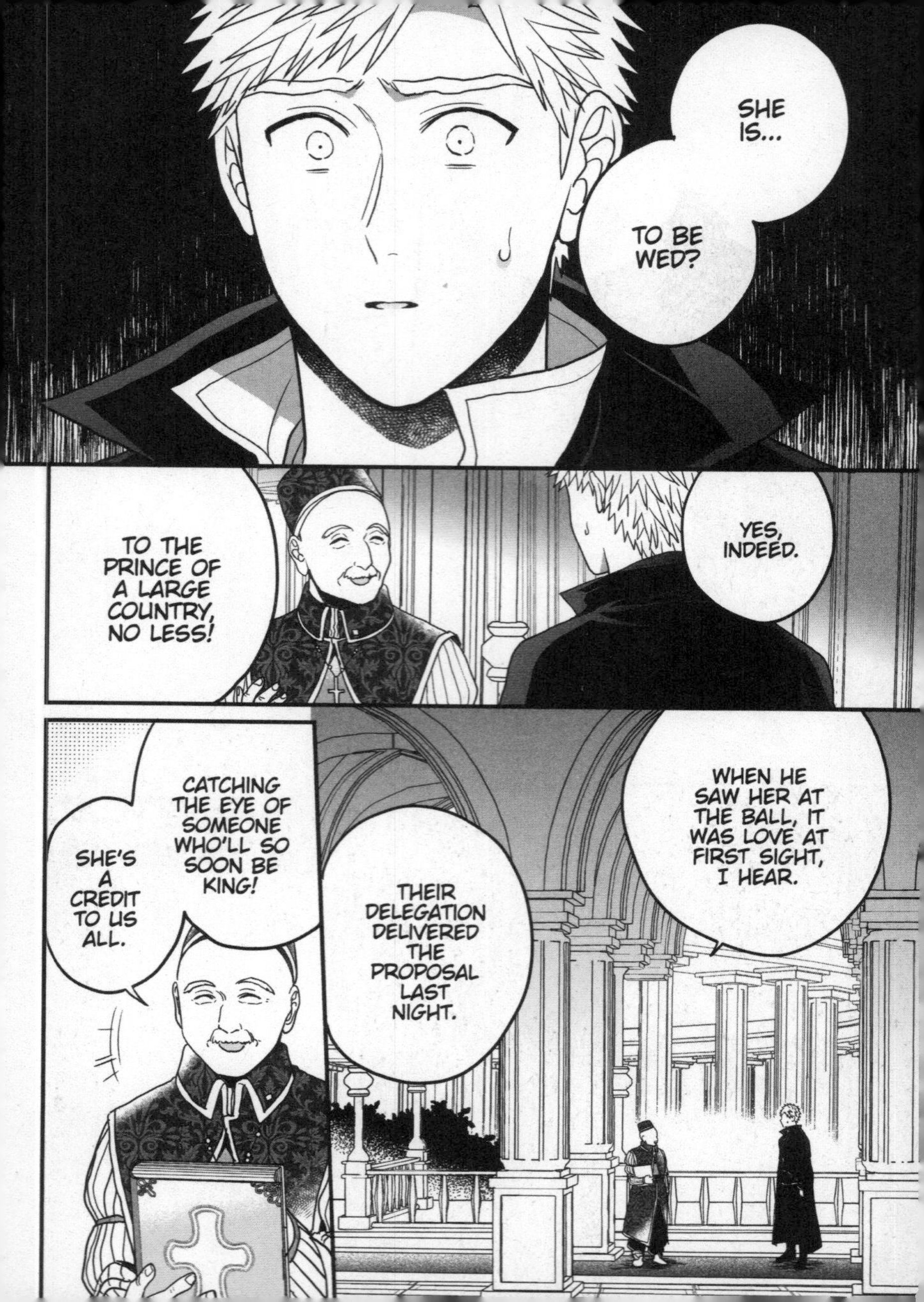
SHE IS...
TO BE WED?
YES, INDEED.
TO THE PRINCE OF A LARGE COUNTRY, NO LESS!
WHEN HE SAW HER AT THE BALL, IT WAS LOVE AT FIRST SIGHT, I HEAR.
THEIR DELEGATION DELIVERED THE PROPOSAL LAST NIGHT.
CATCHING THE EYE OF SOMEONE WHO'LL SO SOON BE KING!
SHE'S A CREDIT TO US ALL.

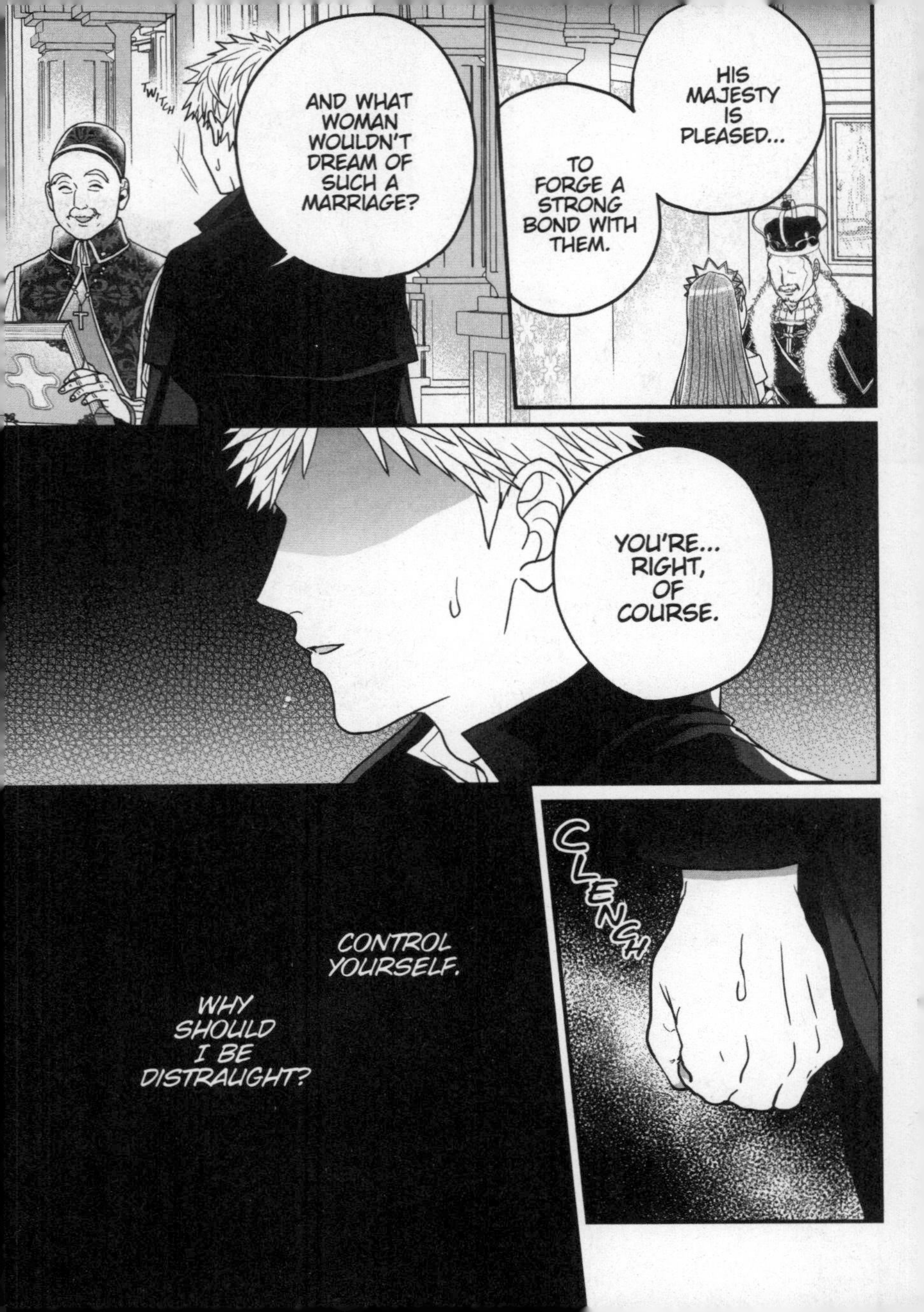
HIS MAJESTY IS PLEASED...
TO FORGE A STRONG BOND WITH THEM.
TWITCH
AND WHAT WOMAN WOULDN'T DREAM OF SUCH A MARRIAGE?
YOU'RE... RIGHT, OF COURSE.
CLENCH
CONTROL YOURSELF.
WHY SHOULD I BE DISTRAUGHT?

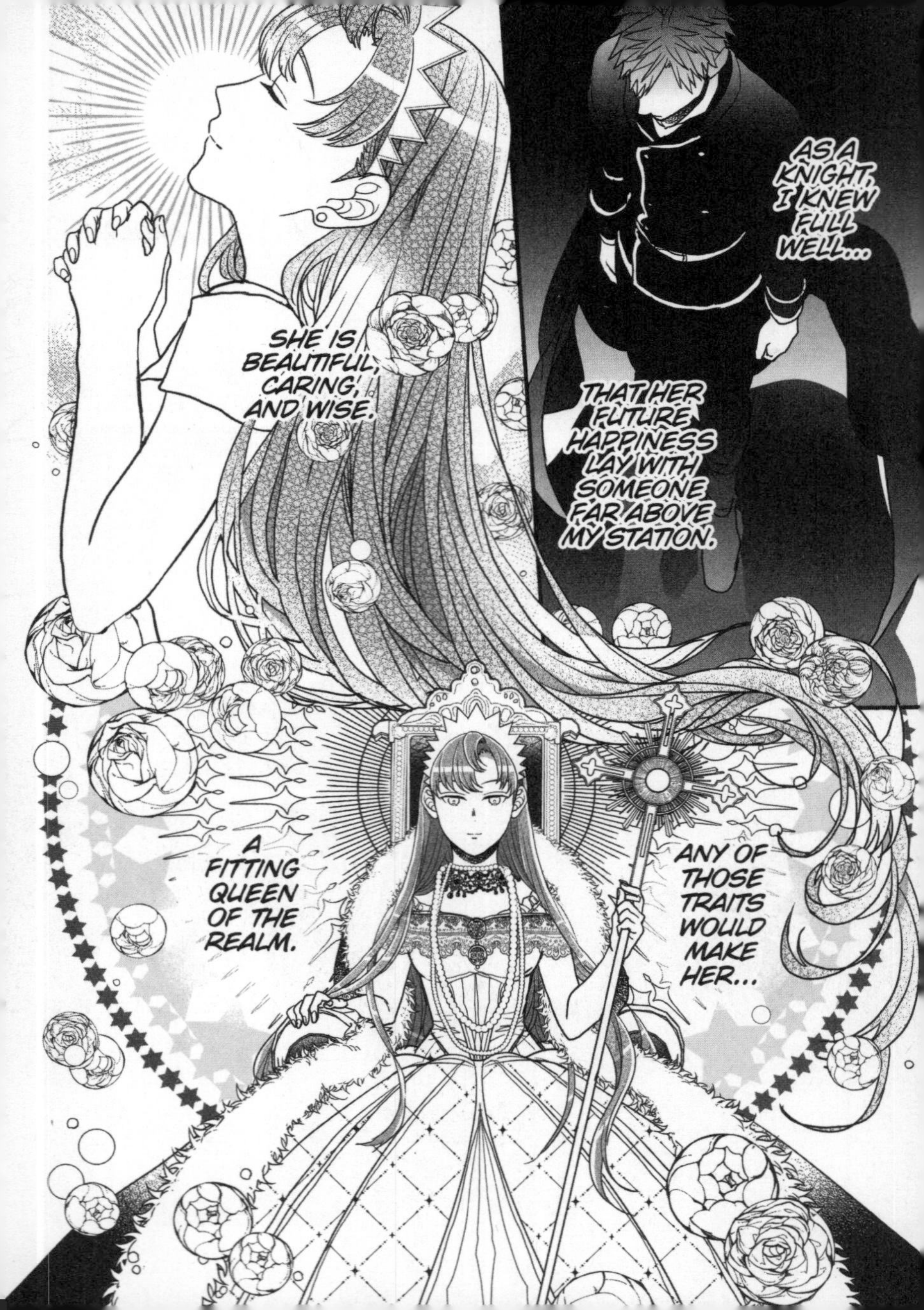
AS A KNIGHT, I KNEW FULL WELL...
THAT HER FUTURE HAPPINESS LAY WITH SOMEONE FAR ABOVE MY STATION.
SHE IS BEAUTIFUL, CARING, AND WISE.
ANY OF THOSE TRAITS WOULD MAKE HER...
A FITTING QUEEN OF THE REALM.

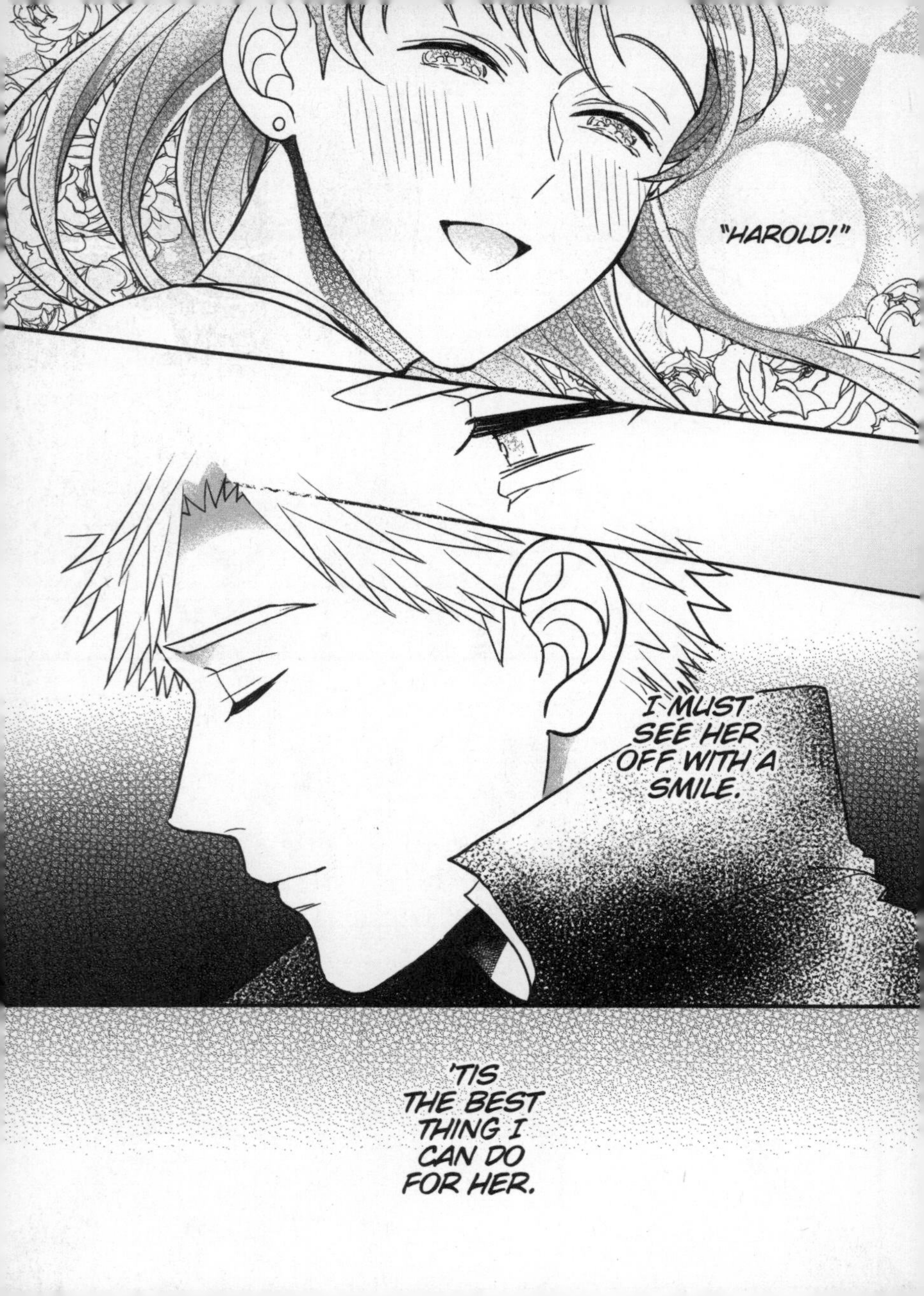
"HAROLD!"
I MUST SEE HER OFF WITH A SMILE.
'TIS THE BEST THING I CAN DO FOR HER.

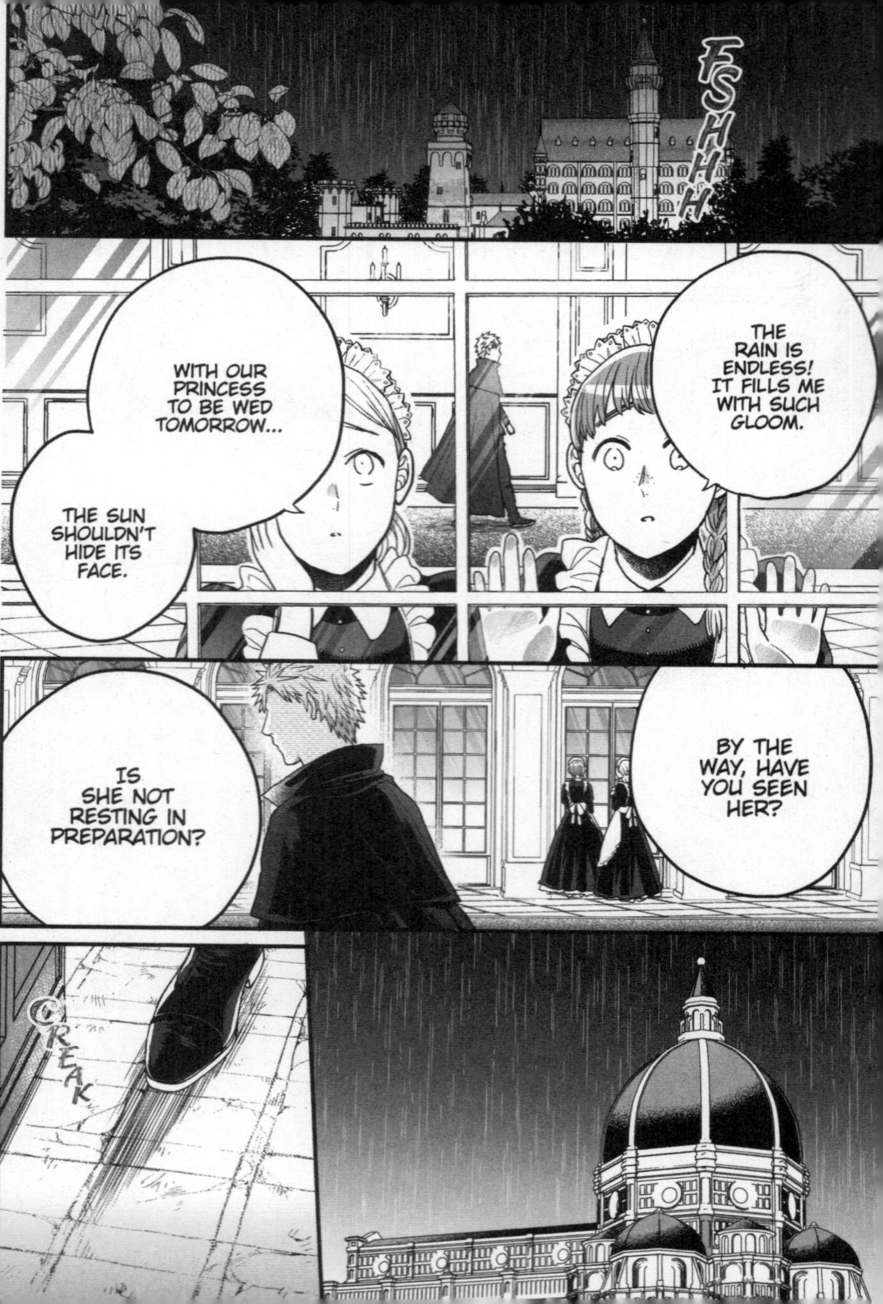
FSHHHH
THE RAIN IS ENDLESS! IT FILLS ME WITH SUCH GLOOM.
WITH OUR PRINCESS TO BE WED TOMORROW...
THE SUN SHOULDN'T HIDE ITS FACE.
BY THE WAY, HAVE YOU SEEN HER?
IS SHE NOT RESTING IN PREPARATION?
CREAK

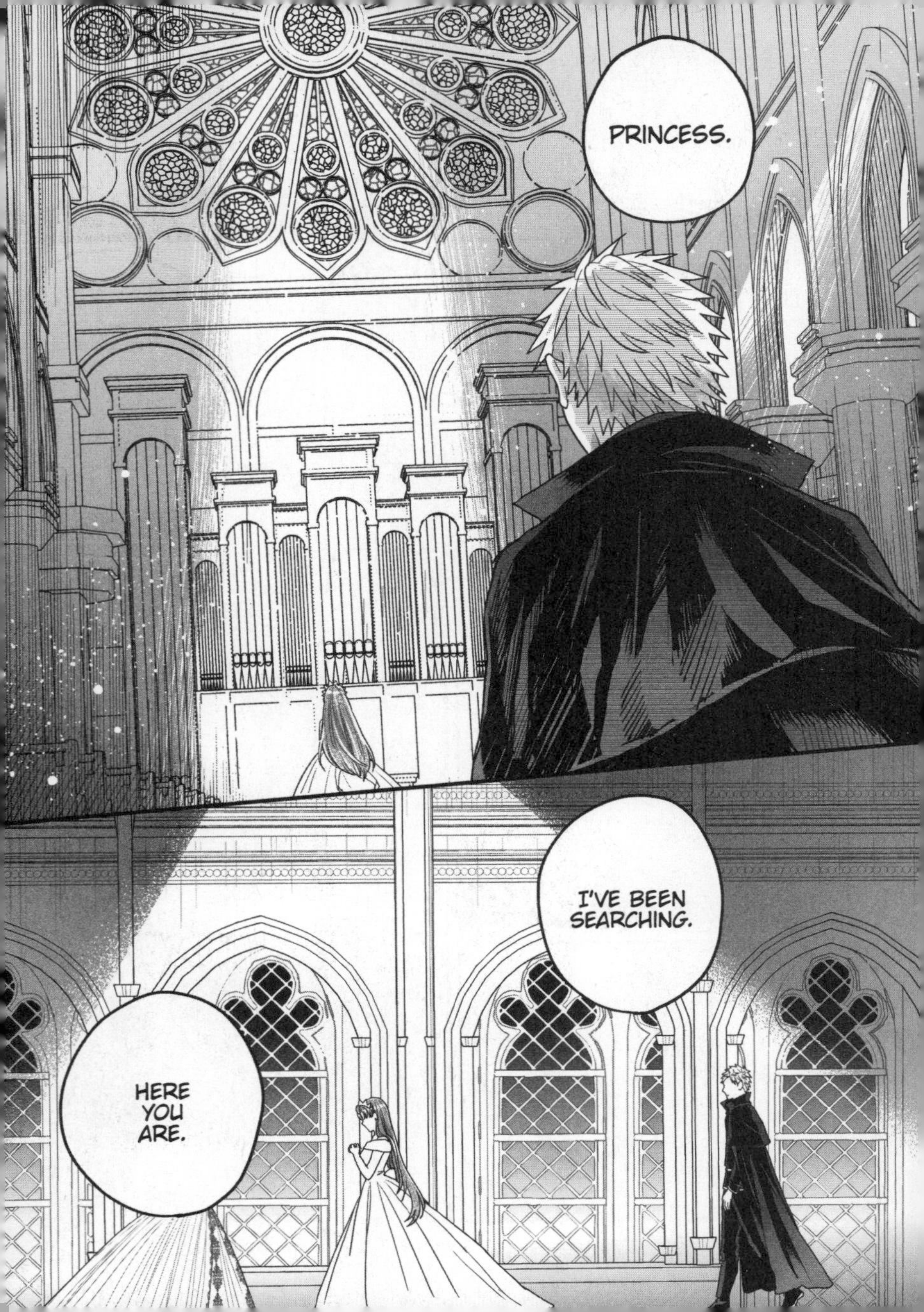
PRINCESS.
I'VE BEEN SEARCHING.
HERE YOU ARE.

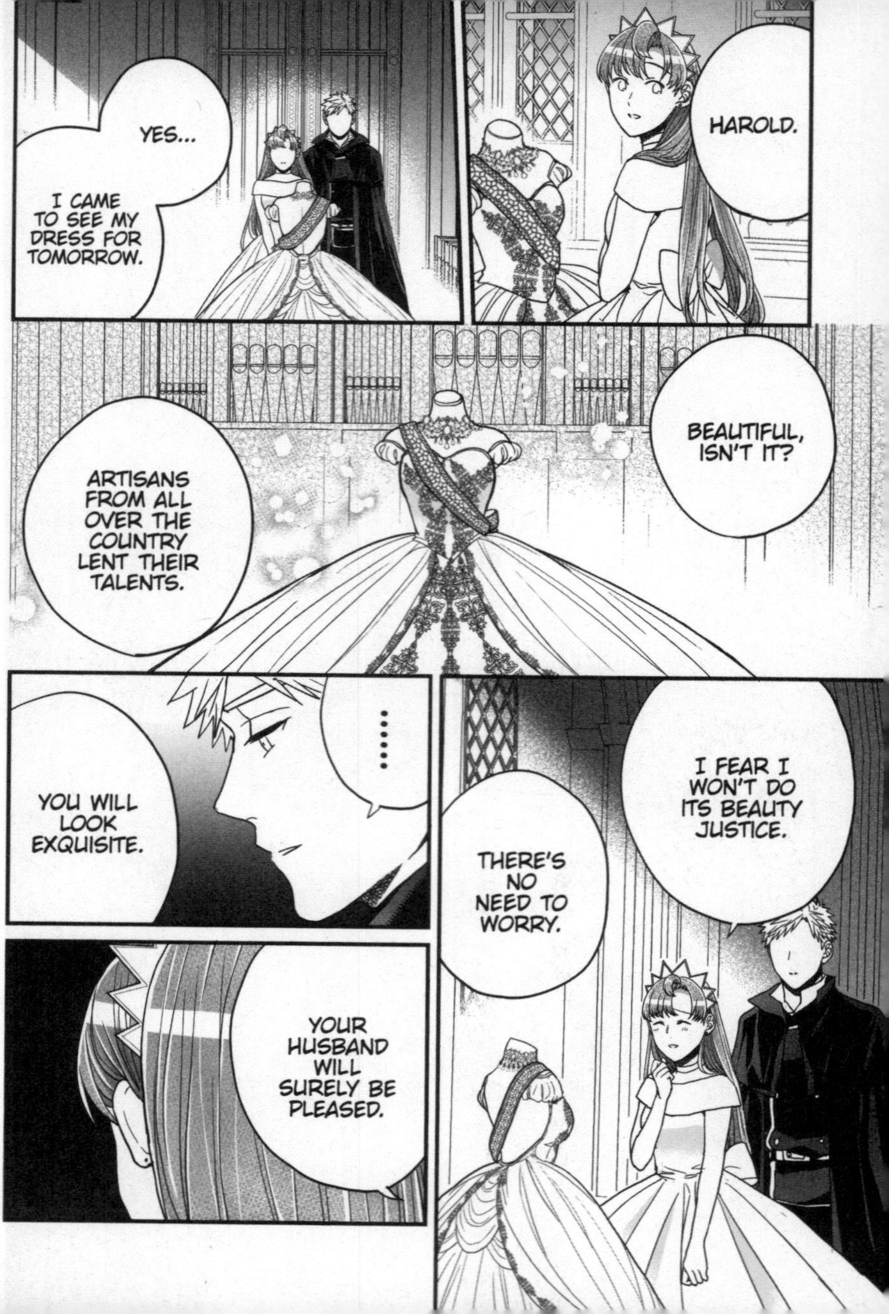
HAROLD.
YES...
I CAME TO SEE MY DRESS FOR TOMORROW.
BEAUTIFUL, ISN'T IT?
ARTISANS FROM ALL OVER THE COUNTRY LENT THEIR TALENTS.
I FEAR I WON'T DO ITS BEAUTY JUSTICE.
THERE'S NO NEED TO WORRY.
......
YOU WILL LOOK EXQUISITE.
YOUR HUSBAND WILL SURELY BE PLEASED.

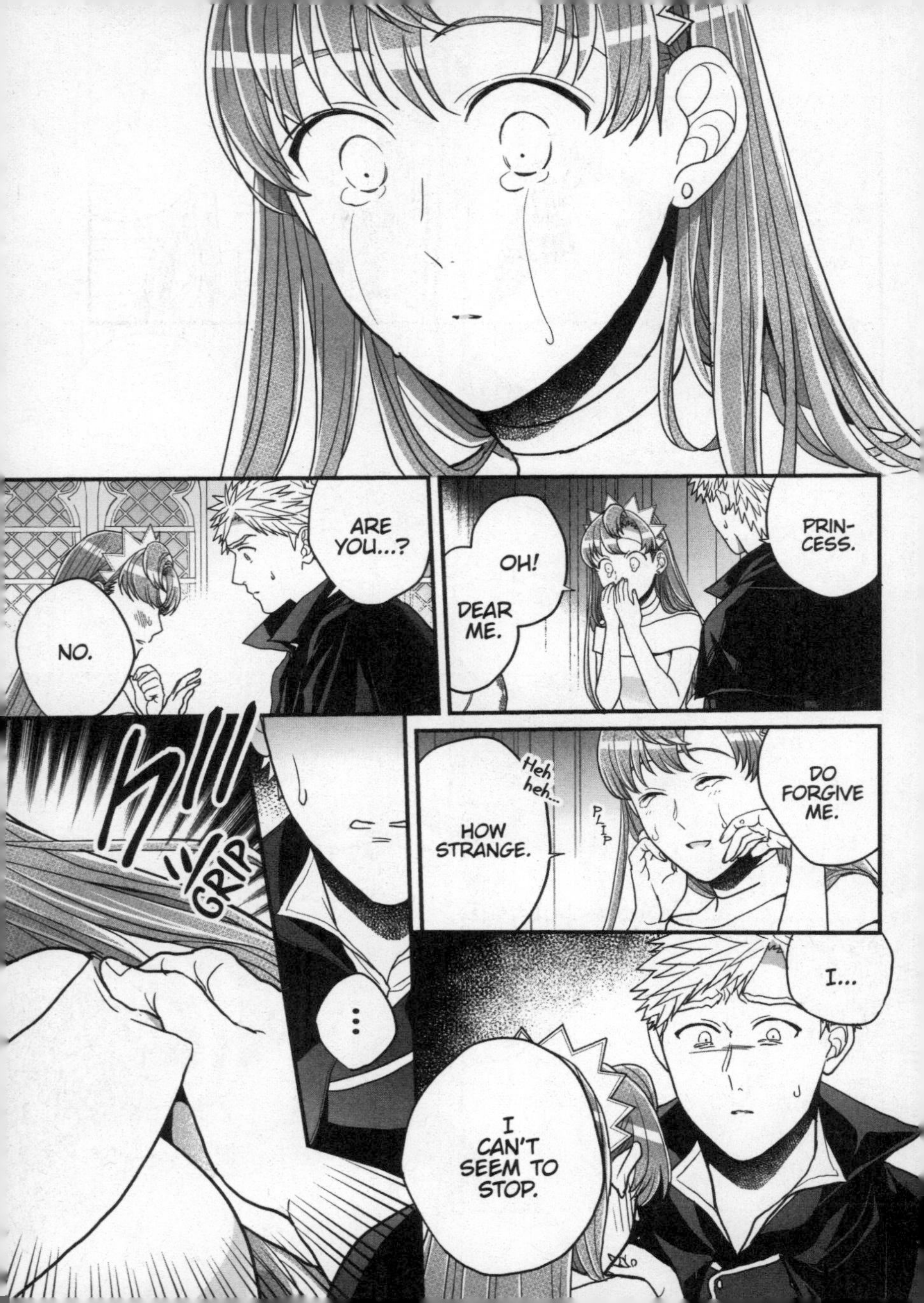
PRIN-CESS.
OH!
DEAR ME.
ARE YOU...?
NO.
DO FORGIVE ME.
Heh heh...
HOW STRANGE.
PLIP
...
GRIP
I...
I CAN'T SEEM TO STOP.

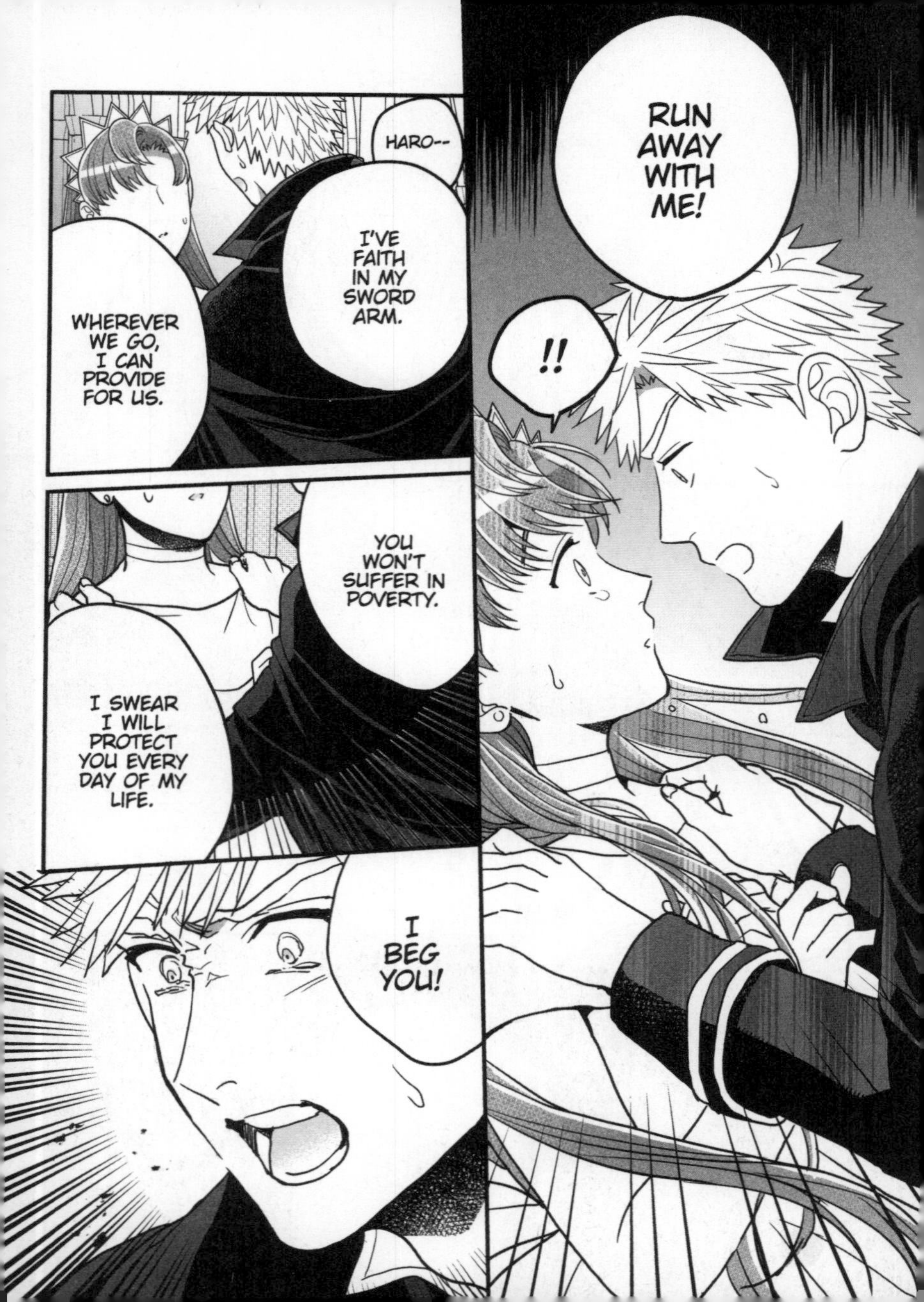
RUN AWAY WITH ME!
!!
HARO--
I'VE FAITH IN MY SWORD ARM.
WHEREVER WE GO, I CAN PROVIDE FOR US.
YOU WON'T SUFFER IN POVERTY.
I SWEAR I WILL PROTECT YOU EVERY DAY OF MY LIFE.
I BEG YOU!

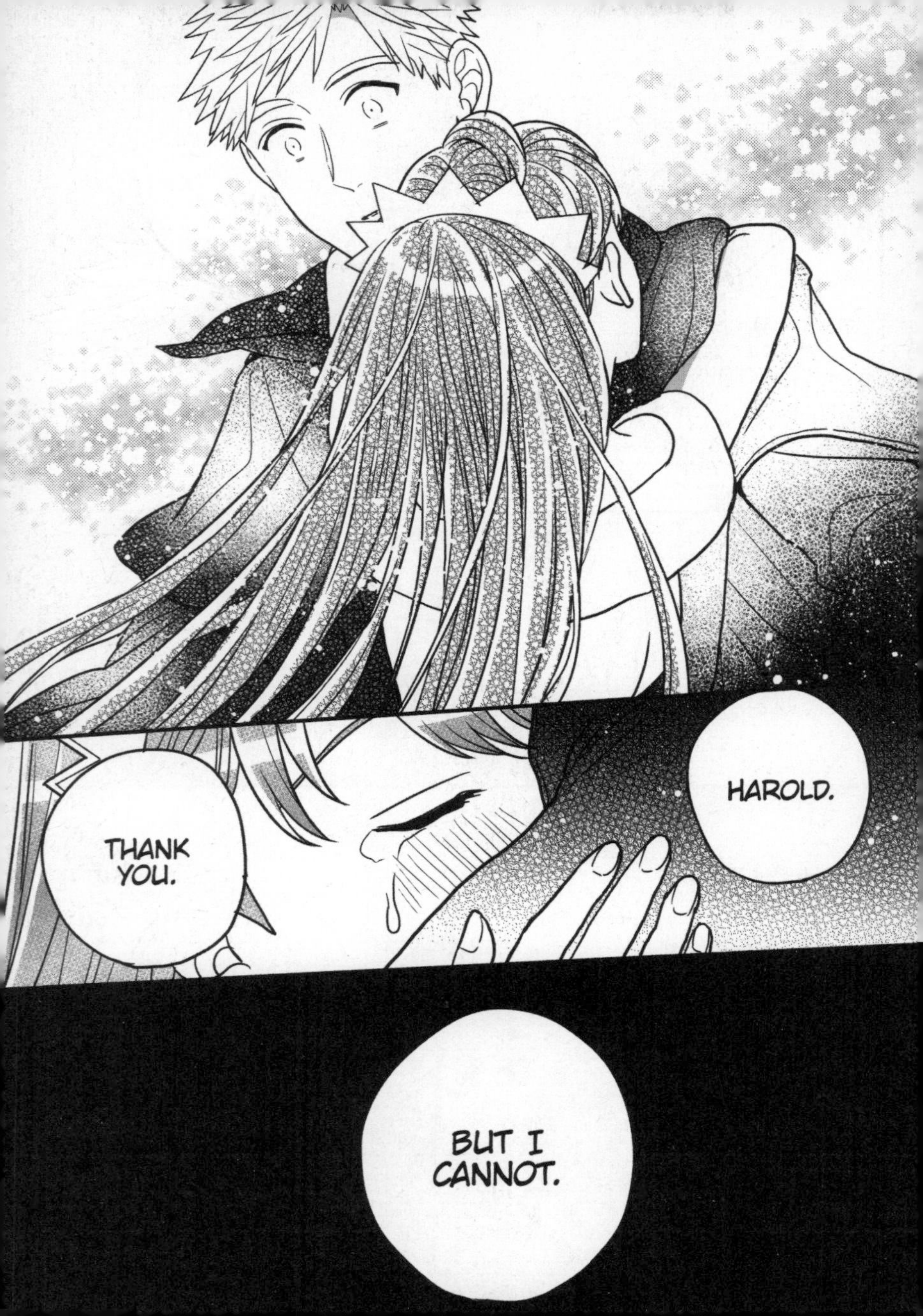
HAROLD.
THANK YOU.
BUT I CANNOT.

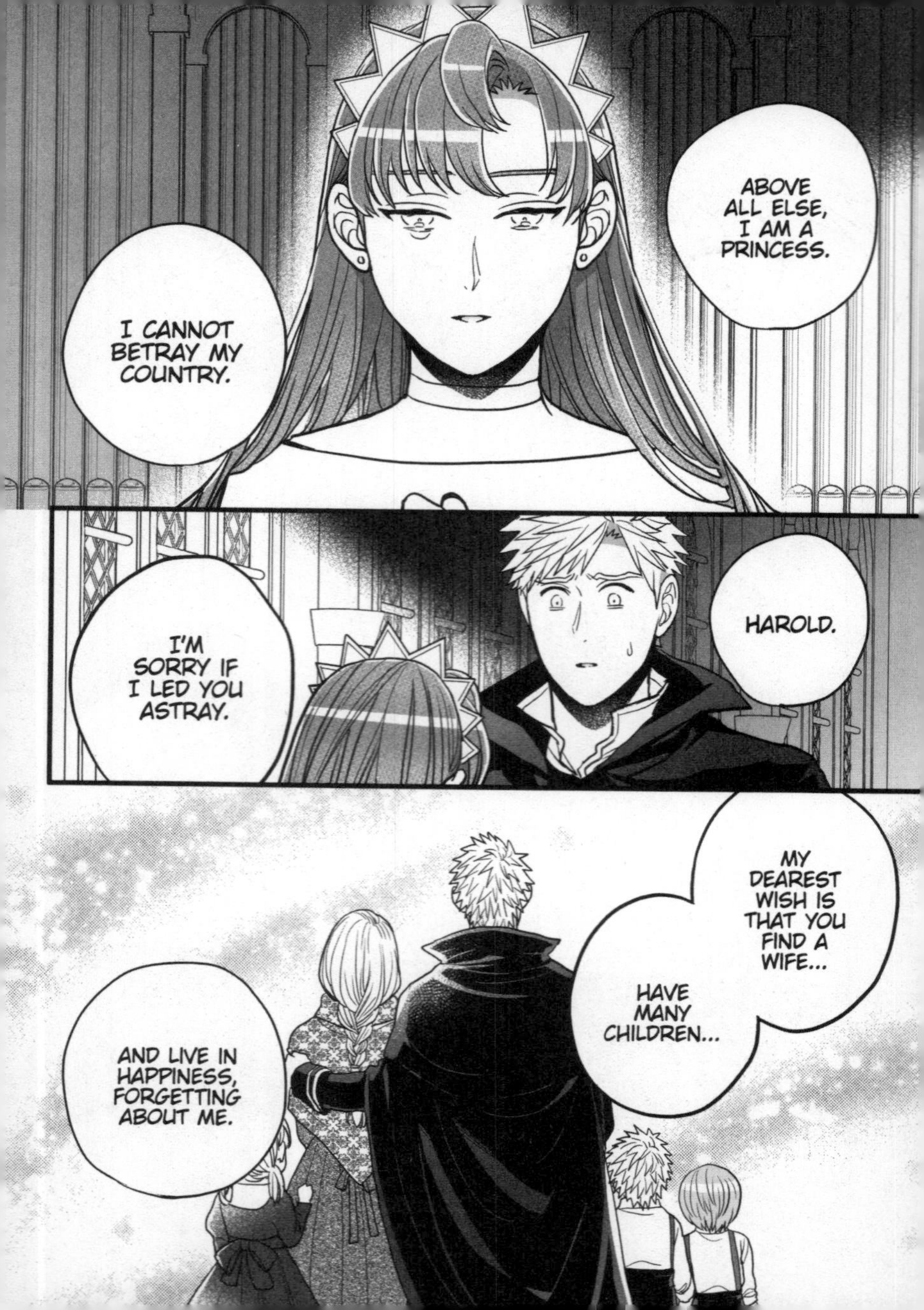
ABOVE ALL ELSE, I AM A PRINCESS.
I CANNOT BETRAY MY COUNTRY.
HAROLD.
I'M SORRY IF I LED YOU ASTRAY.
MY DEAREST WISH IS THAT YOU FIND A WIFE...
HAVE MANY CHILDREN...
AND LIVE IN HAPPINESS, FORGETTING ABOUT ME.

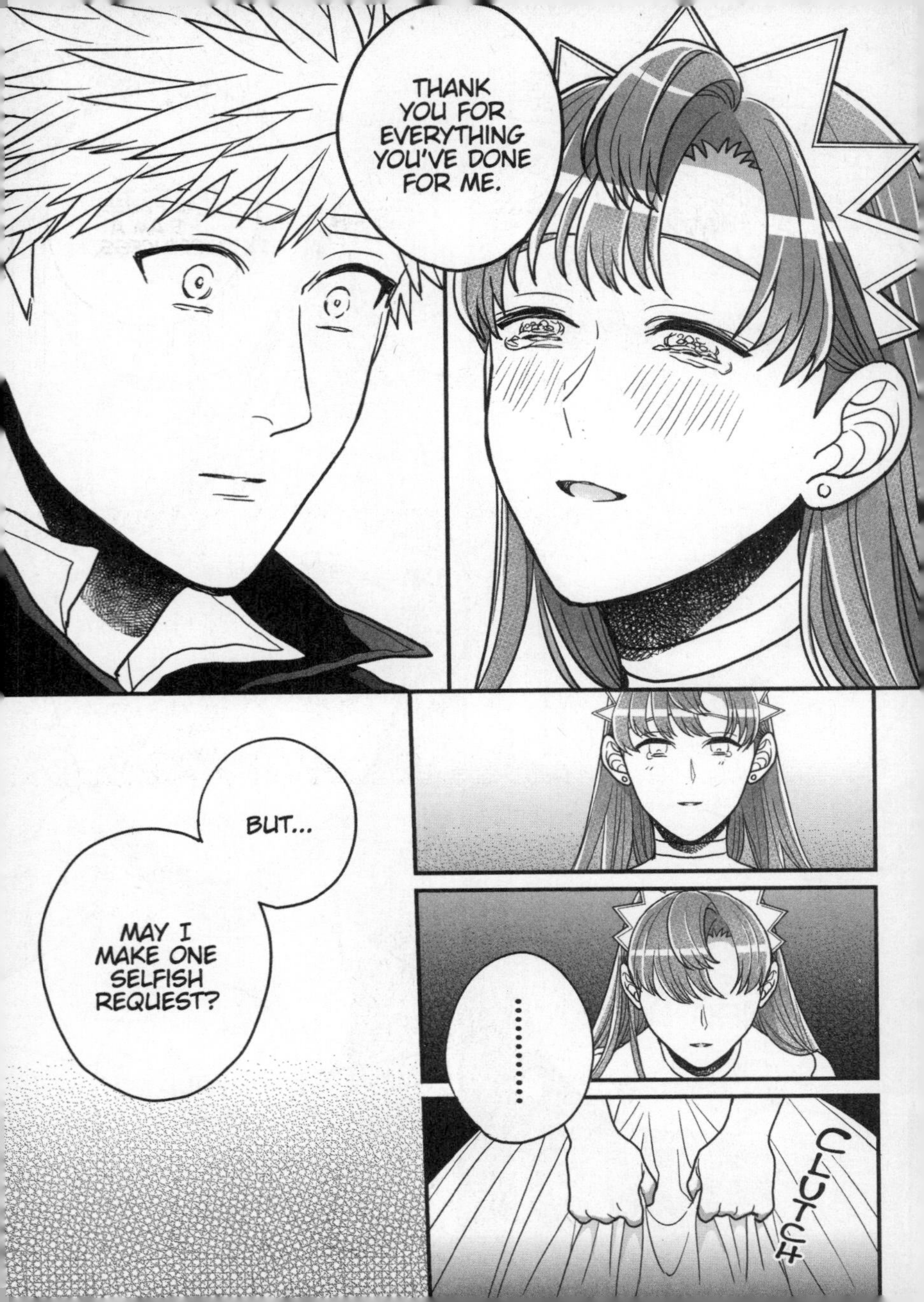
THANK YOU FOR EVERYTHING YOU'VE DONE FOR ME.
BUT...
MAY I MAKE ONE SELFISH REQUEST?
....
CLUTCH

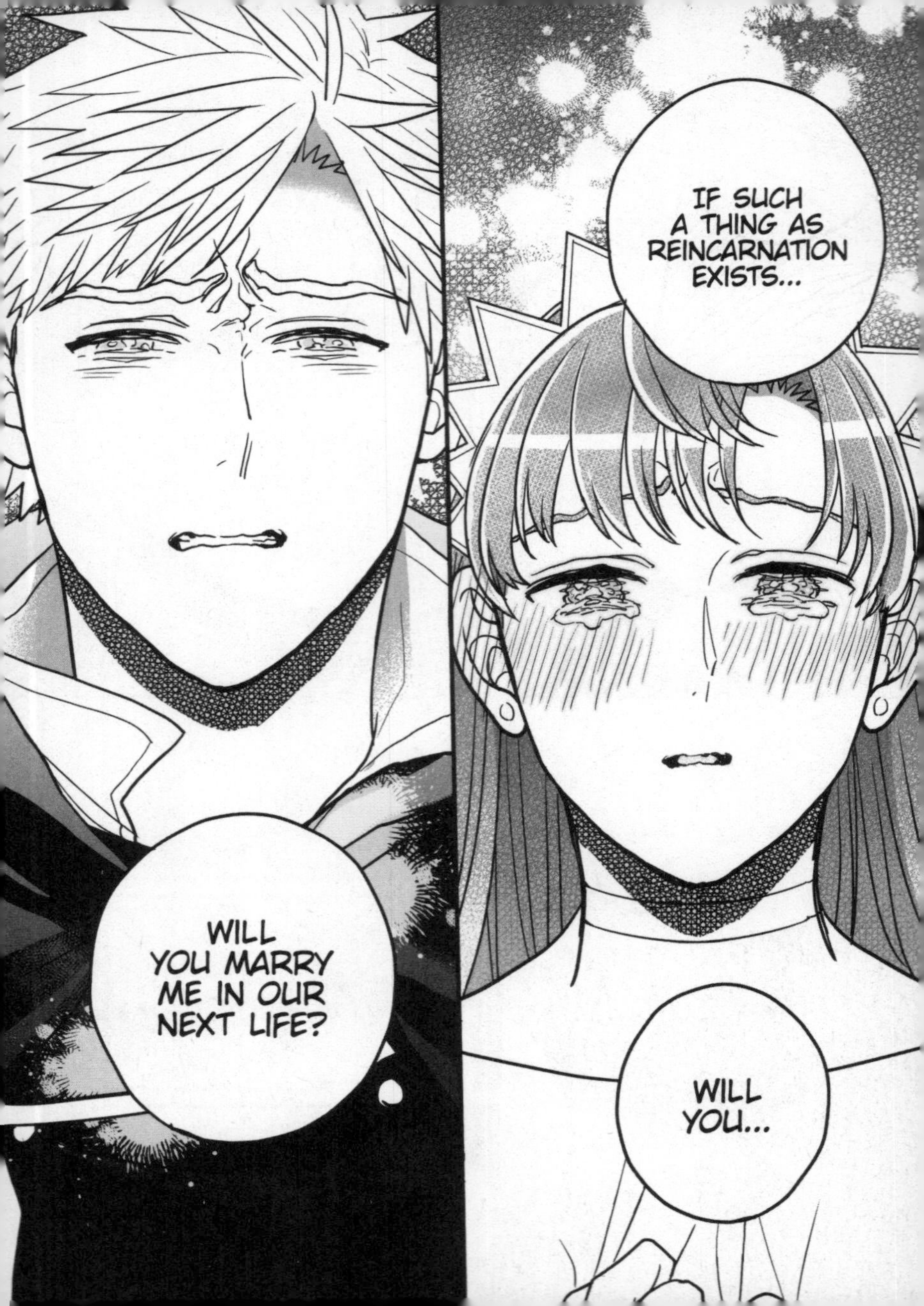
IF SUCH A THING AS REINCARNATION EXISTS...
WILL YOU...
WILL YOU MARRY ME IN OUR NEXT LIFE?

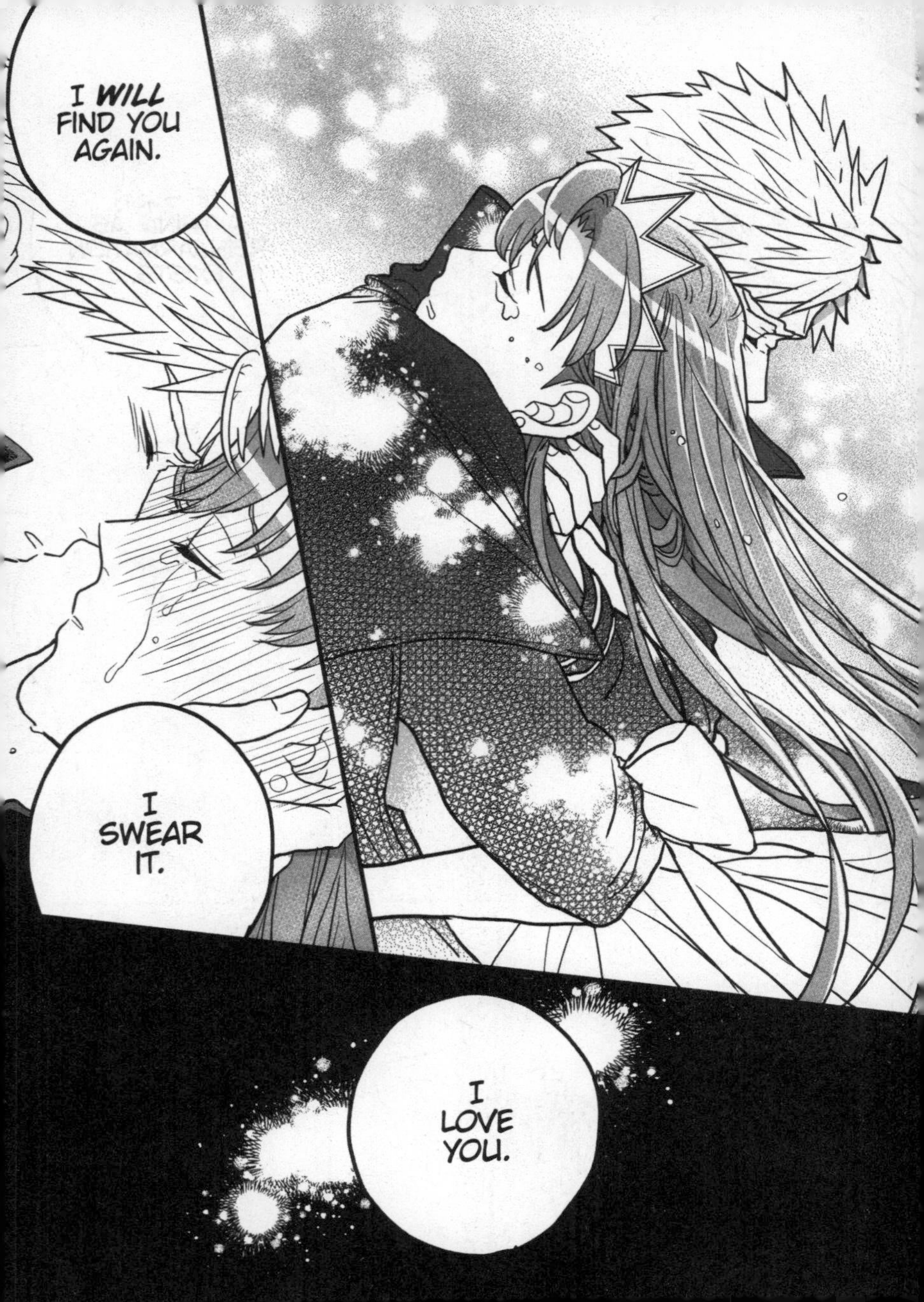
I WILL FIND YOU AGAIN.
I SWEAR IT.
I LOVE YOU.

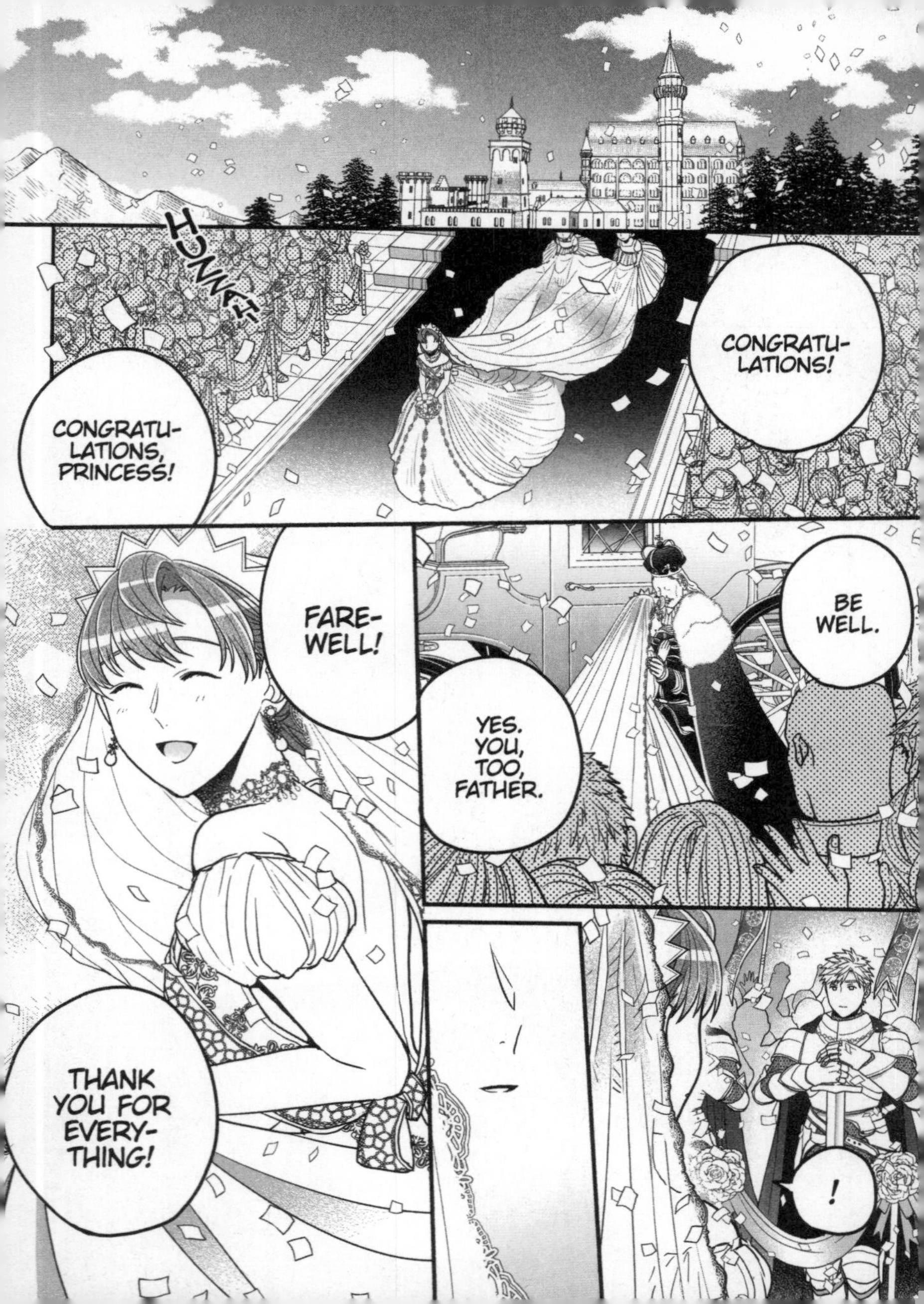
HUWAAH
CONGRATU-LATIONS!
CONGRATU-LATIONS, PRINCESS!
BE WELL.
YES. YOU, TOO, FATHER.
FARE-WELL!
THANK YOU FOR EVERY-THING!
!

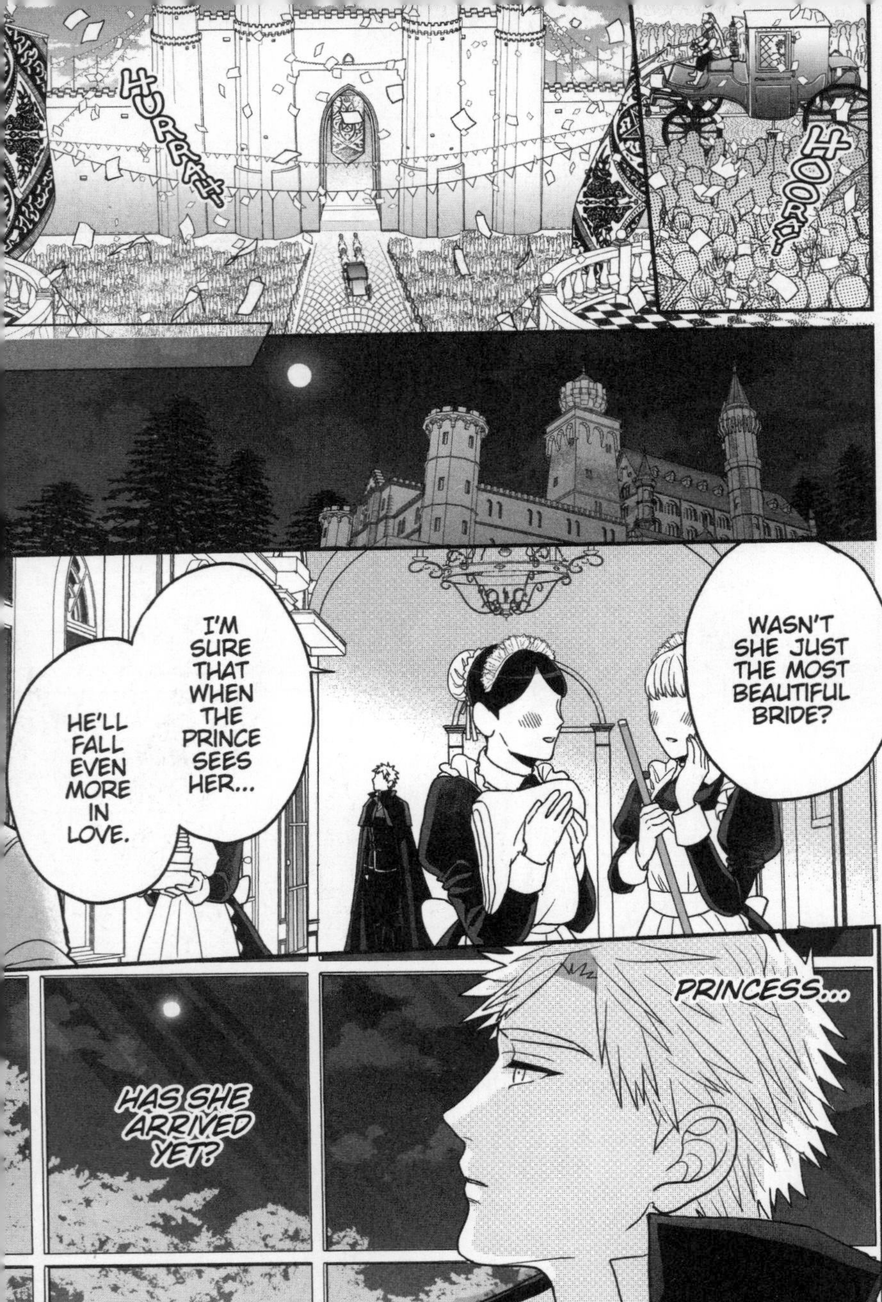
HURRAH
HOORAY
WASN'T SHE JUST THE MOST BEAUTIFUL BRIDE?
I'M SURE THAT WHEN THE PRINCE SEES HER...
HE'LL FALL EVEN MORE IN LOVE.
PRINCESS...
HAS SHE ARRIVED YET?

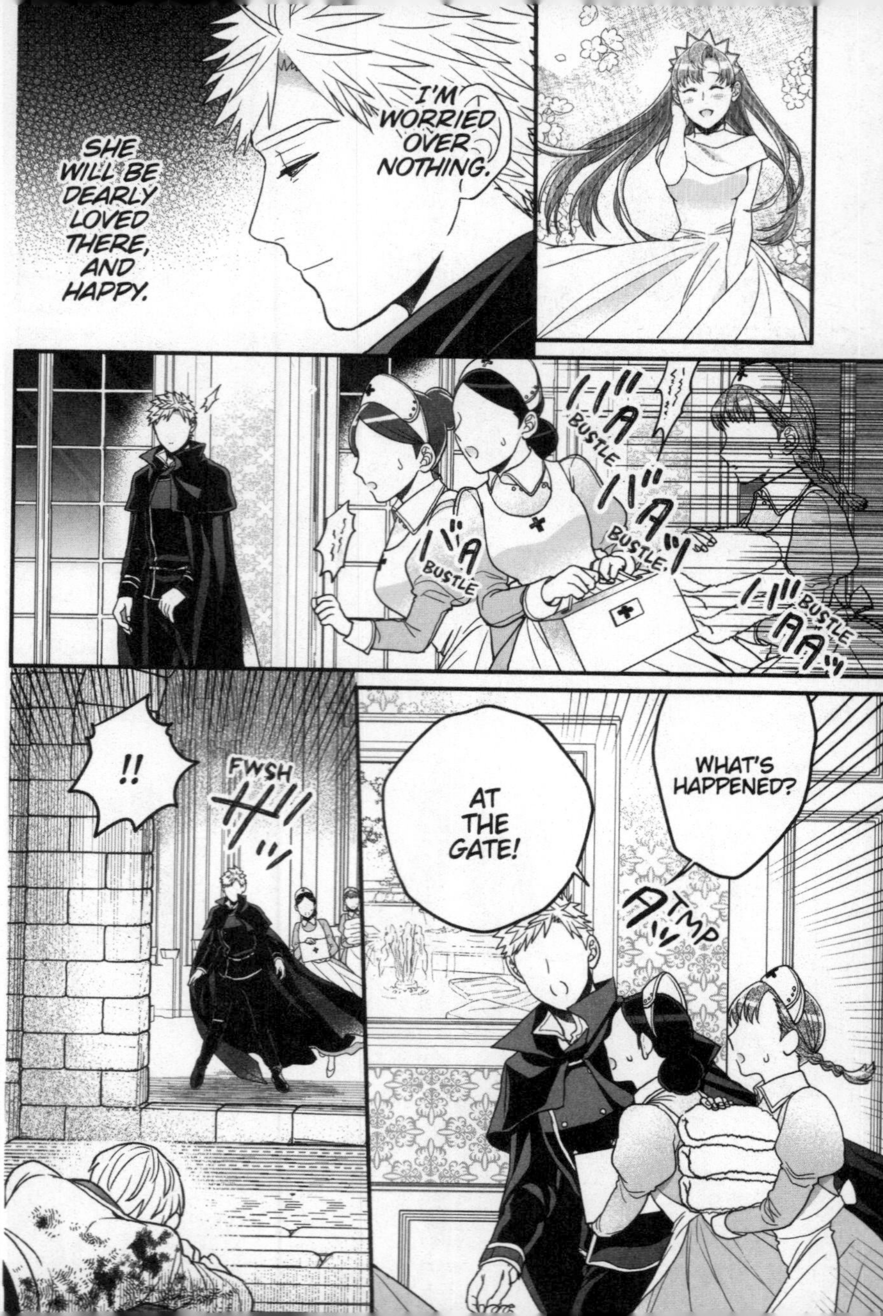

I'M WORRIED OVER NOTHING.
SHE WILL BE DEARLY LOVED THERE, AND HAPPY.
BUSTLE
BUSTLE
BUSTLE
BUSTLE
WHAT'S HAPPENED?
AT THE GATE!
TMP
!!
FWSH

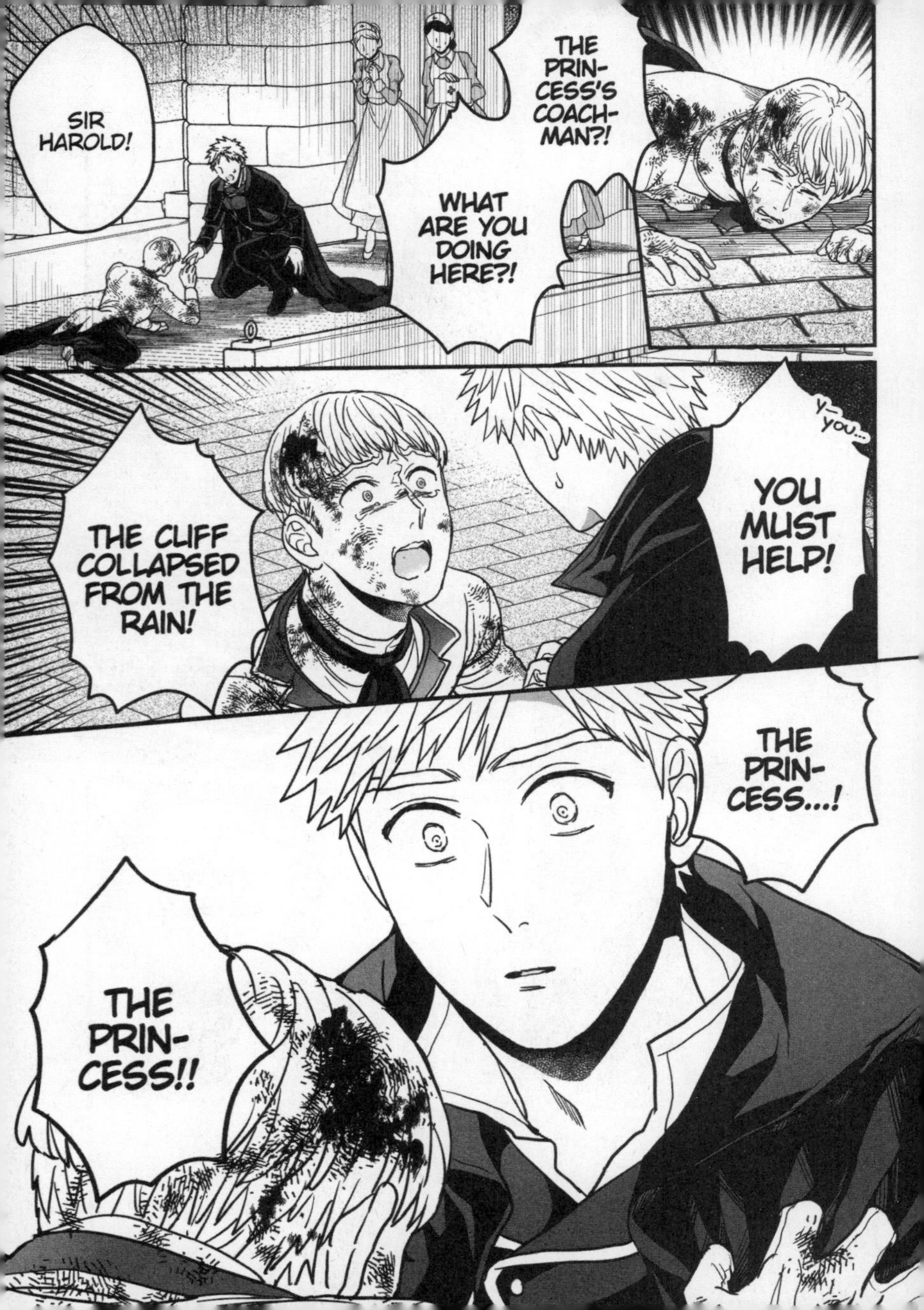
THE PRIN-CESS'S COACH-MAN?!
WHAT ARE YOU DOING HERE?!
SIR HAROLD!
Y—YOU...
YOU MUST HELP!
THE CLIFF COLLAPSED FROM THE RAIN!
THE PRIN-CESS...!
THE PRIN-CESS!!

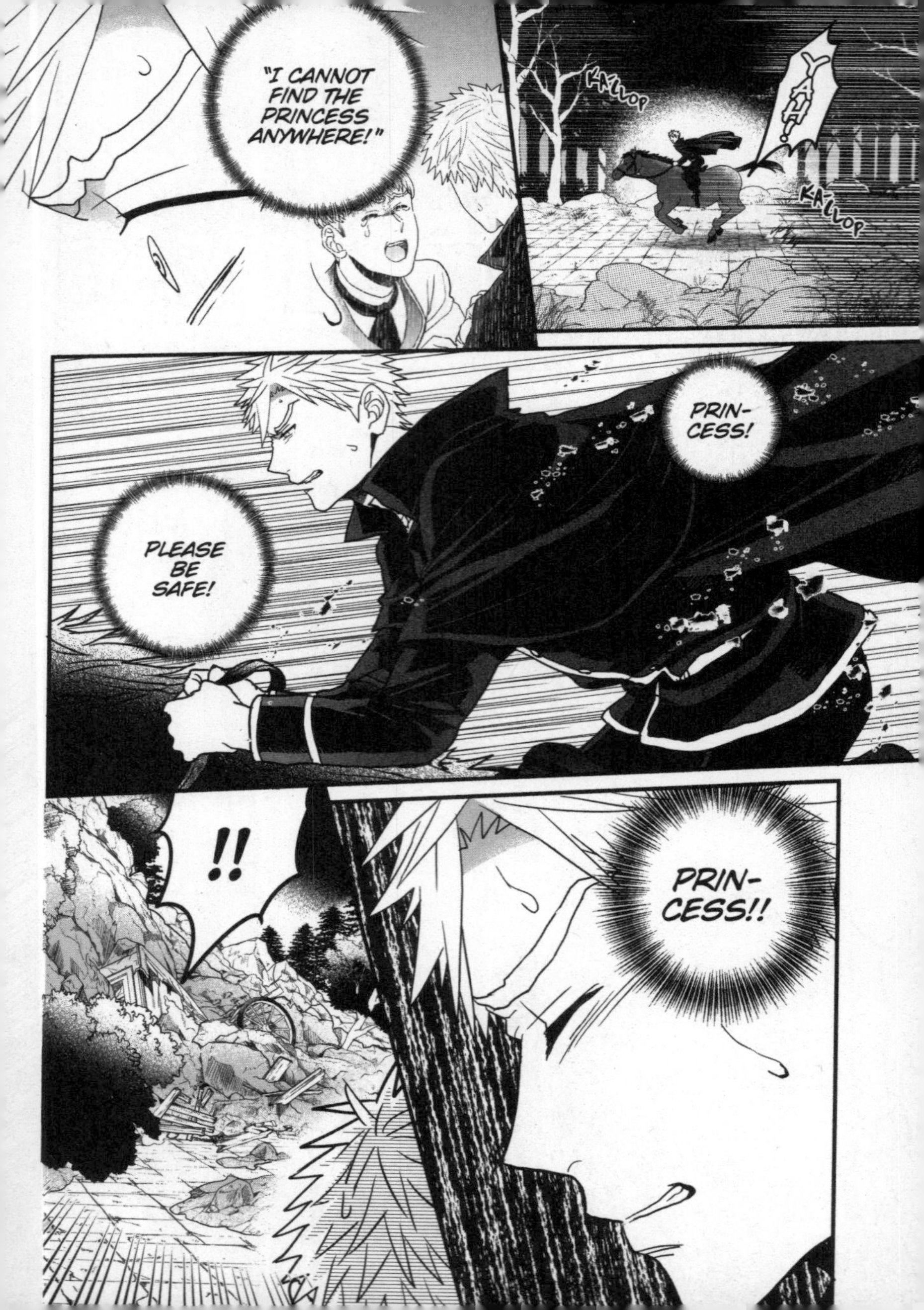
"I CANNOT FIND THE PRINCESS ANYWHERE!"
YAH!
KA-LLOP
KA-LLOP
PRIN-CESS!
PLEASE BE SAFE!
PRIN-CESS!!
!!

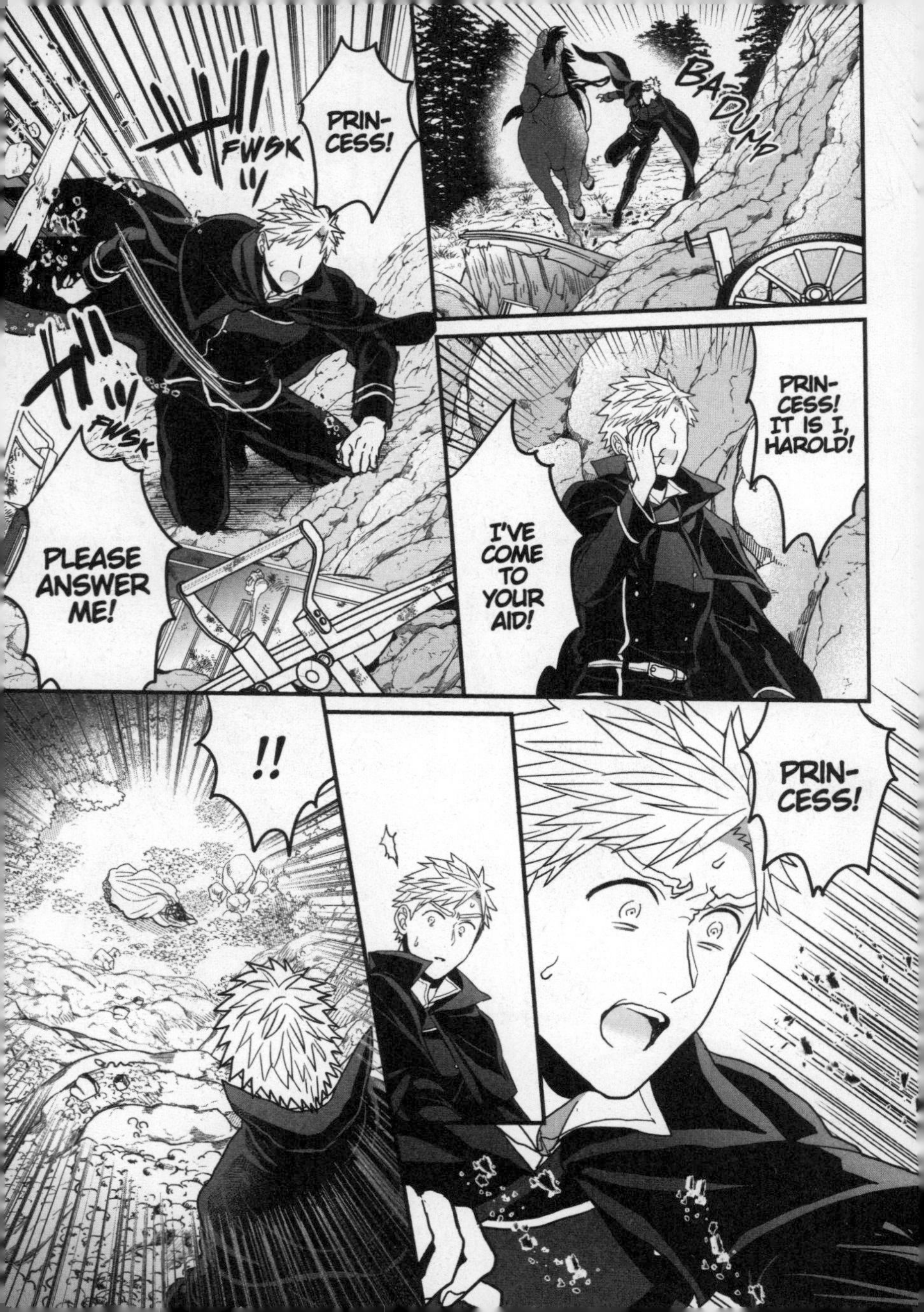
BA-DUMP
PRIN-CESS!
FWSK
FWSK
PLEASE ANSWER ME!
PRIN-CESS! IT IS I, HAROLD!
I'VE COME TO YOUR AID!
PRIN-CESS!
!!

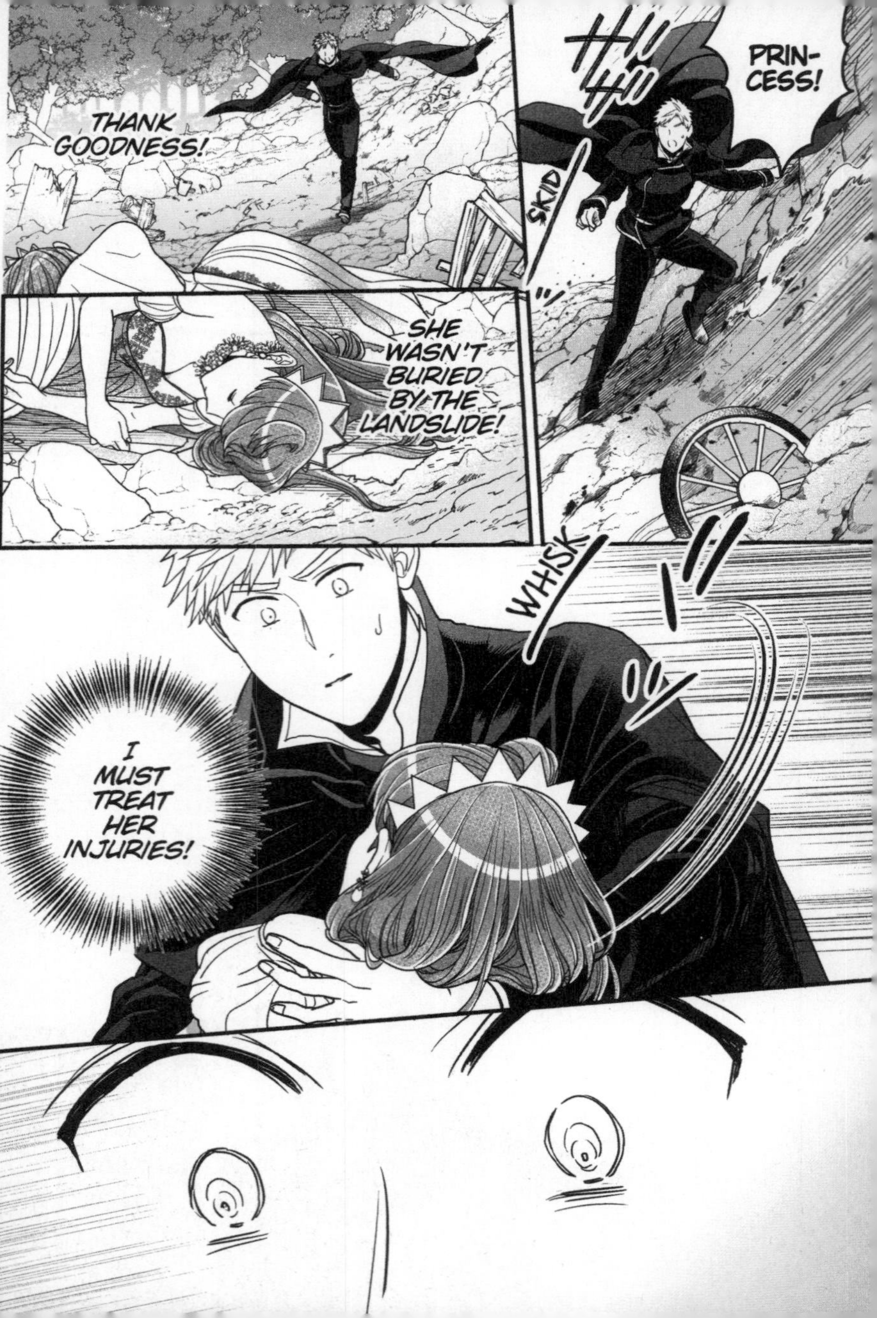
PRIN-
CESS!
SKID
THANK GOODNESS!
SHE WASN'T BURIED BY THE LANDSLIDE!
WHISK
I MUST TREAT HER INJURIES!

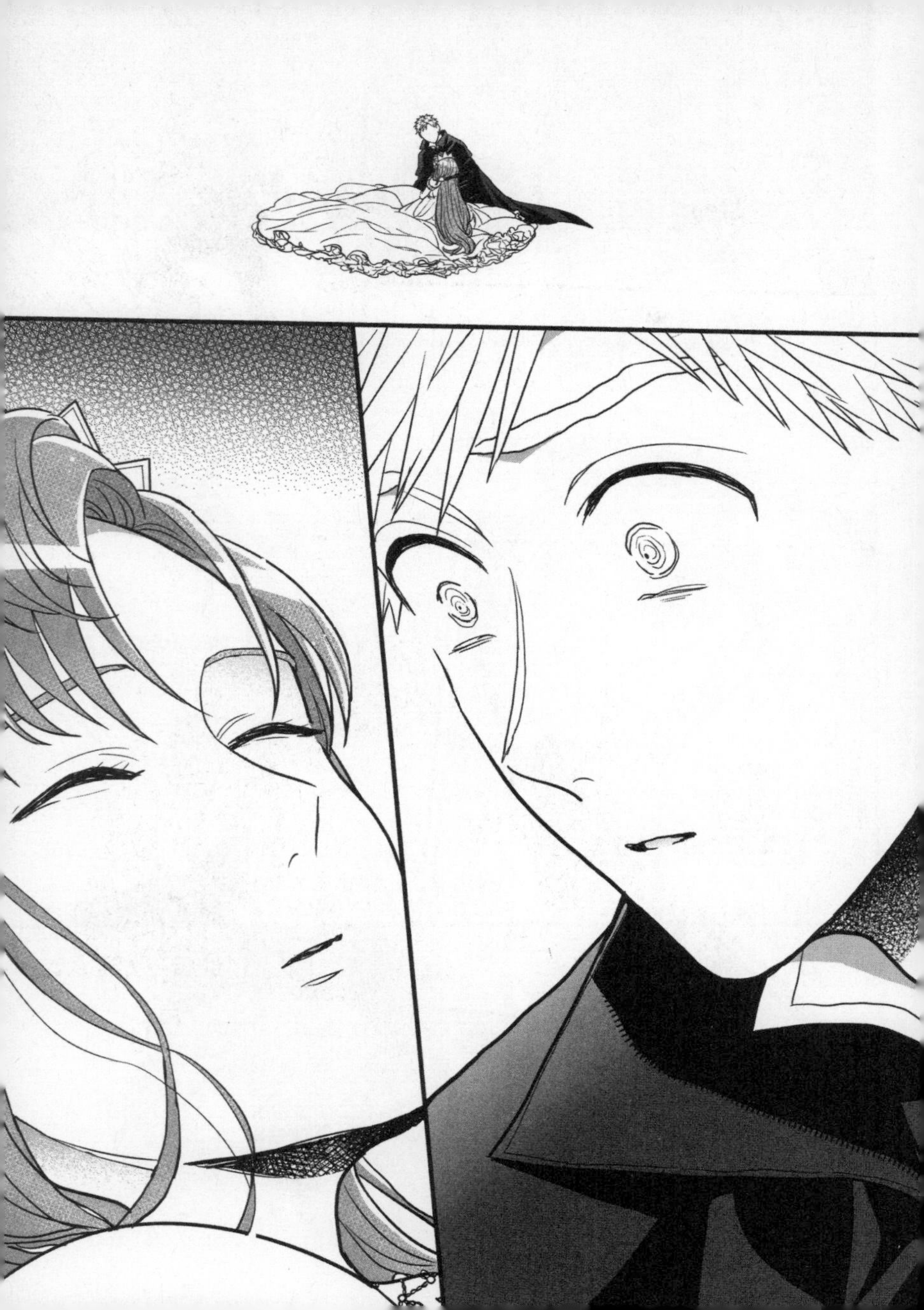

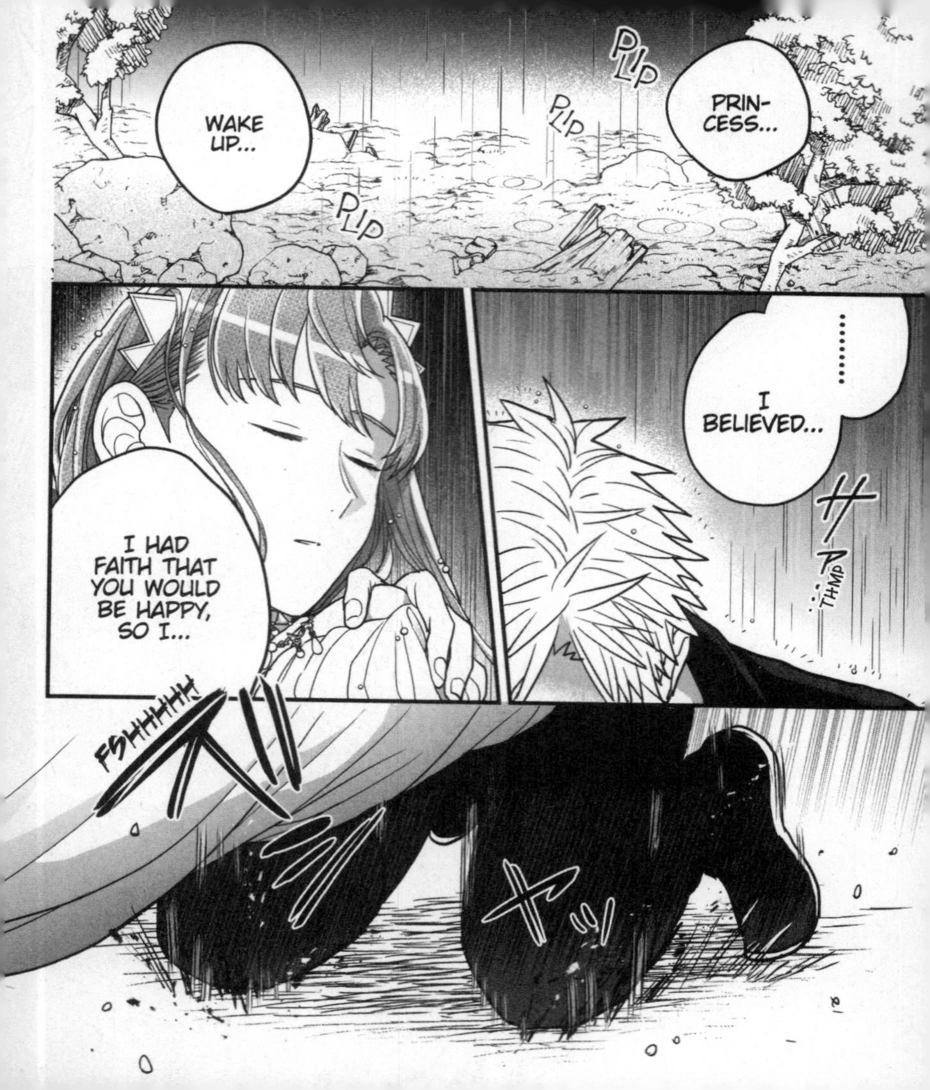
PRIN-
CESS...
PLIP
PLIP
WAKE
UP...
PLIP
......
I
BELIEVED...
THMP
I HAD
FAITH THAT
YOU WOULD
BE HAPPY,
SO I...
FSHHHHH

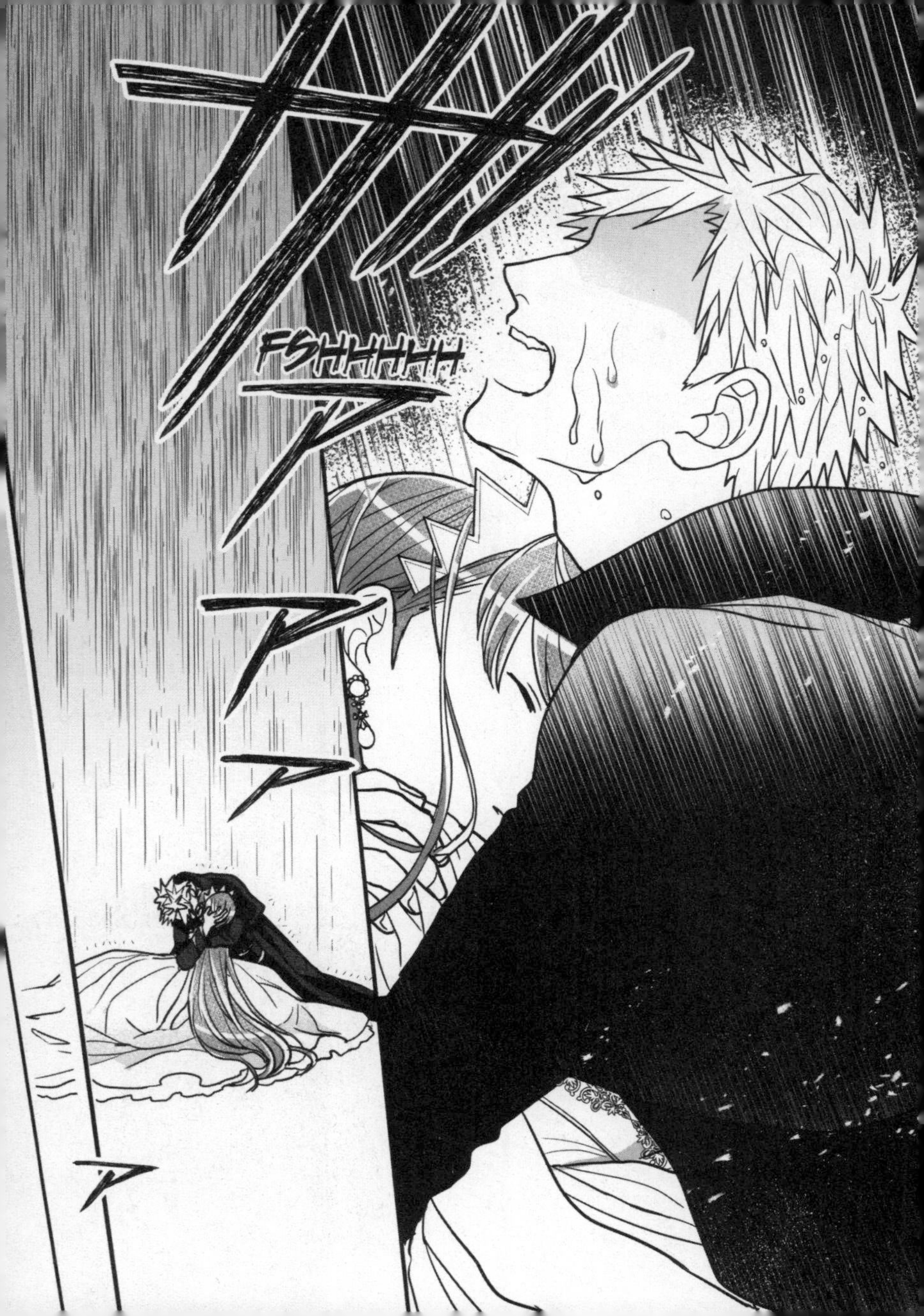
FSHHHHH

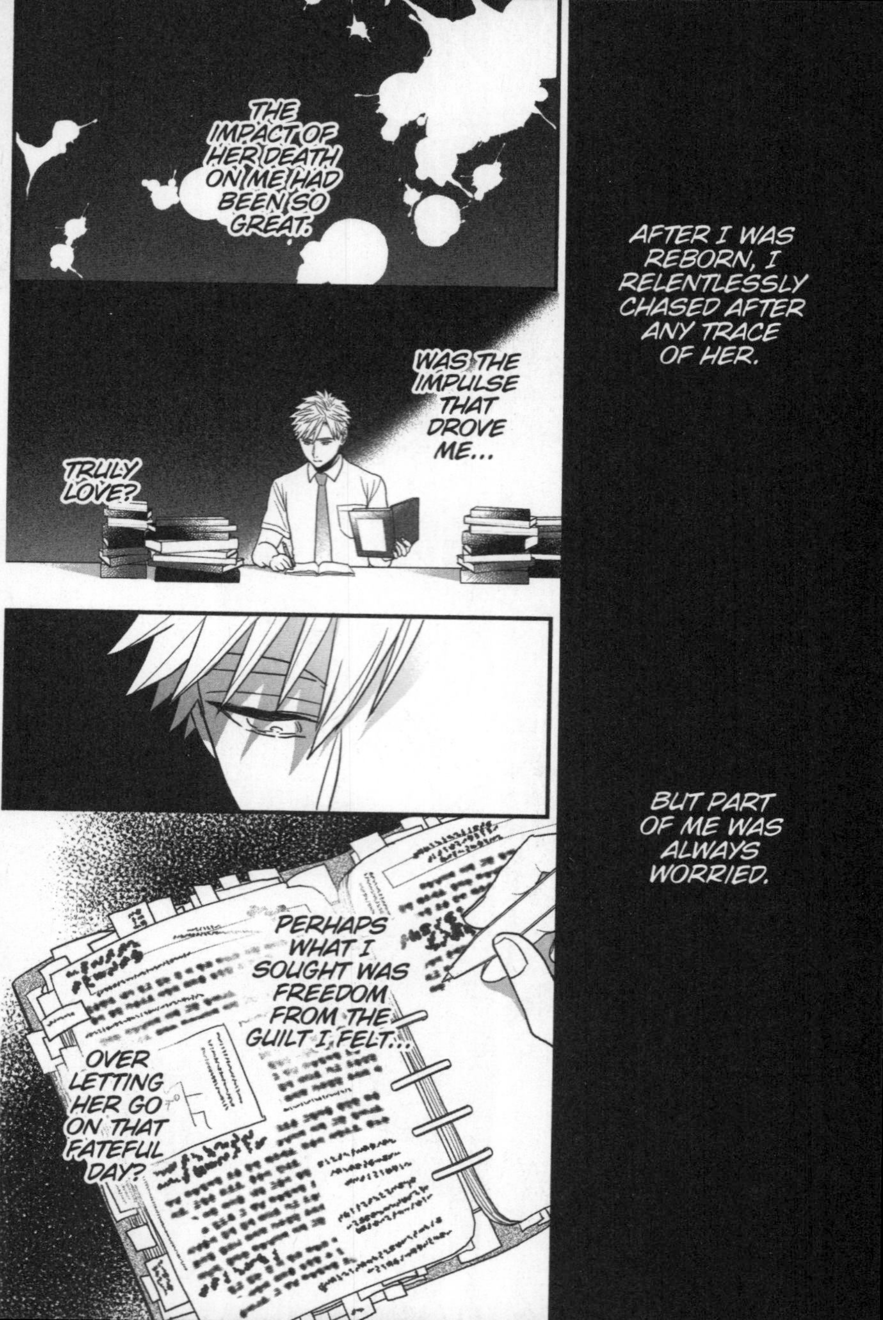
AFTER I WAS REBORN, I RELENTLESSLY CHASED AFTER ANY TRACE OF HER.
THE IMPACT OF HER DEATH ON ME HAD BEEN SO GREAT.
WAS THE IMPULSE THAT DROVE ME...
TRULY LOVE?
BUT PART OF ME WAS ALWAYS WORRIED.
PERHAPS WHAT I SOUGHT WAS FREEDOM FROM THE GUILT I FELT...
OVER LETTING HER GO ON THAT FATEFUL DAY?

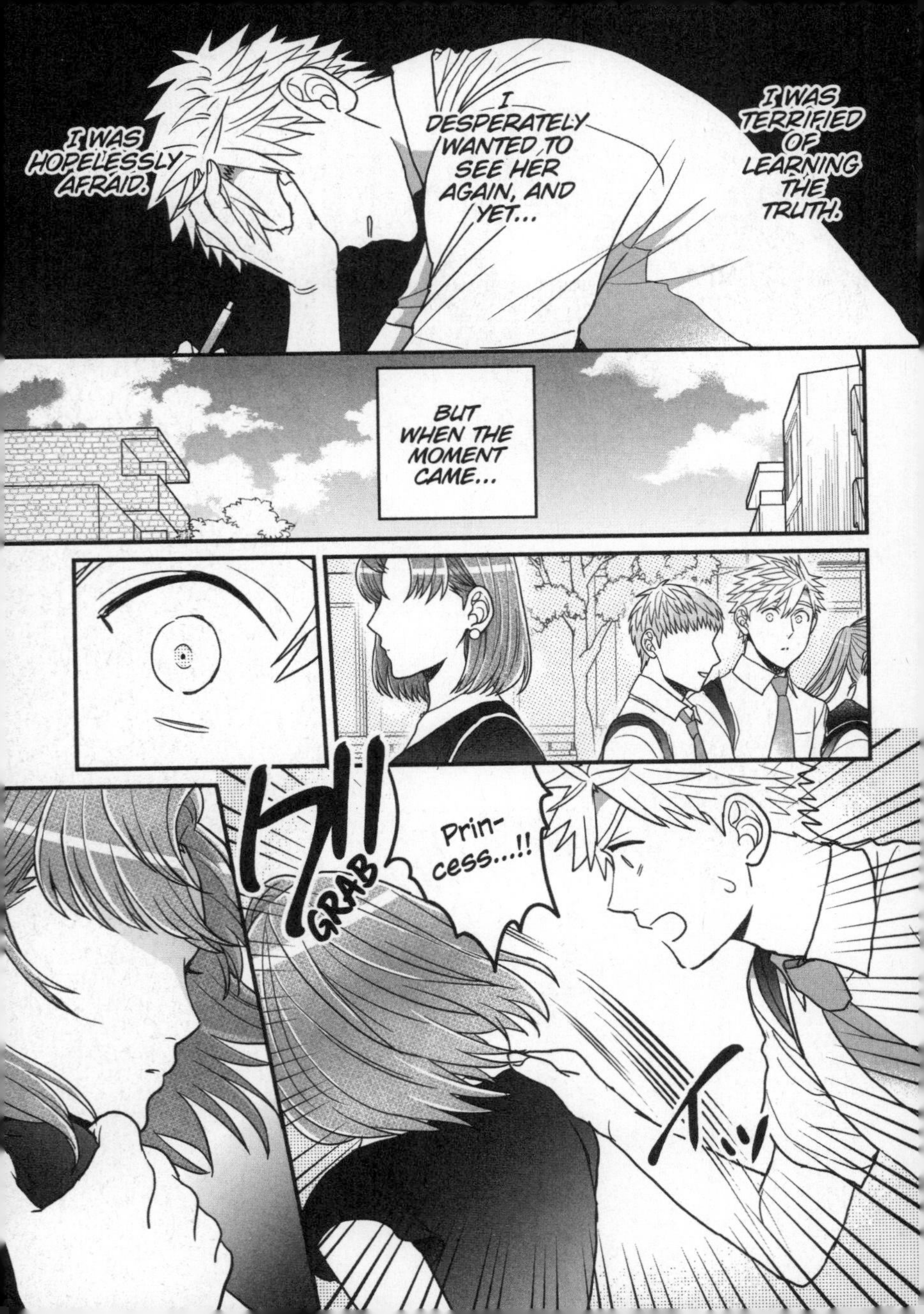
I WAS TERRIFIED OF LEARNING THE TRUTH.
I DESPERATELY WANTED TO SEE HER AGAIN, AND YET...
I WAS HOPELESSLY AFRAID.
BUT WHEN THE MOMENT CAME...
GRAB
Prin-cess...!!

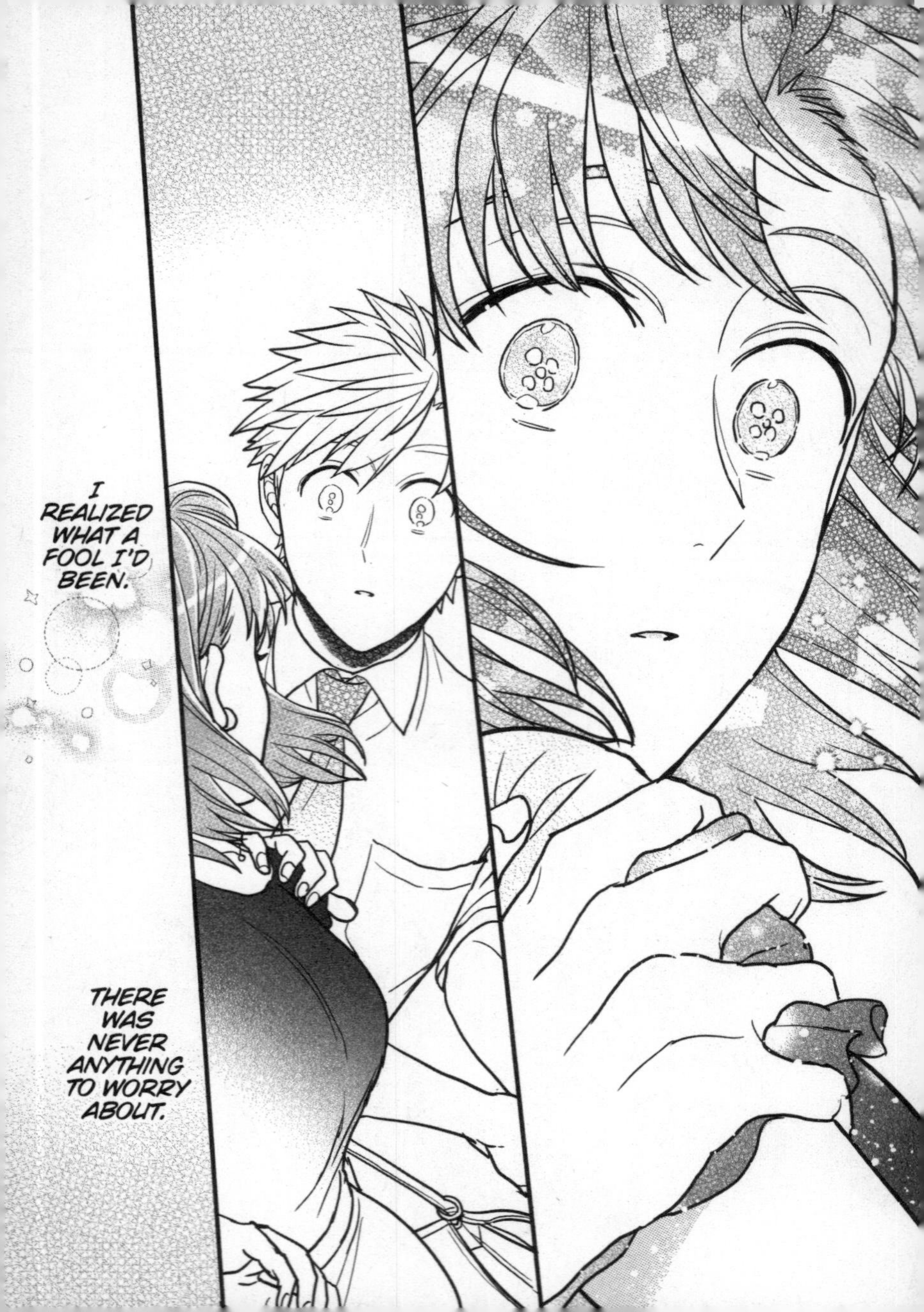
I REALIZED WHAT A FOOL I'D BEEN.
THERE WAS NEVER ANYTHING TO WORRY ABOUT.

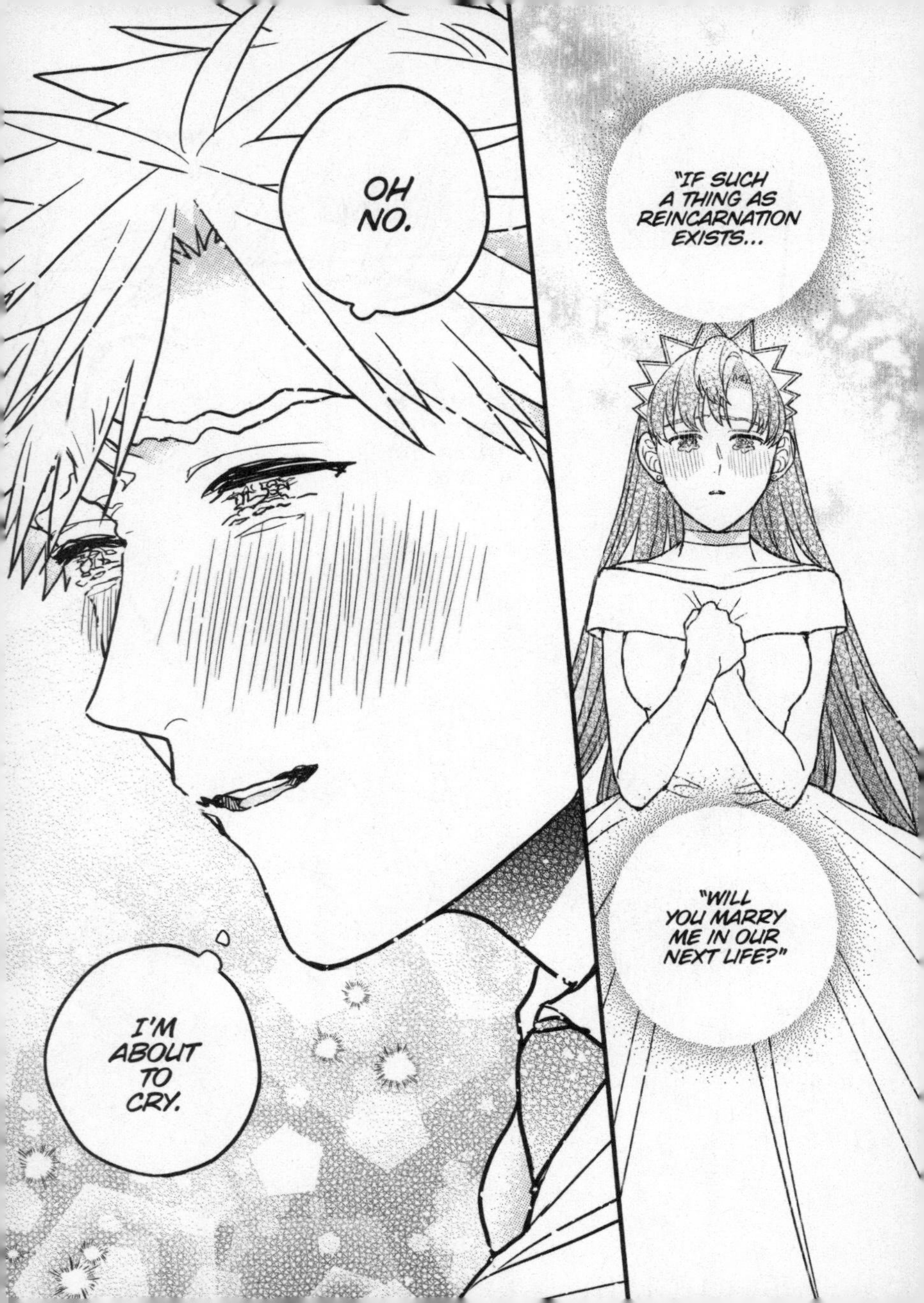
"IF SUCH A THING AS REINCARNATION EXISTS...
"WILL YOU MARRY ME IN OUR NEXT LIFE?"
OH NO.
I'M ABOUT TO CRY.

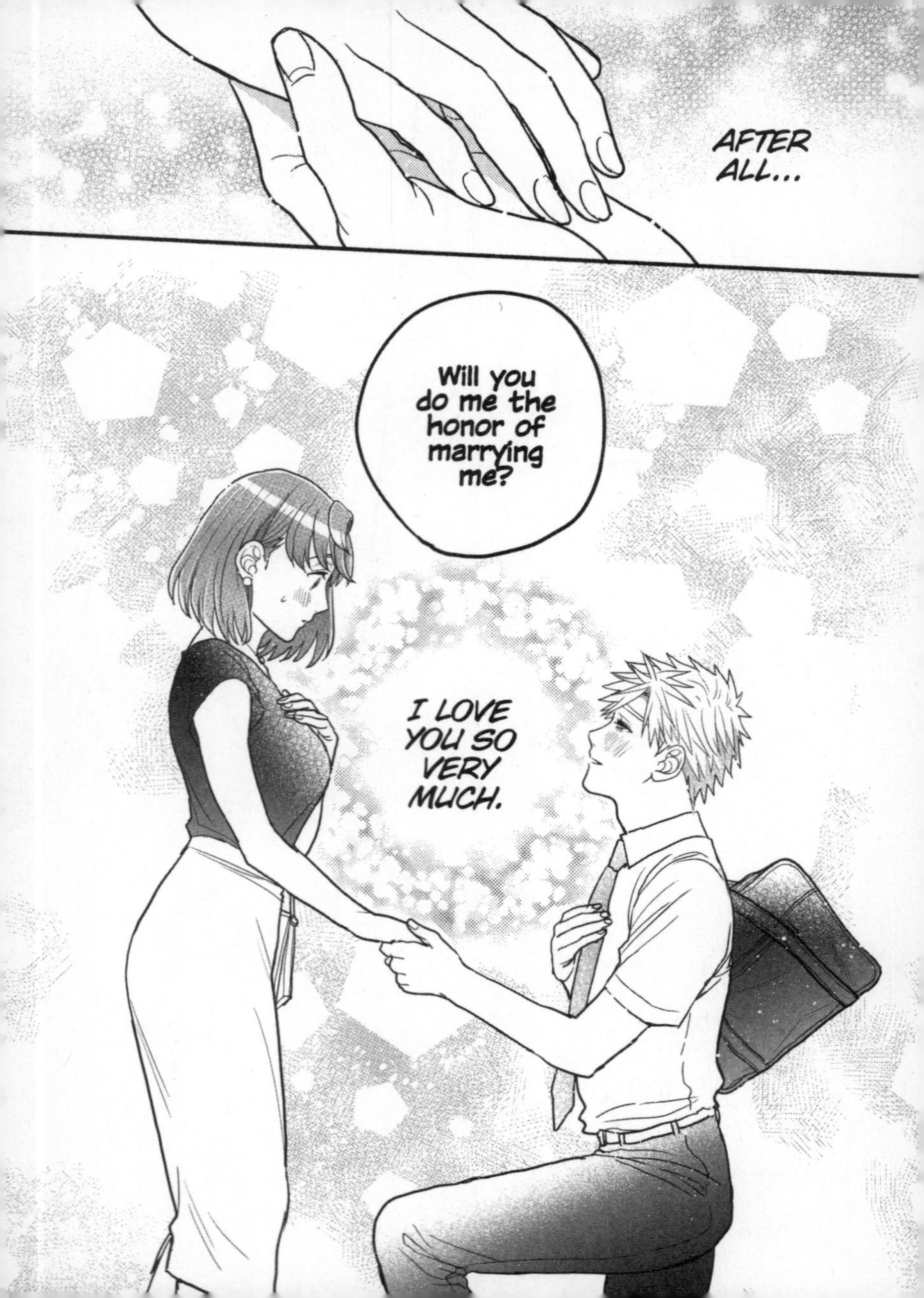
AFTER ALL...
Will you do me the honor of marrying me?
I LOVE YOU SO VERY MUCH.

We Swore to Meet in the Next Life and That's When Things Got Weird!

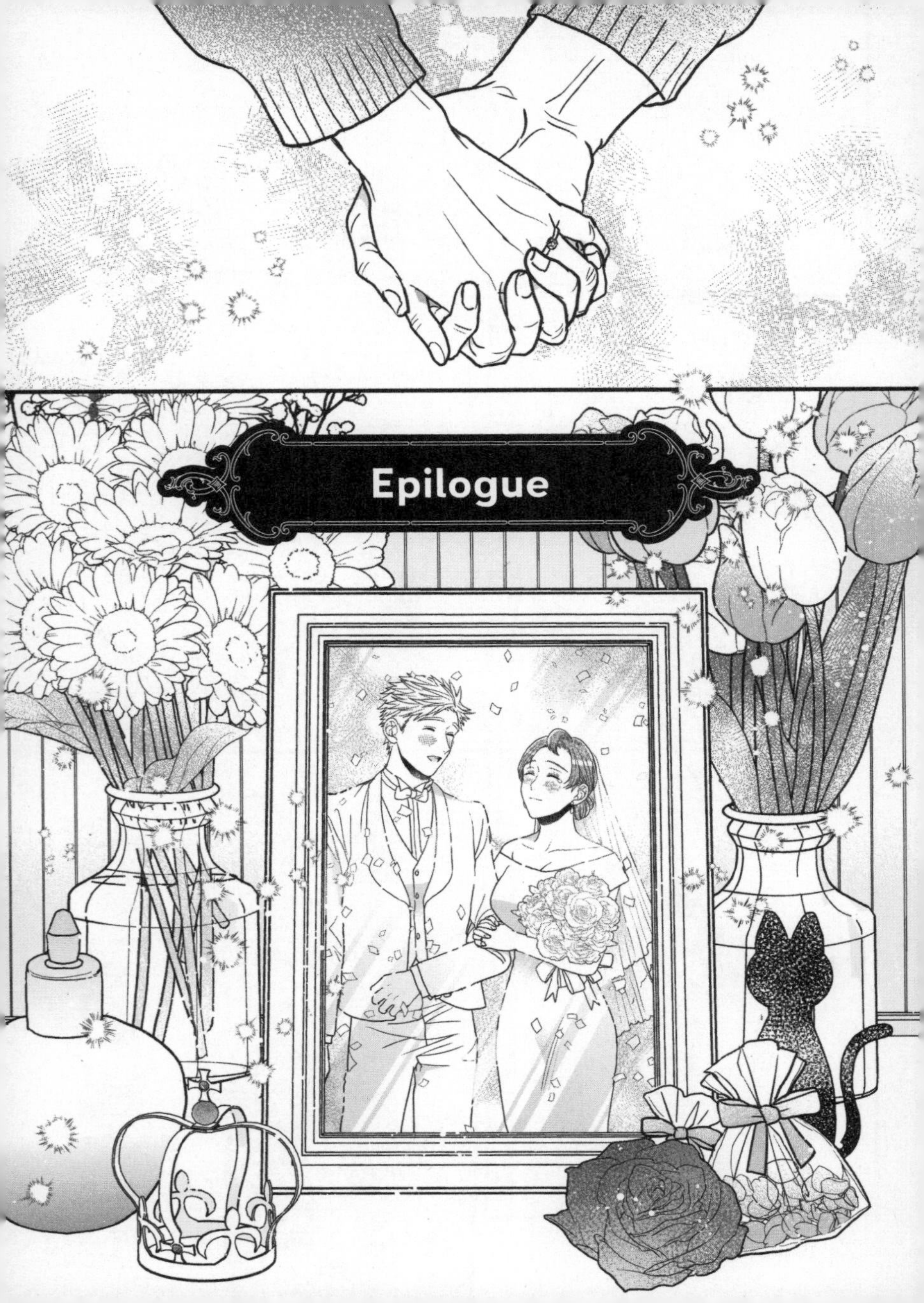
Epilogue

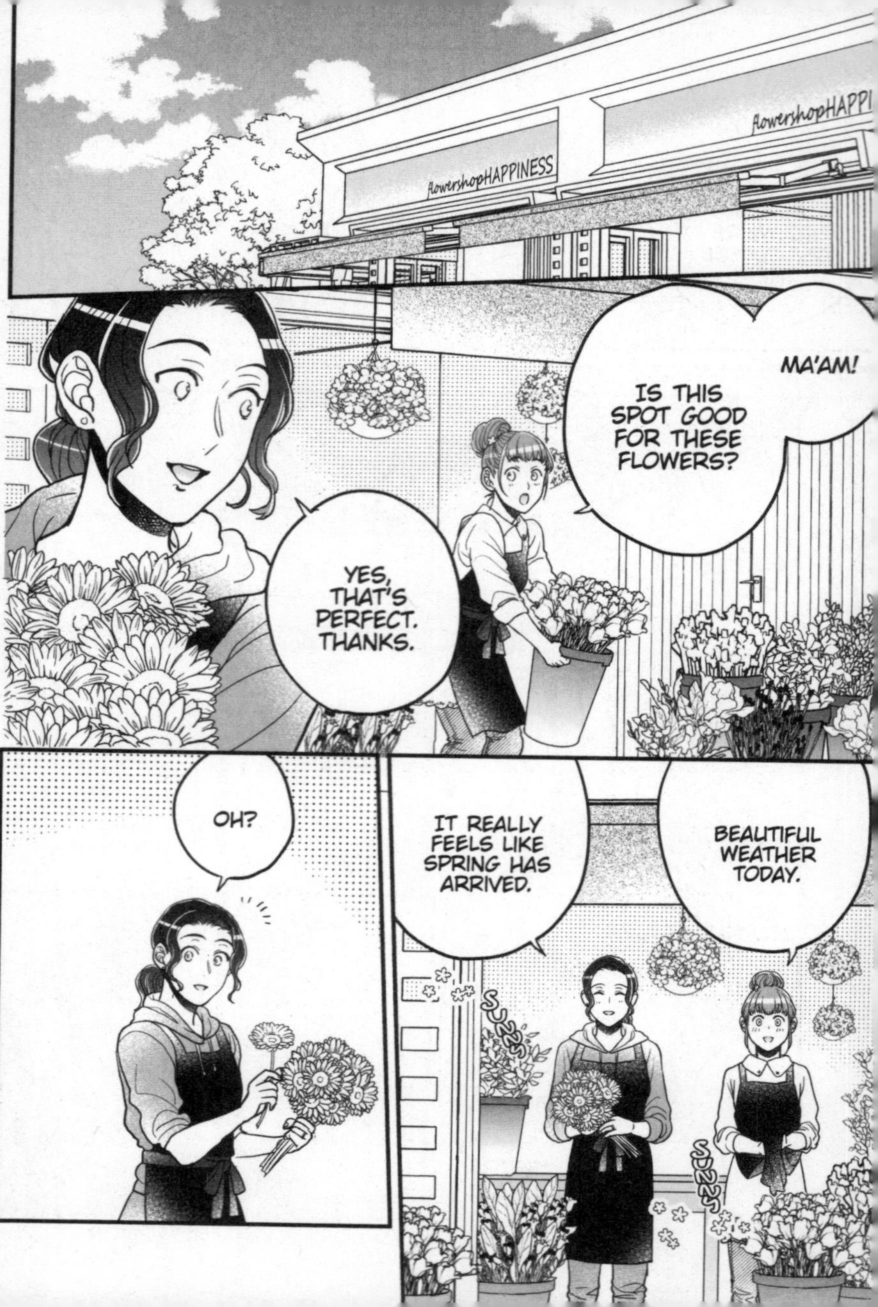

flowershopHAPPI
flowershopHAPPINESS
MA'AM!
IS THIS SPOT GOOD FOR THESE FLOWERS?
YES, THAT'S PERFECT. THANKS.
BEAUTIFUL WEATHER TODAY.
IT REALLY FEELS LIKE SPRING HAS ARRIVED.
OH?

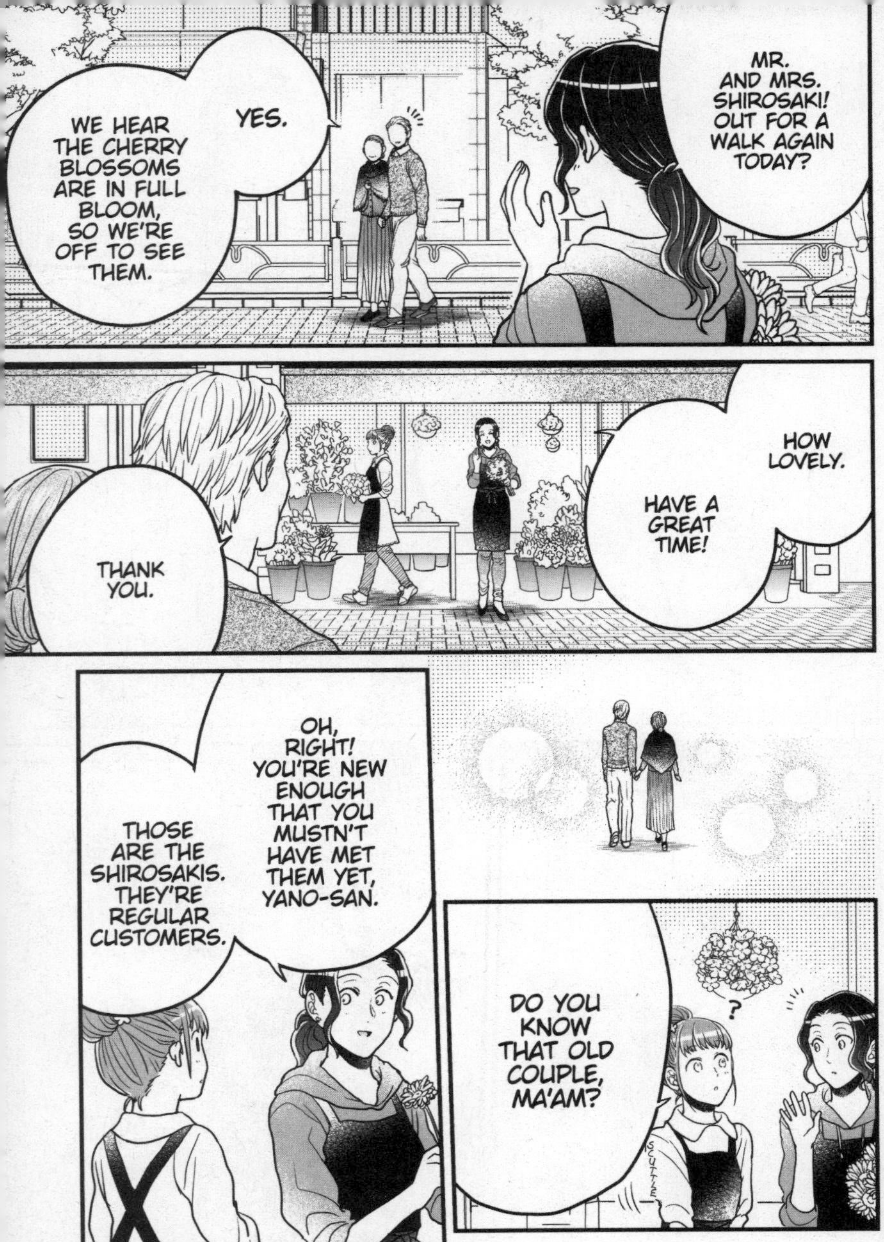
MR. AND MRS. SHIROSAKI! OUT FOR A WALK AGAIN TODAY?
YES.
WE HEAR THE CHERRY BLOSSOMS ARE IN FULL BLOOM, SO WE'RE OFF TO SEE THEM.
HOW LOVELY.
HAVE A GREAT TIME!
THANK YOU.
DO YOU KNOW THAT OLD COUPLE, MA'AM?
SCUTTLE
OH, RIGHT! YOU'RE NEW ENOUGH THAT YOU MUSTN'T HAVE MET THEM YET, YANO-SAN.
THOSE ARE THE SHIROSAKIS. THEY'RE REGULAR CUSTOMERS.

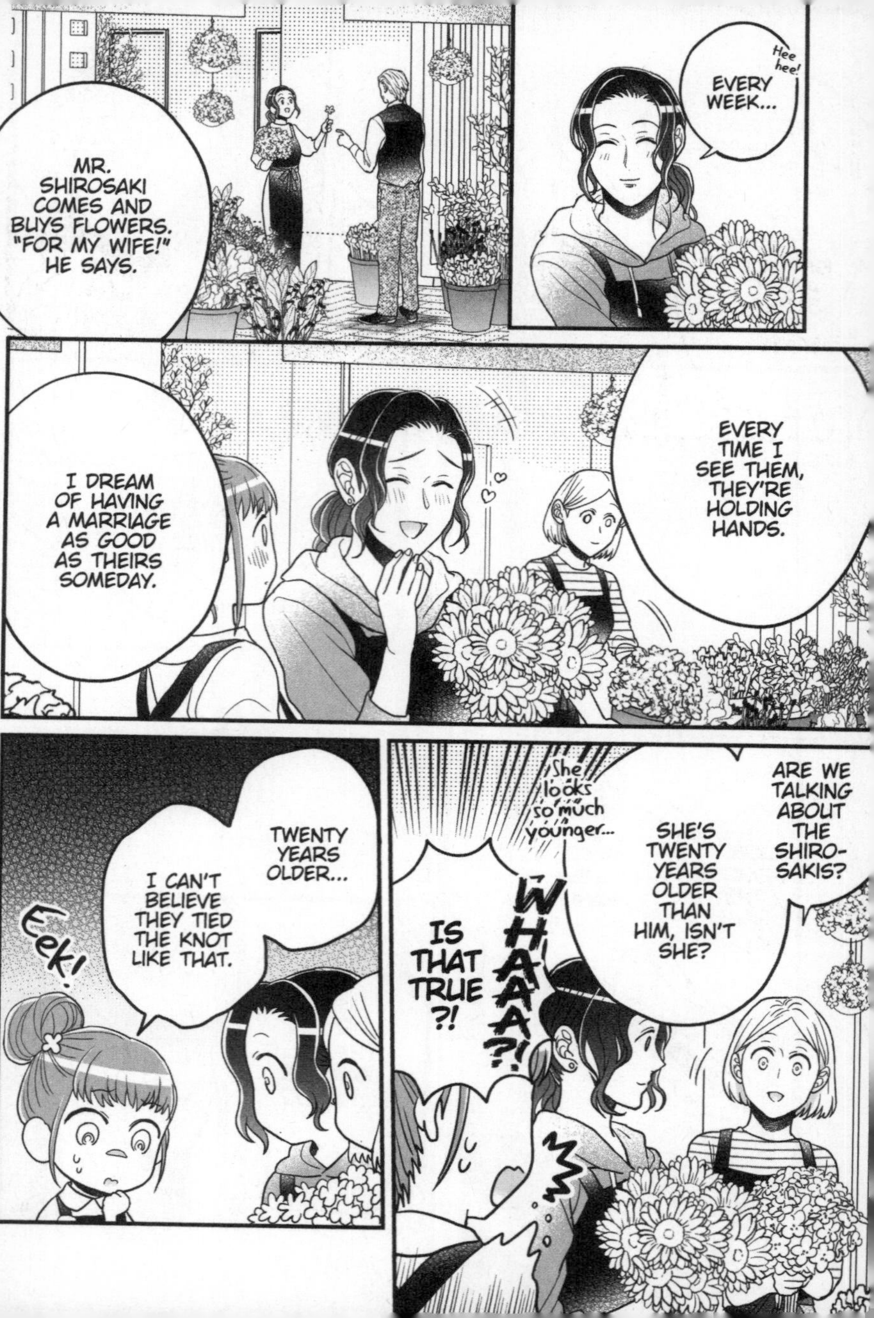

Hee hee!
EVERY WEEK...
MR. SHIROSAKI COMES AND BUYS FLOWERS. "FOR MY WIFE!" HE SAYS.
EVERY TIME I SEE THEM, THEY'RE HOLDING HANDS.
I DREAM OF HAVING A MARRIAGE AS GOOD AS THEIRS SOMEDAY.
ARE WE TALKING ABOUT THE SHIRO-SAKIS?
SHE'S TWENTY YEARS OLDER THAN HIM, ISN'T SHE?
She looks so much younger...
WHAAAA?!
IS THAT TRUE?!
TWENTY YEARS OLDER...
I CAN'T BELIEVE THEY TIED THE KNOT LIKE THAT.
Eek!

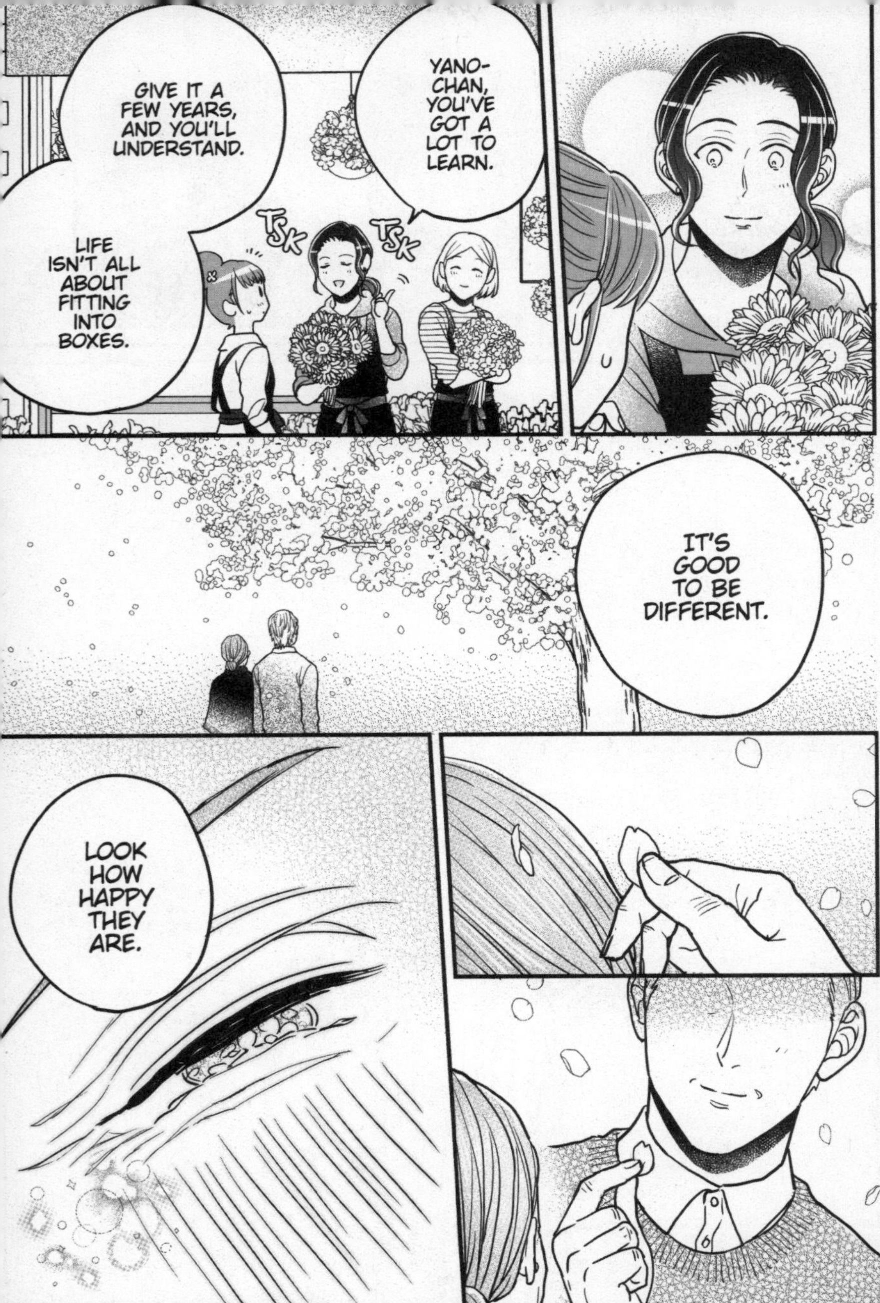

YANO-CHAN, YOU'VE GOT A LOT TO LEARN.
TSK TSK
GIVE IT A FEW YEARS, AND YOU'LL UNDERSTAND.
LIFE ISN'T ALL ABOUT FITTING INTO BOXES.
IT'S GOOD TO BE DIFFERENT.
LOOK HOW HAPPY THEY ARE.

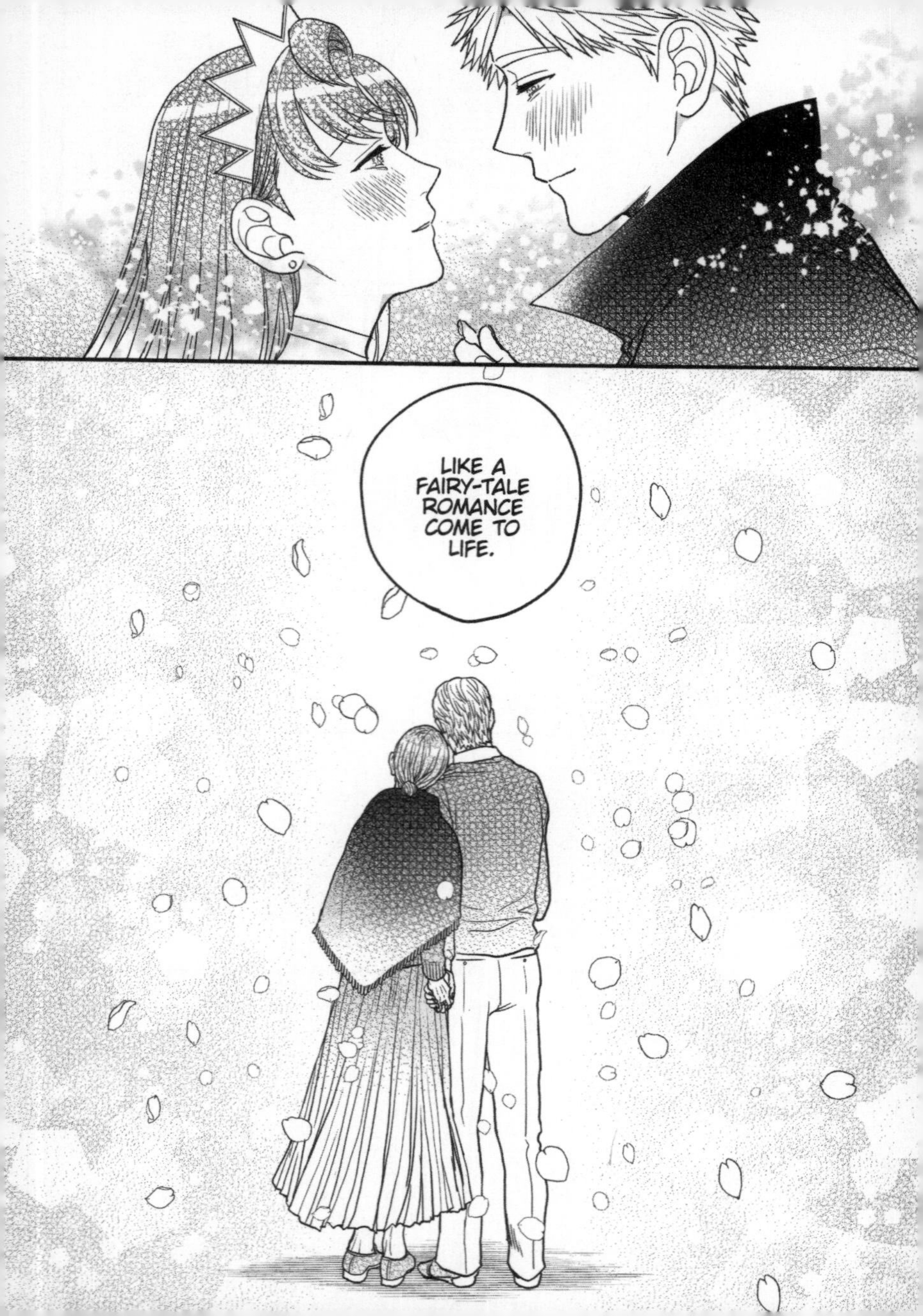
LIKE A FAIRY-TALE ROMANCE COME TO LIFE.

We Swore to
Meet in the Next Life
and That's When
Things Got
Weird!

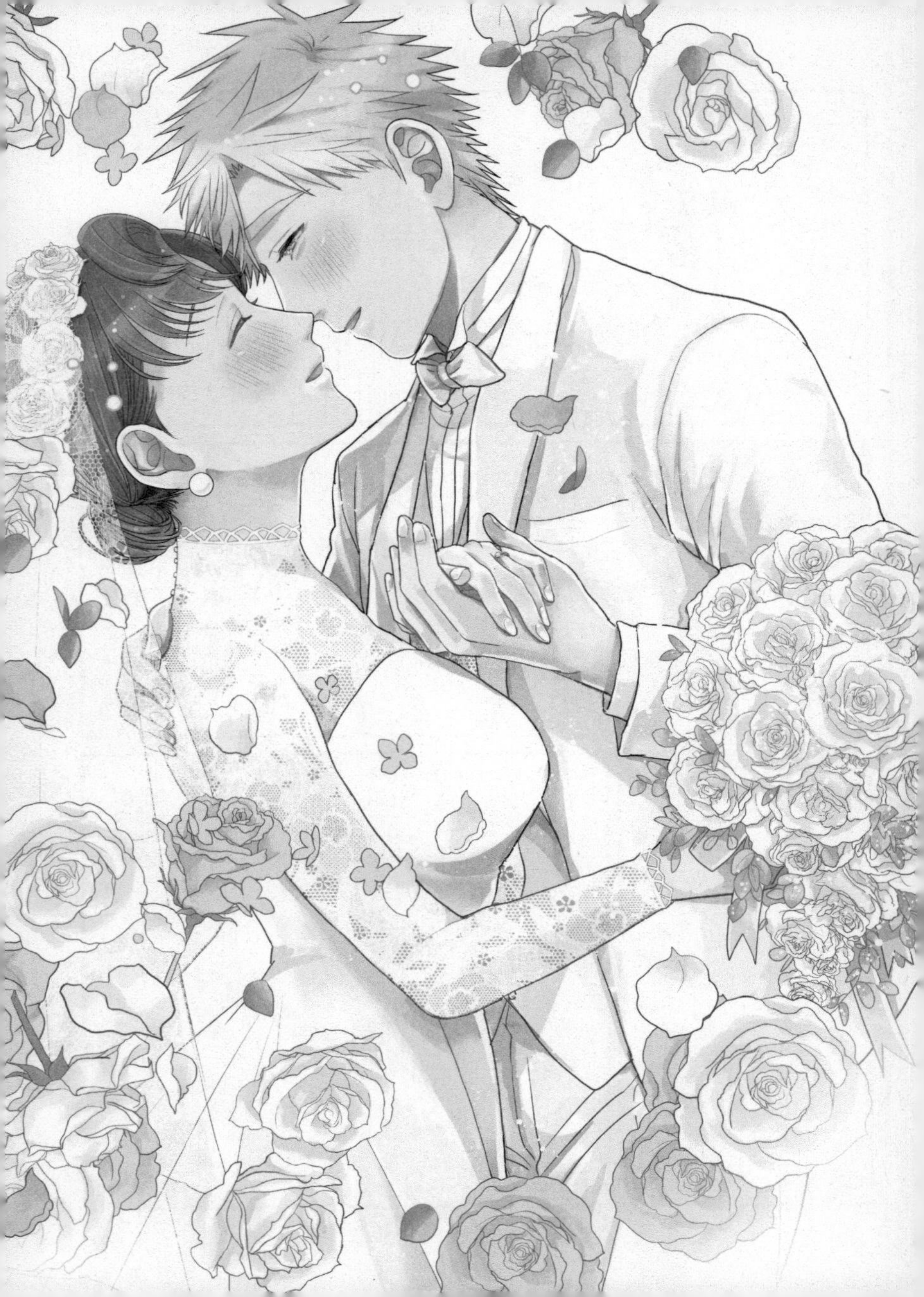

Them Until Now

Read after finishing!

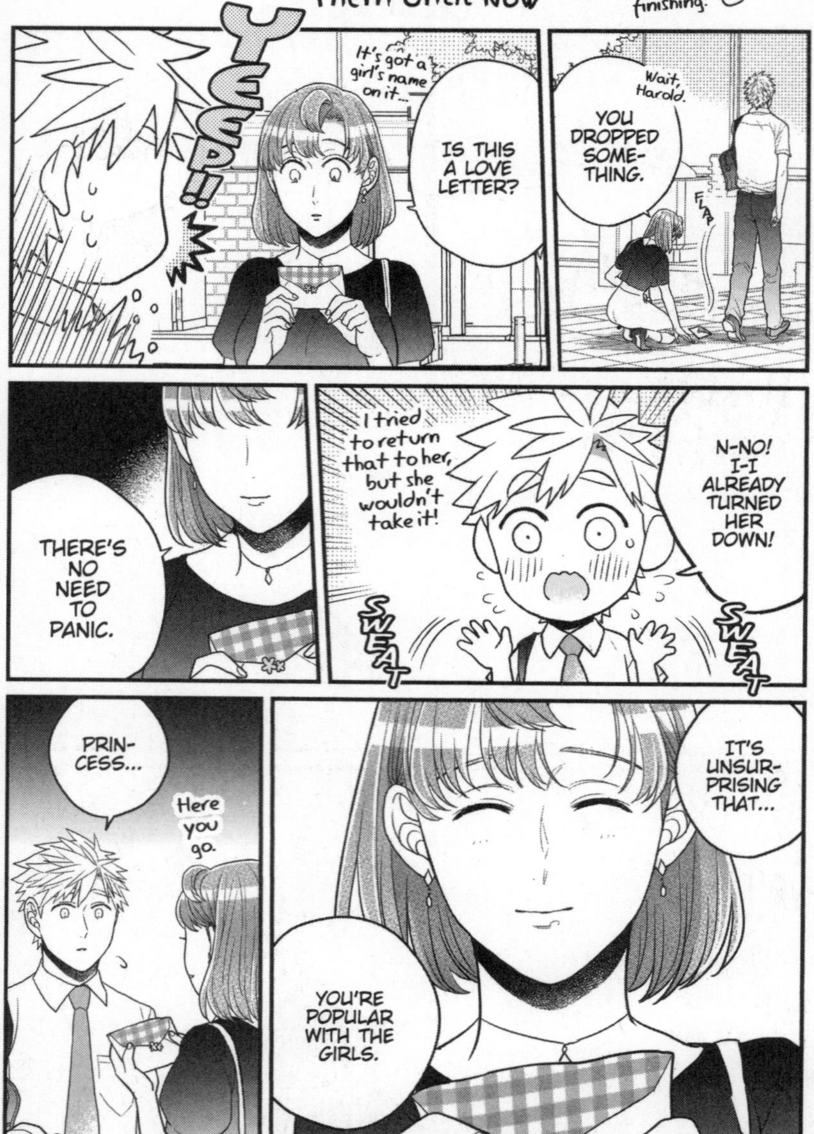

Wait, Harold.
YOU DROPPED SOME-THING.
FLAP
It's got a girl's name on it...
IS THIS A LOVE LETTER?
YEEP!!
N-NO! I-I ALREADY TURNED HER DOWN!
I tried to return that to her, but she wouldn't take it!
SWEAT
SWEAT
THERE'S NO NEED TO PANIC.
IT'S UNSUR-PRISING THAT...
YOU'RE POPULAR WITH THE GIRLS.
PRIN-CESS...
Here you go.

Them Three Years Later

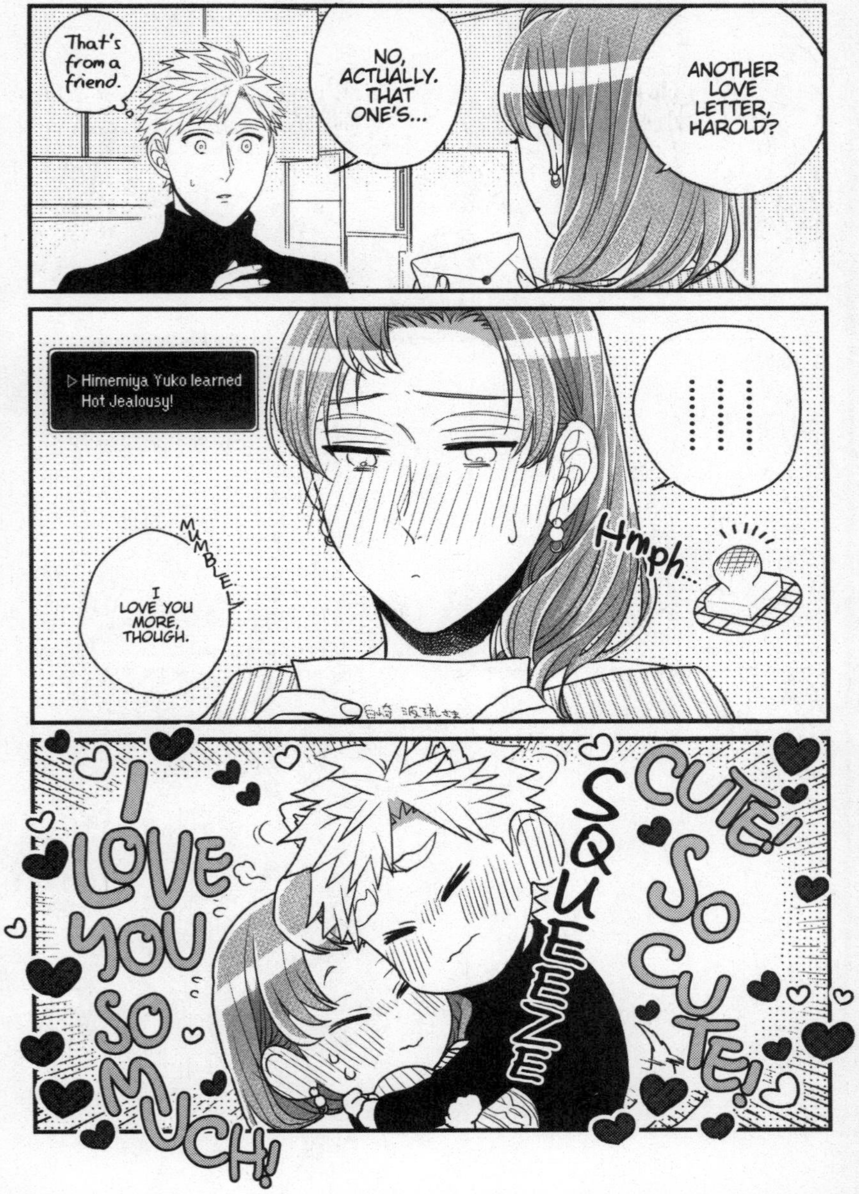
ANOTHER LOVE LETTER, HAROLD?
NO, ACTUALLY. THAT ONE'S...
That's from a friend.
▷ Himemiya Yuko learned Hot Jealousy!
Hmph...
MUMBLE
I LOVE YOU MORE, THOUGH.
CUTE! SO CUTE!
SQUEEEEZE
I LOVE YOU SO MUCH!

Thank ♥ you

for reading!